Outsourcing Crimmigration Control

CLARENDON STUDIES IN CRIMINOLOGY

Published under the auspices of the Institute of Criminology, University of Cambridge; the Mannheim Centre, London School of Economics; and the Centre for Criminology, University of Oxford.

RECENT TITLES IN THIS SERIES:

Facial Recognition Surveillance: Policing and Human Rights in the Age of Artificial Intelligence
Fussey and Murray

Domestic Violence in Pakistan: The Legal Construction of 'Bad' and 'Mad' Woman
Kamal

Transforming Justice Responses to Non-Recent Institutional Abuses
McAlinden, Keenan, and Gallen

Mafia Expansion: The 'Ndrangheta in Established Democracies
Hauser

Constructing Victimhood: Beyond Innocence and Guilt in the Transitional Justice
Lawther

Crime and Civilization: The Birth of Criminology in the Early Nineteenth Century
Kivivuori

Palestinian Political Organizations in Israeli Prisons
Bernstein

Victims and the Labour of Justice at the International Criminal Court: The Blame Cascade
Ullrich

Law and Personality Disorder: Human Rights, Human Risks, and Rehabilitation
O'Loughlin

Outsourcing Crimmigration Control

Digital Borders, the IOM, and Biometric Statehood

Samuel Singler

Lecturer in Criminology, Department of Sociology and Criminology, University of Essex, UK

OXFORD
UNIVERSITY PRESS

OXFORD
UNIVERSITY PRESS

Great Clarendon Street, Oxford, OX2 6DP,
United Kingdom

Oxford University Press is a department of the University of Oxford.
It furthers the University's objective of excellence in research, scholarship,
and education by publishing worldwide. Oxford is a registered trade mark of
Oxford University Press in the UK and in certain other countries.

Published in the United States of America by Oxford University Press
198 Madison Avenue, New York, NY 10016, United States of America.

British Library Cataloguing in Publication Data
Data available

Library of Congress Control Number: 2025937226

ISBN 9780198927495

DOI: 10.1093/9780198927525.001.0001

Printed and bound by
CPI Group (UK) Ltd., Croydon, CR0 4YY

MIX
Paper | Supporting responsible forestry
FSC® C013604

The manufacturer's authorised representative in the EU for product safety is
Oxford University Press España S.A., Parque Empresarial San Fernando de Henares,
Avenida de Castilla, 2 – 28830 Madrid (www.oup.es/en or product.safety@oup.com).
OUP España S.A. also acts as importer into Spain of products made by the manufacturer.

For my parents
Anne and Hannu Laakkonen

Series Editor's Preface

The Clarendon Studies in Criminology series aims to provide a forum for outstanding theoretical and empirical work in all aspects of criminology and criminal justice, broadly understood. The Editors welcome submissions from established scholars, as well as manuscripts based on excellent PhD dissertations. The series was inaugurated in 1994, with Roger Hood as its first General Editor, following discussions between Oxford University Press and Oxford's then Centre for Criminological Research. It is edited under the auspices of three centres: the Institute of Criminology at the University of Cambridge, the Centre for Criminology at the University of Oxford, and the Mannheim Centre for Criminology at the London School of Economics. Each supplies members of the Editorial Board and, in turn, the Series General Editor or Editors.

In *Outsourcing Crimmigration Control,* Samuel Singler explores the development and deployment of border control technologies in the context of an increasing digitalisation of border controls. Sitting within the field of border criminology, this book discusses the role of States and non-state institutions, including Southern actors, in shaping global practices of 'crimmigration' control. The case study presented, focused on the implementation of the Migration Information and Data Analysis System (MIDAS) in Nigeria, provides interesting insights into power relations, strategic goals, and agency of state and non-state institutions. Undoubtedly, the digitalisation of borders serves the purposes of Western States in governing (stemming?) migration flows into their territory. Crucially, Southern actors also play an important role in this field, using the deployment of border technology to achieve their own (internal and external) strategic goals and interests. Technology becomes an instrument to generate new dynamics of power relations within Southern actors and vis-à-vis international organisations and other State actors.

Migration and migration controls are topical, highly debated, and often divisive issues. The merging of migration control and criminal justice highlights the need for criminologists to engage with such questions. As inherently complex phenomena, migration and its regulation raise profound ethical dilemmas and involve policy goals and interests that are often in tension—if not outright conflict. This book provides a critical reflection on these dynamics, and we are pleased to welcome it into the Clarendon Studies in Criminology series.

Paolo Campana and Kyle Treiber
General Editors
Institute of Criminology, University of Cambridge
April 2025

Acknowledgements

An everyday wisdom is expressed in these lines once written by the Finnish poet, Eino Leino: 'Hyvä on hiihtäjän hiihdellä, / kun ystävä häll' on myötä, / kun latu on aukaistu edessään' ('It's good for the skier to ski along, / when joined by a friend, / when the path has been opened ahead').[1] Writing this book would never have been possible without the countless thinkers and authors who charted the intellectual trail before me, as well as the teachers, family members, and friends who accompanied me along the way. Although I authored this book alone—and any errors found within are mine—any insights it might contain arose from the collective wisdom and support of several wonderful people.

I owe a profound debt of gratitude to my teachers and mentors. Mary Bosworth first guided me down the path of criminological research and has supported me in my academic career ever since. As a teacher and researcher, she combines intellectual rigour with empathy and genuine curiosity; as a friend, her care and kindness know no bounds. A decade ago, Jef Huysmans ignited my interest in thinking critically about security and mobility. Our discussions since then have provided deeply challenging and stimulating food for thought, and I am thankful for each of these exchanges of ideas.

I'm deeply grateful to several colleagues for providing me with guidance as well as an intellectually stimulating and challenging environment in which to work through the ideas presented in this book. My former colleagues at Oxford helped me work on my book proposal and some of the early chapters; special thanks go to Ian Loader, Leila Ullrich, and Lucia Zedner. At Essex, several incredible colleagues have supported me in thinking through the theoretical ideas presented in this book, and have made me feel welcome and appreciated by showing me around the cosy pubs of Colchester. I'm thankful to Eamonn Carrabine, Anna Di Ronco, Pete Fussey, Nigel South, Jason Sumich, and Giacomo Vagni for their academic guidance and their friendship.

[1] Author's translation from Finnish. The Finnish version is quoted from Haukio (2017: 33).

Several other academic colleagues have also assisted me with this book in various ways. Katja Franko and Carolyn Hoyle provided excellent, thoughtful feedback on my PhD thesis and were the first to encourage me to write this book. Sami Pihlström and Henrik Rydenfelt both know much more than I ever will about philosophical pragmatism; their insights were remarkably helpful when finalizing the theoretical framework presented in this book. My colleagues involved in the Border Criminologies network, in particular the Technology & Digital Futures thematic group, provide an endless source of intellectual inspiration as well as the motivation to engage in the politics of border control beyond the confines of academia. I am deeply thankful to Sanja Milivojevic, who inspires me with her ceaseless optimism and who constantly reminds me why border control technologies are a fascinating and crucially important field of research.

This book would never have materialized without generous funding from the Economic and Social Research Council and Wolfson College, Oxford. The University of Essex Library covered the entire costs of publishing this work fully open access; special thanks are due to Sean Andersson and our wonderful social sciences librarian, Sandy Macmillen. Hannaleena Heiska—an extremely talented artist and wonderfully empathetic human being—kindly gave permission to use her stunning art on the cover of this book. I owe the entirety of the empirical material presented in later chapters to the generosity of my interlocutors at the International Organization for Migration. I greatly appreciate their openness to my critical remarks, their willingness to engage with my ideas, and their support in facilitating my interviews and fieldwork. Parts of Chapters 3 and 5 of this book were previously published in a journal article (see Samuel Singler (2021) 'Biometric statehood, transnational solutionism and security devices: The performative dimensions of the IOM's MIDAS', *Theoretical Criminology*, 25(3): 454–473).

I'm also thankful to my editors at Oxford University Press—especially Fiona Briden, Kezia Johnson, and Kate Plunkett—and the anonymous reviewers for their supportive feedback and insightful suggestions.

Words cannot express the full extent of my gratitude to my friends and family, whose emotional support has been invaluable throughout this book project and whose love and support make life worth living. I am exceedingly thankful for years of loyalty and camaraderie to Tapio, Henri, Marcello, and Matt. These incredible friends have brought me endless joy and an abundance of unforgettable and invaluable life experiences. Olly deserves a special thanks not only for his friendship but also for providing helpful feedback on the book proposal. Nea has patiently listened to my despair, comforted me, and lifted my spirits whenever the writing process has been difficult. I cherish the time we spend together, as she keeps reminding me what is truly important in life. Grunde never fails to calm me down and cheer me up.

My brother Akseli is my most profound inspiration for viewing the world with openness and treating others with kindness; each day, he exemplifies what it means to be humane. My sister Sofia has inspired me since childhood to reach for the stars; my admiration for her intellectual ability, artistic eye, and loyalty knows no bounds. I am incredibly happy that Girish has joined our family, brightening our lives with his laughter and love. This book is dedicated to my loving parents. One of the happiest days of my life was when my father Hannu agreed to adopt me. His absolutely unconditional love and acceptance are invaluable gifts that I treasure dearly. My mother Anne has unyieldingly supported me throughout my life, and I am forever grateful for the boundless motherly love and devotion that has made me who I am today.

Contents

Abbreviations

ACBC	African Capacity Building Center
API	Advance Passenger Information
BMIS	Border Management Information System
DSS	Department of State Services
ECOWAS	Economic Community of West African States
EU	European Union
FR	Foreigner Registration
MIDAS	Migration Information and Data Analysis System
MoJ	Ministry of Justice
NAPTIP	National Agency for the Prohibition of Trafficking in Persons
NBIC	National Biometric Identity Card
NCAA	Nigeria Civil Aviation Authority
NDLEA	National Drug Law Enforcement Agency
NDPA	Nigeria Data Protection Act
NDPR	Nigeria Data Protection Regulation
NGO	Non-governmental organization
NIS	Nigerian Immigration Service
NTWG	New Technologies Working Group
IBM	Immigration and Border Management
ICAO	International Civil Aviation Organization
ILO	International Labour Organization
IO	International Organization
IOM	International Organization for Migration
ISO	International Organization for Standardization
OHCHR	Office of the United Nations High Commissioner on Human Rights
ONSA	Office of the National Security Advisor
PIRS	Personal Identification and Registration System
PNR	Passenger Name Record
STS	Science and Technology Studies
UN	United Nations
UNHCR	United Nations High Commissioner for Refugees
UNOCT	UN Office of Counter-Terrorism
UNODC	UN Office on Drugs and Crime
UNOICT	UN Office on Information and Communications Technology
WAPIS	West Africa Police Information System

PART I

CRIMINAL JUSTICE, BORDER CONTROL, AND DIGITAL TECHNOLOGIES

1
Introduction: Digital Borders and Social Exclusion

> *Technology captivates. Capturing bodies.*
>
> —Ruha Benjamin (2019: 1)

> *Governments and non-state actors are developing and deploying emerging digital technologies that are uniquely experimental, dangerous, and discriminatory in the border and immigration enforcement context [. . .] Not only is technology not neutral, but its design and use typically reinforce dominant social, political and economic trends.*
>
> —UN Special Rapporteur E. Tendayi Achiume (2020: 3)

The mundane practices of border surveillance

Contemporary border zones are characterized by a web of high-tech surveillance technologies, and digital border control tools have become an everyday part of the experience of international travel on a global level. After a recent visit to Helsinki, I arrived at London Stansted Airport and observed the mundane operation of automated biometric passport gates, which have become ubiquitous at airports in the Global North. These gates consist of a passport scanner and an automated facial recognition camera, replacing the need for identity verification by human border control officers. The gates identify individual passengers by conducting a 'one-to-one' verification process, confirming that the passport holder's facial characteristics match the biometric information found in the passport chip, and validate the traveller's arrival in the country by checking their visa status and conducting a 'one-to-many' identification process against domestic and international police alert lists (ICAO, 2017: 7).

Outsourcing Crimmigration Control. Samuel Singler, Oxford University Press. © Samuel Singler 2025.
DOI: 10.1093/9780198927525.003.0001

These gates are primarily viewed as convenient technical tools that allow for 'quicker entry' than the more time-consuming method of border control officers manually checking each traveller and passport (UK Border Force, 2021). They are not often the subject of political controversy, and instead have receded into the mundane background of airport infrastructure. Yet, automated passport control gates quietly enact a global hierarchy of trustworthiness and mobility. In the UK, they are only available to citizens of wealthier states[1] as well as 'Registered Travellers' who visit the country frequently, have a biometric chip in their passport, and are able to pay the £70 annual membership fee (UK Government, n.d.). At London Stansted Airport and elsewhere, this hierarchy of trustworthiness is materially apparent in the separation of passport control queues according to citizenship: quicker automated controls for the privileged, increased scrutiny for everyone else.

As I stood in line waiting for my turn to step in front of the automated facial recognition camera that would allow my entry into the UK, I observed others placing their passports onto the scanners and waiting for the camera to verify their identity. For some, this process was smooth and quick, lasting only a couple of seconds, while for others the facial recognition process took much longer, and was only successful after repeated attempts at removing and reapplying the passport onto the scanner. A few individuals were turned away entirely, as the automated gates told them to head over to the border control desks staffed by human officers instead. There was no discernible trend among the travellers whose faces apparently could not be read. However, as the passport booth lit up my face and verified my identity nearly instantaneously, I recalled that researchers have demonstrated how the most popular facial recognition algorithms on the market consistently produce lower error rates for white men—such as myself—than for darker-skinned individuals and women (Buolamwini and Gebru, 2018; El Khiyari and Wechsler, 2016). My sex and skin tone likely contribute to the ease with which I pass through these gates each time I encounter them, but such racial and gender-based privileges operate discreetly underneath the veneer of facilitation and technical progress that automated passport controls represent.

The preceding account is a mundane example of a broader ongoing process of digitalizing migration control practices. In other contexts, the

[1] These are the Member States of the EU, Australia, Canada, Iceland, Japan, Liechtenstein, New Zealand, Norway, Singapore, South Korea, Switzerland, and the United States.

deployment of novel border control technologies has been much more spectacular and controversial. As of September 2024, according to the International Organization for Migration's (IOM) 'Missing Migrants Project',[2] 30,614 migrants have been recorded missing in the Mediterranean Sea since 2014. These deaths at sea have periodically become highly politicized; in response to the tragic death of more than 350 migrants in 2013—when an overloaded vessel sank off the coast of the Italian island of Lampedusa—the European Union (EU) set up search-and-rescue operations to reduce migrant fatalities. Later, in the context of the 'migrant crisis' of 2015–2016, such operations were halted by EU agencies, and criminalized for non-governmental organizations (NGOs), resulting in an increased death rate yet again (Lloyd-Damnjanovic, 2022).

In 2019, the EU again decided to invest resources into dealing with the issue of migrant crossings in the Mediterranean, but this time the response was markedly different from the 2013 initiative. Instead of expanding search-and-rescue capacities, or even establishing more maritime patrols, the bloc invested approximately €100 million into unmanned aerial drones (Howden et al., 2019). These drones are unburdened by the responsibility enshrined in the United Nations Convention on the Law of the Sea to intervene to preserve the life of those in need, and are instead used for 'real-time monitoring' and to 'assess risks at the borders and then to reduce vulnerability to challenges' (Frontex, 2022). On the other side of the Atlantic, the United States continues to expand its digital border surveillance network that consists of drones, blimps, facial recognition cameras, licence plate readers, surveillance towers, and ground sensors (Hellerstein, 2021). Although the two main political parties disagree on the desirability and utility of building a physical wall at the border, both sides agree that—either in addition or as an alternative to physical walls and fences—the US–Mexico border must be monitored by a 'smart wall' consisting of a plethora of digital border control technologies (Greer, 2019). Digital technologies, as Ruha Benjamin (2019: 1) has explained, exert political influences not only by 'capturing bodies' but also by captivating our imaginations and shaping how we think about appropriate responses to the problems of border control.

The example of automated passport gates shows that, while the political nature of novel border control technologies is readily apparent in the

[2] The Missing Migrants Project can be accessed online at: https://missingmigrants.iom.int/ (Accessed 29 September 2024).

'spectacle' of highly visible and exceptional moments of politicization, the politics of unequal mobility and social exclusion also underpin the everyday practices of border control (Bosworth and Singler, 2022; De Genova, 2013). This book does not focus on the surveillance tools deployed in the life-and-death contexts of the Mediterranean Sea or the Sonoran Desert, but rather the more mundane digital tools that operationalize what the IOM terms 'migration management'. In the organization's parlance, this term refers to 'the policy, legislation, operational systems, human resources and administrative and technical structures' that are required to 'facilitate orderly, safe and regular migration and mobility' (IOM, 2022b). In recent years, the IOM's 'migration management' practices globally have centred on the development and deployment of a novel biometric border control technology, the Migration Information and Data Analysis System (MIDAS). The organization provides this rather unspectacular technical system—which is primarily meant to digitalize the everyday practices of traveller identification at border crossing checkpoints—to states in the Global South free of charge, funded by its wealthier Global North donor states.

Despite the mundane nature of MIDAS, critical journalists and civil society organizations have characterized this system as a crucial component in 'the EU's strategy in the war on migration' (Privacy International, 2019). In this view, MIDAS is one among many tools within an expanding global network enabling the surveillance and policing of migrants, involving actors such as Frontex, the US Department of State, and Interpol in addition to local government agencies (Zandonini, 2019). In 2024, Privacy International referred to MIDAS as part of a wider network of systems that 'entrench externalized EU borders in West Africa', which also includes regional law enforcement databases such as Interpol's West Africa Police Information System (WAPIS) (Privacy International, 2024).

These critical accounts are alarming, but they are also somewhat perplexing. If MIDAS operates as a tool for border externalization, meant to ease deportations and limit South–North migration, why have so many states in the Global South not only willingly adopted this system, but actively requested it from the IOM? If the IOM deploys MIDAS to uphold global hierarchies of mobility and enact Northern-produced practices of biometric surveillance, how can the organization simultaneously present itself as a neutral, UN-affiliated agency whose 'capacity-building' practices directly benefit its Southern member states? If MIDAS simply digitalizes border control authorities' analogue practices of passport stamping and manually checking passport photographs, why has the deployment of this system raised concerns regarding expansive surveillance by law enforcement agencies, whose remit lies outside of the field of border control?

Criminology, migration management, and border control technologies

The development and deployment of border control technologies is not a classically criminological research topic. Even within the context of contemporary research by border criminologists (Bosworth, 2017a; Brandariz, 2022; Franko Aas and Bosworth, 2013), only limited work has been done to tease out the interconnections between digital migration management tools and broader criminological questions relating to criminal justice and social exclusion. This book is underpinned by three analytical assumptions that explain its focus on a border control technology developed by a large international organization, which has been deployed primarily in the Global South.

First, this book is underpinned by the assumption that border control practices generally constitute a criminologically relevant topic. Several border criminologists have demonstrated the increasing importance of immigration law and migration control practices in shaping contemporary forms of punishment, control, and social exclusion (Barker, 2017; Bosworth et al., 2018b). In an age of globalization—characterized by the intensified cross-border mobility of people, goods, and information—sovereign states have increasingly deployed the criminal justice system to control migration and to discipline migrants, while conversely resorting to the legal and administrative frameworks of immigration control to enact their penal power (Bosworth, 2008; Hernández, 2018; Stumpf, 2006). The example of migration surveillance practices in the Mediterranean highlights how criminalization—whether of 'illegal' arrival or search-and-rescue missions—has been deployed by EU Member States to influence migration trends and soothe domestic political concerns. This merger of the legal and practical frameworks of criminal justice and migration control is now regularly referred to as 'crimmigration control' (Bowling and Westenra, 2018). The upshot of this critical field of scholarship is that the use of 'criminal-justice-like powers' is no longer confined to the criminal justice system itself, and that answering classical criminological questions relating to social exclusion and penal power now necessitates an examination of migration and border control (Weber, 2002: 24; Bosworth et al., 2018b).

The second guiding assumption of this book is that non-state actors have become increasingly influential in shaping crimmigration control practices in the Global South. Although penal power and migration control are in many ways the most classical sovereign prerogatives of modern states, border criminologists have demonstrated that crimmigration control is enacted by a complex network of public and private agencies and organizations (Ford and Lyons, 2013; Infantino, 2016; Lemberg-Pedersen, 2012; Walsh, 2020). It is no longer sufficient to examine the actions of state institutions when critically analysing the practices of border control and criminal justice, as the 'expanded border includes law enforcement agencies other than state police, industry regulators, service providers and private citizens' (Weber, 2013: 114). Critical authors have illuminated how border control functions have become geographically detached from the physical border, emanating both inward and outward through diffuse processes of 'outsourcing border control' (Infantino, 2016). Domestic non-state actors and private citizens are now forced to carry out border control practices on an everyday basis. For instance, employers, universities, landlords, and banks are now 'responsible for conducting immigration status checks, refusing people services/jobs/accommodation, and sharing migrants' data with the Home Office' (Griffiths and Yeo, 2021: 526). Externally, a range of private companies, NGOs, and international organizations are now in charge of issuing visas, carrying out forced returns, and operating offshore immigration detention centres on behalf of states (Hirsch and Doig, 2018; Infantino, 2019; Koch, 2014).

Although still relatively overlooked in the field of border criminology (although see, e.g., Lee, 2022; Stambøl, 2021a), scholars of International Relations and migration studies have argued that international organizations such as the IOM and UN High Commissioner for Refugees (UNHCR) are particularly influential in shaping border control practices in the Global South (Koch, 2014; Molnar, 2021). Their influence is underpinned by socioeconomic and epistemic postcolonial hierarchies, reflected in making aid conditional on the adoption of Northern logics and practices of migration control (Andrijasevic and Walters, 2010; Frowd, 2018; Pécoud, 2018; Stambøl, 2021b). Such hierarchies constitute a central analytical theme throughout this book; I examine the dynamics of post-imperial influence, dependence, and Southern agency in detail in later chapters.

The final assumption underpinning this research is that novel technologies can shape human actions and social life in politically important ways that are not always intended or foreseen by their human developers and operators. Criminologists have already suggested that the proliferation of new digital policing tools can have unintended effects. For instance, Alpa Parmar (2019: 948) has argued that although initially developed to 'limit discriminatory practices', digital information systems in UK police custody contexts have resulted in 'increased levels of scrutiny for target groups such as foreign nationals or black and minority ethnic suspects'. Similarly, Robert Werth (2019: 342) has argued that actuarial risk assessment technologies designed to provide more objective predictions of reoffending have had the unintended consequence of justifying further criminal justice interventions by presenting all 'parolees as subjects who are definitely risky and in need of penal intervention'.

I draw on scholarship in Science and Technology Studies (STS) and the philosophy of technology to argue that the development of new technical tools is a social endeavour—imbued with human interests and values—and conversely that material objects enact power relations and shape both individual and collective identities (Matthewman, 2011). Exceptional and highly visible cases, such as the deployment of drones to observe people drowning in the Mediterranean, present us with stark choices regarding our collective values. Yet, more mundane technologies can also shape dominant views about migration and criminal justice by enacting specific logics of suspicion and trustworthiness as well as social inclusion and exclusion at the border. As UN Special Rapporteur E. Tendayi Achiume (2020: 3) has argued, new border surveillance technologies are often 'uniquely experimental, dangerous, and discriminatory', yet their seeming neutrality can mask how their 'design and use typically reinforce dominant social, political and economic trends'. For this reason, it is productive to critically examine not only exceptional uses of surveillance technologies, but also the everyday operation of supposedly neutral and mundane technical tools. These technologies 'can reinforce interlocking forms of discrimination, especially when we assume they are insulated from human influence' (Benjamin, 2019: 17).

Outsourcing crimmigration control: Biometric statehood, pedagogical performances, and digital technologies

This book demonstrates that the ongoing digitalization of border controls globally is intimately linked to the contemporary merger of border control and criminal justice, which has resulted in a diffuse set of crimmigration control practices. These practices reflect a process of 'outsourcing' in the sense that they are often underpinned by the political motivations of wealthy states and the technical and legal norms produced in the Global North, and materially enabled by Northern donor funds and technical infrastructures (Infantino, 2016). However, a critical analysis of the IOM's MIDAS brings into view how this process of outsourcing—while underpinned by postcolonial socioeconomic and epistemic hierarchies—has been mediated by the agency of Southern state authorities, the organizational goals of the IOM, and the affordances of the technical components of MIDAS itself.

Southern state agencies in Nigeria and elsewhere have not passively acquiesced to external interventions aimed at reshaping their sovereign territorial authority. Instead, they have actively utilized MIDAS to pursue their own political goals. Although the material impact of the system has varied widely between empirical contexts, state-level authorities in countries such as Burkina Faso, Niger, Nigeria, Tanzania, and Uganda have all widely publicized their adoption of MIDAS to both domestic and international audiences. As this book demonstrates in more detail with reference to Nigeria, state agencies such as the Nigeria Immigration Service (NIS) have utilized MIDAS to reaffirm their territorial political authority vis-à-vis domestic audiences by centralizing border control at the federal level, and by symbolically presenting themselves as the preferred and legitimate partner of the United Nations-affiliated IOM. Internationally, these state agencies have deployed MIDAS to affirm their membership in the international society of states by enacting contemporary legal and technical norms of territorial sovereignty. I characterize the set of norms that these state agencies have enacted as 'biometric statehood', centred on the collection and analysis of digital biometric data in border control contexts. These data can be simultaneously used to facilitate travel for 'legitimate' travellers while identifying and excluding 'suspicious' and 'risky' would-be border crossers (Longo, 2018; Muller, 2010). Regardless of whether new technologies actually work on the ground, states deploy digital biometric border controls to avoid the label of a 'failed state' by 'creating an image of a modern, efficient, depoliticized, and professionally bureaucratized state' (Markó, 2016: 115).

The IOM, through its 'capacity-building' interventions that include its MIDAS-related projects, has promoted the legal and technical norms of biometric statehood in the Global South (Frowd, 2018). Because these norms were developed by wealthy Global North states and technology companies in the context of the post-9/11 securitization of migration, the IOM's interventions have periodically risked being politicized, criticized, and rejected as forms of 'post-imperial' influence (Andrijasevic and Walters, 2010). The process of outsourcing crimmigration control through MIDAS has been mediated by the organizational goals of the IOM itself, which simultaneously relies on the monetary support of Global North donor states and the political support of recipient states in the Global South. In this book, I show that the IOM has used MIDAS to present itself as a politically neutral 'teacher' of 'modern' digital border control practices. Through what I term 'pedagogical performances', the IOM has pre-empted criticisms and depoliticized its capacity-building projects by presenting MIDAS as underpinned by apolitical legal and technical norms relating to human rights and digital border control. Nonetheless, the organization's officials were aware that these capacity-building interventions were not neutral. The system was underpinned by postcolonial hierarchies and enacted potentially exclusionary forms of crimmigration control that resulted in new risks in terms of human rights violations, intrusions of individual privacy, and exclusionary border control practices.

Although the expansion of MIDAS in Nigeria was often the result of explicit deliberation by IOM and Nigerian federal officials regarding the risks and benefits of the system, its effects were not always predictable or reducible to the political goals of the IOM or the NIS. The final key insight of this book is that the materiality of the various components of MIDAS itself—cameras, fingerprint readers, databases, file formats, and data processing algorithms—shaped the expansion of crimmigration control in Nigeria. The various components of this technology created technical feedback loops tending towards interoperability with law enforcement databases, materially enacted norms and standards that required reconfiguring other national biometric databases, reshaped ideas about suspicion and reliable identification, and materialized particular views about 'progress' and 'modernization' while foreclosing political alternatives. This argument accords with an expanding body of interdisciplinary literature that has highlighted the independent—and, often, unpredictable—impacts of new digital technologies in reshaping practices of border security and law enforcement as well as the socio-technical imaginaries that underpin these practices (Amicelle et al., 2015; McGuire and Renaud, 2023). To better understand these dynamics, a deeper theorization and empirical understanding of the digital technologies of crimmigration control is direly needed. This book offers both a novel theoretical framework for analysing digital crimmigration control tools in a range of empirical contexts, and an in-depth analysis of one important but overlooked technology, the IOM's MIDAS.

Democratizing and Southernizing criminology

Due to its focus on mechanisms of social exclusion that are based on racialized hierarchies of citizenship (Zedner, 2010), research in the field of border criminology inherently raises questions regarding postcolonial global hierarchy, privilege, and racial exclusion. Recently, some authors have called for a more sustained effort to explicitly democratize and decolonize this field (Aliverti et al., 2021). This book aims to contribute to this broader project.

Following postcolonial theorists such as Dipesh Chakrabarty, Achille Mbembe, Gayatri Spivak, Aníbal Quijano, and others, I understand 'democratization' in this context to mean the widening of Northern epistemological horizons to accommodate more voices and experiences from the Global South (Chakrabarty, 2008; Mbembe, 2011; Quijano, 2007; Spivak, 2013). As Boaventura de Sousa Santos (2016: 42) has argued: 'it is imperative to go to the South and learn from the South.' The process of epistemological democratization implies more than the incorporation of Southern empirical examples into a Northern-dominated corpus of criminological knowledge. In the context of the globalization of crimmigration control practices (Šalamon et al., 2020), democratization necessitates engaging with how Southern actors and their worldviews actively contribute to shaping contemporary practices of migration control and criminal justice on a global level. As Katja Franko (Franko Aas, 2012b: 16) has put it: 'Developing more democratic epistemologies is not only a question of epistemological justice, but increasingly also an analytical imperative and an opportunity for theoretical innovation.' Several authors have recently drawn on this view to highlight how Southern actors have resisted and reshaped crimmigration control practices in various local contexts (see, e.g., Badalič, 2019; Lee, 2013; Mehta, 2016; Vigneswaran, 2013). Drawing on this existing literature—in pursuit of expanding the democratic horizons of border criminology—I not only take Nigeria as a case study but specifically highlight how the agency of Nigerian federal authorities was crucial to the IOM's capacity-building interventions in the country, and how local political interests directly shaped the expansion of crimmigration control practices.

The decolonization of border criminology, in turn, implies both an empirical and theoretical endeavour to illuminate the continuities of colonial hierarchies in contemporary practices of migration control and criminal justice, as well as in knowledge production regarding these topics (Agozino, 2019; Aliverti et al., 2021). As Walter Mignolo and Catherine Walsh (2018: 17) have explained, decoloniality

> implies the recognition and undoing of the hierarchical structures of race, gender, heteropatriarchy, and class that continue to control life, knowledge, spirituality, and thought, structures that are clearly intertwined with and constitutive of global capitalism and Western modernity.

Empirically, such an endeavour requires a critical appraisal of how contemporary practices of crimmigration control are underpinned by postcolonial inequalities that result in differential access to global mobility as well as a division of border crossers into 'trusted travellers' and inherently suspicious 'crimmigrant others' (Franko, 2020; Gundhus, 2021; Zedner, 2019). Moreover, as this book demonstrates, postcolonial hierarchy is also empirically reflected in the extent to which Global North actors have disproportionately shaped the international standards, practices, and technologies that are deployed to control migration on a global level. Theoretically, decolonization requires mounting an epistemic challenge to theories and worldviews regarding migration control and criminal justice that were developed in the Global North and primarily based on Northern experiences. As Ana Aliverti and colleagues (2021: 300) have argued, 'decolonizing [criminological] scholarship involves not only a shifting of the criminological gaze to places and subjects long forgotten [. . .] but also unveiling the ideological dimensions through which the "North" has been predominantly theorized and researched'.

I deploy the terminology of Global South and North in this book to highlight continuities between colonial and postcolonial socioeconomic and epistemic hierarchies. My use of these terms accords with ongoing projects to Southernize academic research, in which this terminology has been used to empower previously marginalized populations (Carrington et al., 2018; Dal Santo and Sepúlveda Penna, 2024; Sud and Sánchez-Ancochea, 2022). Nonetheless, it is important to note that my analysis of 'Southern' agency in the Nigerian context focuses on the agency of federal state authorities, rather than Nigerian migrants or civil society actors. I focus on state elites not because migrants and non-state actors are unimportant, but because federal agencies have been the primary actors shaping the deployment of MIDAS in the country thus far. Federal state elites were able to strategically leverage their international partnerships with Global North states and the IOM to enact the norms of biometric statehood both domestically and internationally. Their enactment of norms that are potentially exclusionary toward Nigerian migrants accords with Nandita Sharma's (2020, 2022) critical analysis of the limits of national liberation movements in postcolonial contexts. In her analysis, 'nationalism became the main form of anti-colonial action across imperial colonies', yet post-independence national elites have often failed to deliver on their promises of democratization and economic empowerment; instead, 'inequalities between people within nation-states and across the new global system of nation-states' have only grown (Sharma, 2022: 644–645). Although Nigerian federal authorities shaped the deployment of MIDAS in important ways, they ultimately sought to reaffirm the broader norms of territorial sovereignty, which are not always compatible with expanded rights and protections for migrants themselves.

The technopolitics of digital borders and the limits of critique

While this book presents a series of arguments relating to border control, criminal justice, and postcolonial hierarchies, these claims are all anchored by a focus on a specific technical system, the IOM's MIDAS. This focus on a single digital border control technology raises critical questions about the nature of technology and its role in shaping social practices. By answering these questions, this book provides insights that are relevant to understanding how digital surveillance and security technologies can reshape criminal justice and policing practices beyond the context of border control as well.

A rapidly expanding interdisciplinary literature has documented how digital surveillance technologies have become central to contemporary practices of law enforcement and border control (Beduschi, 2021; Fussey and Sandhu, 2022; Jeandesboz, 2016; Miller, 2019; Molnar, 2024; Parmar, 2019; Werth, 2019). Criminologists and social scientists in other fields have presented a broad range of perspectives that can be used to understand how exactly technology relates to social change (Amicelle et al., 2015; Matthewman, 2011; Wood, 2021). Recently, several authors have drawn on 'hybrid' and 'posthumanist' theories of technology to conceptualize digital border control and criminal justice technologies as 'socio-technical' networks or 'assemblages' composed of both human and non-human actors or 'actants' (Brown, 2006; Leander, 2021; Madianou, 2019; Müller, 2015; Sayes, 2014). In contrast to earlier theories that posited fundamental ontological differences between humans and non-humans, posthumanist theories instead level the ontological terrain by conceptualizing agency as 'distributed' across socio-technical networks: 'There was never a time when human agency was anything other than an interfolding network of humanity and nonhumanity' (Bennett, 2010: 31).

Such perspectives have been useful for highlighting the complexity of contemporary processes of digitalization in border control and criminal justice contexts. However, levelling the ontological playing field between humans and non-humans risks depoliticizing technology, as the agency and accountability of human actors can get lost underneath the complexity of distributive agency (Lemke, 2018; Singler, 2023). In Chapter 3, I offer an extended critique of posthumanist theories of technology and develop a novel framework for theorizing crimmigration control technologies, based on the insights of performativity and the philosophical tradition of pragmatism. This perspective allows us to conceptualize the expansion of crimmigration control as the product of 'technopolitics', which refers to 'how diverse material objects are mobilized by human actors in pursuit of political goals, as well as how these objects, in turn, can reshape social and political dynamics' (Müller and Richmond, 2023: 8). By drawing specifically on humanist perspectives on pragmatism, I argue that although novel technologies can shape human practices in unpredictable and unintended ways, the capacity to normatively deliberate and choose between several technological alternatives remains a uniquely human activity, for which humans need to be held responsible and accountable.

The upshot of this framework is that crimmigration control technologies are material representations of the values and logics that guide normative decisions relating to the proper scope and orientation of border control and criminal justice practices. On one hand, the developers of new crimmigration control technologies constitute an epistemic community guided by particular social and political understandings of the problems these new tools are meant to address. On the other hand, new digital technologies can reshape the boundaries of criminal justice and border control in unintended and unexpected ways as well. The power of these technologies to shape human practices only increases as they recede into the mundane background of everyday border control practices, at which point 'it becomes difficult to rediscover the contested assumptions that were freely in play before stability was effected' (Jasanoff, 2004b: 279).

This framework offers critical analytical tools for expanding the boundaries of critique regarding digital border control and criminal justice technologies. Existing criticisms of surveillance technologies as potentially inaccurate and biased are hugely important (Fussey et al., 2020; Johnson et al., 2022), but these criticisms risk being reappropriated and reframed by the proponents of these systems as temporary setbacks or glitches, while affirming the fundamental normative desirability of expanded surveillance practices (Jaffe and Pilo', 2023; Lisle, 2018; Obendiek and Seidl, 2023). In addition to interrogating how accurate these tools are—and whether they accurately reflect the '*actual dangers* posed by various kinds of border crossers' (Wonders, 2006: 65, emphasis added)—critical researchers should question the problem formulations that motivated the development of new technical systems in the first place. Analysing processes of technological development and the deployment of new systems on the ground can raise critical political questions regarding who has the power to develop new technologies, who these tools impact and in what ways, what social and political assumptions guide their deployment, and which alternative values and worldviews are marginalized.

The case study: The IOM's MIDAS in Nigeria

In view of the considerations outlined above, in this book I develop a novel theoretical framework for assessing the political impacts of crimmigration control technologies in the Global South, and then utilize this framework to analyse an empirical case study. I focus specifically on the development and deployment of the Migration Information and Data Analysis System (MIDAS) by the IOM in Nigeria.

The IOM is one of the most influential and multidimensional transnational actors operating in the field of what it calls 'the global governance of migration' (IOM, 2019: 291; Frowd, 2018). An intergovernmental organization with 173 member states, the IOM employs more than 20,000 staff members across 590 offices in over 100 countries globally (IOM, 2021c, 2024c). The organization is a key intermediary between wealthier donor states in the Global North and 'beneficiary' states in the Global South, providing border management trainings, humanitarian support, and technical and material assistance 'to support governments to build capacity for the governance of migration' (IOM, 2021c: 1). The vast majority of the organization's $3.3 billion annual budget is project-based and decentralized, meaning that field offices are responsible for securing funds by identifying new potential projects that donor states are willing to fund (IOM, 2023b; Pécoud, 2018: 1629).

In the context of significant organizational expansion in the 2000s, the IOM sought to engage in new migration management initiatives that would accord with the interests of its Northern donor states as well as beneficiary states in the Global South (Georgi, 2010). Reflecting the broader digitalization of border control tools in the Global North (Frowd, 2024; Muller, 2010), the organization developed a digital border management system called the Personal Identification and Registration System (PIRS) in 2007 (IOM, 2011), which was renamed MIDAS in 2013 (IOM, 2018b). MIDAS is a digital border management information system (BMIS), which the IOM offers to its member states free of charge.

The system consists of a centralized digital database of passenger information, into which data are collected using a document reader, a facial recognition camera or webcam, and a fingerprint scanner. The organization's internal documentation explains that collecting this data at the border allows states to 'process and record traveller information upon entering and exiting border crossing points to identify travellers, verify biometrics, inspect and authenticate travel documents, and collect and analyse data' (Field diary, 28 August 2021). Each time a traveller passes through a MIDAS-equipped border crossing point, the system collects and stores their 'biographic data, biometric data (photographs and fingerprints), travel document images examined under infrared, Ultraviolet and White Light, entry and exit data, visa data, and vehicle/flight/vessel data' (IOM, 2018b: 2). These data can also be checked against national alert lists as well as Interpol's I-24/7 global alert list (Interpol, 2022), although the extent of such interoperability varies by country. Each MIDAS setup consists of a country-wide 'Wide Area Network' which is made up of the individual 'Local Area Networks' installed at border crossing points and at the headquarters of the primary immigration control agency, meaning that all data are stored in a central server (Field diary, 28 August 2021). The system can also accommodate the installation of additional 'modules' that expand its functionality to include processing Advance Passenger Information (API) data, issuing visas, collecting travel document information via barcode rather than a machine-readable chip, and communicating with other national and international identity databases (IOM, 2018b).

For the purposes of this research, MIDAS combines the analytical focal points highlighted above, in that it is a comprehensive border control technology that most often operates in a mundane register, which has been developed by an international organization and is deployed by Southern state agencies. Moreover, the system directly brings into view the interconnections between the logics of migration control and criminal justice, by requiring 'secondary inspection' of traveller data by law enforcement agencies in the case of a hit in national or international alert lists (IOM, 2018b: 2).

In Nigeria, as I outline in more detail in later chapters, cooperation between the Nigerian Immigration Service (NIS) and law enforcement agencies is a novel development, as is the deployment of a centralized digital border management system as such. MIDAS was first rolled out in the country in 2010. Before the introduction of the system, the NIS checked border crossers' travel documents and identities manually. As NIS officer Gabriel explained to me, before MIDAS 'we had nothing, we had pen and paper' (Field diary, 26 August 2021). Due to the federal governmental structure of Nigeria, its individual states had significant autonomy in managing the country's external borders. Data sharing between border posts and NIS headquarters in Abuja was virtually nonexistent before the introduction of the IOM's border management system. As of 2021, MIDAS had been equipped at 13 land border posts, 3 sea borders, 6 NIS State Commands, and all 5 international airports in Nigeria (Field diary, 3 September 2021). These local installations all connected to the central server at NIS headquarters in Abuja, where data were stored in a centralized database. Information on border crossers and alert lists were previously not often shared between border crossing points, and border control officers relied on checking passport stamps to validate a traveller's immigration or visa status. After the deployment of MIDAS, such information was shared and updated either automatically through a real-time internet connection, or via regular manual data transfer using an external physical hard drive.

In this book, I demonstrate that the rollout of MIDAS resulted in the introduction of new technical, operational, and legal frameworks that intensified the merger of migration control and criminal justice. However, the extent and direction of future transformations remain open questions, as the rollout of MIDAS proceeds on the basis of time- and resource-limited capacity-building projects that are often contested by local agencies and dependent on continued funding from the IOM's donor states. Although some actors in the field assumed that the continued expansion of the system was a foregone conclusion, the future of crimmigration control in Nigeria is not yet set in stone. These future developments are contingent on continued political choices made by officials from Nigerian federal agencies as well as the IOM; MIDAS has reached a point of technical maturity and an established status as the preferred tool for border management in the country, but its future technical makeup has not yet been entirely determined. The next few years represent a critical juncture that will determine how the landscape of crimmigration control in Nigeria will look in years to come. In this book, I aim to illuminate the contingency and the underlying politics of these future developments.

Methodology

This book builds on and contributes to a wide range of interdisciplinary scholarship on migration control, digital technologies, and criminal justice from the fields of criminology, International Relations, critical security studies, STS, and the philosophy of technology. I synthesize insights from these fields to produce, in Part I, a novel theoretical framework for analysing the role of digital technologies in shaping practices of border control and criminal justice. The empirical analysis in Part II of this book is based on a qualitative research approach combining document analysis, elite interviews, and non-participant field observations. This approach is common to qualitative case studies (Mabry, 2008), as the combination of different kinds of qualitative data sources allows researchers to produce rich descriptions and to triangulate findings, or in other words alleviate potential data bias by cross-checking whether, for instance, interview findings accord with official documentation (Gadd, 2012).

Qualitative document analysis involves 'locating, identifying, retrieving, and analyzing documents for their relevance, significance, and meaning' (Altheide and Schneider, 2013: 5; Wach and Wach, 2013). My analysis focused on all official, publicly available documentation published by the IOM that related to digital border control technologies. These sources included policy papers, technical briefing documents, promotional news stories, and tweets that were publicly available online. Later, while I was based in the IOM field offices in Abuja, Nigeria, I gained access to internal IOM and NIS documentation and included these in my analysis as well.

The primary qualitative data analysed in this book does not focus on the lived experiences of those subject to border control. Many others, far more qualified than I am to conduct ethnographic research among vulnerable migrants, have written about those experiences (see, e.g., Andersson, 2014; Canning, 2020; de Noronha, 2019; Milivojevic, 2019a). I focused instead on the views of policymakers and practitioners who were intimately involved in the development and deployment of MIDAS. This attention to elites stemmed from my original feeling of unease towards how border control technologies were presented in a policy context, particularly by international organizations. Moreover, in criminological research, a focus on elites can be justified due to 'the fact that much of the social problems faced by the "powerless" (e.g., poverty, precariousness, crime, violence, drug use, migration) are, in many respects, closely intertwined with actions and omissions of the powerful' (Petintseva et al., 2020: 4).

As Katherine Smith (2006: 645) has highlighted, although the term 'elite' is often only vaguely defined, it is generally used to denote individuals who control significant epistemic, financial, or political resources. In this book, interviewees are defined as elites due to their 'important social networks, social capital and strategic positions' within the field of global migration management (Harvey, 2011: 433). More specifically, the individuals I interviewed were all directly involved either in the development of MIDAS, or in its deployment in the various IOM Member States that currently use the system. In total, I carried out 28 qualitative, semi-structured elite interviews between January and April 2021. In a politically contested field such as migration control, the information elicited through elite interviewing was 'cast in terms of the exploration of respondents' perceptions and sensibilities rather than the factual accuracy of those perceptions' (Davies, 2001: 77). In other words, not only was I interested in gaining new empirical information on the complex topic of border control technologies, but I was also directly focused on how exactly IOM officials would speak of their work and describe their role in the global crimmigration control system. The interview data was transcribed and anonymized directly after the interview process, and I use pseudonyms to refer to participants in this book.

Interviewing elites presents a specific set of challenges, not least of which is simply 'getting in the door', that is, gaining access to elites who are willing to discuss their work for the purposes of academic research (Goldstein, 2002). In highly politicized fields such as border control, attempting to arrange interviews by 'cold calling' participants is unlikely to work due to a lack of trust between the elites and a previously unknown researcher. In Chapter 4, I explain in detail how I was able to gain access to IOM elites through a combination of privilege, luck, and successfully earning the trust of my earliest IOM interlocutors. Another challenge, once elite interviews were under way, was gaining the trust of and establishing rapport with the interviewees. Academics effectively present themselves to research participants as experts in their fields of study. As expert practitioners, elite participants will sometimes 'consciously or sub-consciously challenge them on their subject and its relevance' (Harvey, 2011: 434). In my interviews, I often faced situations where my interviewees asked if I knew what a particular acronym or initialism stands for, if I was familiar with some of the technical specifications of MIDAS, and whether I could recount specific articles of the IOM constitution. Passing these 'tests' nearly always resulted in a more relaxed discussion afterwards, as evidenced by statements such as 'I'll be very honest with you, Samuel . . .' (Interview, 3 March 2021) and 'I'm gonna get in so much trouble for this one' (Interview, 2 March 2021), followed by the interviewee disclosing highly interesting and potentially sensitive information.

The final data collection method deployed in this research can be characterized as non-participant observation (Pollock, 2009). As I sought to better understand the relationship between postcolonial global hierarchies and border control technologies, researching the impact of Southern agency constituted a key component of this research project. To avoid making claims about Southern agency from afar and perpetuating Northern-centric forms of knowledge creation, I wanted to observe how MIDAS was rolled out on the ground in the Global South. Between July and September 2021, I was based in the IOM field offices in Abuja, Nigeria. There, I observed the daily work of IOM officials working together with officials from Nigerian federal state agencies, particularly the NIS and the Ministry of Justice (MoJ). Field observations consist of 'spending long periods watching people, coupled with talking to them about what they are doing, thinking and saying, designed to see how they understand their world' (Delamont, 2004: 206). Observations remain 'the methodological touchstone' of criminologists seeking to better understand particular social and cultural environments (Kane, 2004: 306). The aim of carrying out field observations in Abuja was to collect information on how IOM officials interacted with Nigerian officials, how a system like MIDAS was actually rolled out in practice, and whether and to what extent the implementation of such a system impacted crimmigration control practices on the ground.

A central ethical and methodological issue arising from this research related to my positionality as a white, male, Global North-based academic conducting research in Nigeria with the aim to better understand postcolonial hierarchies and racialized forms of social exclusion at the border. I discuss my positionality in more detail in Chapter 4, where I explain how a personal sense of unease motivated this research, and how the normative orientation of this book has been inspired by critical feminist epistemology and the projects of decolonizing and democratizing criminology. I have taken on board contemporary critiques of positionality, according to which performative positionality statements risk reifying postcolonial hierarchies unless accompanied by both intellectual humility and reparatory actions (Gani and Khan, 2024).

The research for this book formed the basis for engagement with civil society actors to produce fairer, more limited, and rights-oriented digital border controls and humanitarian practices (Singler, 2024b; Tsui et al., 2023). In my other academic work, I have actively sought out opportunities to collaborate with Nigerian academics in order to directly engage with and promote local expert knowledge (Oxford Law Faculty, 2023; Singler and Babalola, 2024). Despite such engagements, Leila Ullrich (2024: 45–46) has rightly stressed that 'decolonizing knowledge production is important, but so is the admission that global knowledge production under conditions of global capitalism is always exploitative and extractive. [. . .] Building non-exploitative relationships and solidarity between intellectual, manual, and socially reproductive workers globally is hard work.' Nonetheless, my hope is that this book can contribute, to however limited an extent, to critiquing global postcolonial hierarchies in mobility and epistemic authority, and I remain engaged in practical efforts to do so outside of academia as well.

Structure of the book

This book is divided into two main parts. Part I critically engages with the contemporary interdisciplinary literature on criminal justice, border control, and surveillance technologies and develops a new framework for analysing these digital tools. Part II turns to an empirical application of this framework, by analysing the IOM's MIDAS on a global level, before turning to an analysis of how the system was deployed on the ground in Nigeria.

Chapter 2 situates this research within contemporary debates about state power, postcolonial hierarchies, and border control technologies.

I discuss the key findings of existing research regarding the deterritorialization of sovereign power in the context of globalization, the postcolonial dimensions of crimmigration control, and the role of digital technologies in shaping practices of punishment and exclusion. I also identify remaining research lacunae that this research addresses: examining the role of Southern actors in the global merger of migration control and criminal justice, illuminating the relationship between postcolonial hierarchies and the IOM's capacity-building practices in the Global South, and empirically interrogating the independent role of novel border control technologies in shaping and enacting logics of crimmigration control.

Chapter 3 draws upon interdisciplinary literature on state power, border control, and the philosophy of technology to develop the theoretical framework that underpins the remainder of this book. I present a novel synthesis of the framework of performativity and the philosophical tradition of pragmatism, arguing that this framework is useful for analysing contemporary border control practices in the Global South. Analytically, it can be used to problematize methodological nationalism and state-centric conceptions of territorial sovereignty, and to highlight the independent political effects of novel technologies while guarding against the depoliticizing tendencies of 'assemblage' theories and other posthumanist perspectives. This framework highlights that non-human technologies can exert performative effects of their own, which are irreducible to the intentions of their developers and operators, yet only humans possess the capacity to normatively deliberate about alternative political practices and intentionally choose between them.

In Chapter 4 I discuss the methodological orientation of the book. I consider how my positionality and my pre-existing beliefs and assumptions shaped this research project, and I outline how pragmatism can be understood not only as a specific theory of technology, but more broadly as a research paradigm within which to carry out critical research into criminal justice and border control. This chapter also engages with ongoing debates regarding researcher positionality and outlines the normative goals of the book in terms of democratizing and decolonizing criminology. In pursuit of what Enrike van Wingerden (2022) has recently called 'unmastering research', I resist claims to authoritative expertise by contextualizing the knowledge claims put forth in this book and highlighting the unpredictability and subjectivity of the research process. In this vein, the chapter also includes a discussion of the role of privilege and luck in shaping the research process.

Part II of the book turns to an empirical analysis of the IOM's MIDAS. Chapter 5 begins the task of applying the theoretical framework proposed in Chapter 3 to primary empirical evidence by analysing interviews with IOM officials. I suggest that, independently of the extent to which MIDAS has transformed border control practices on the ground, the system exerts performative effects that can be analysed from the perspective of beneficiary states, the IOM, and the technical devices themselves. This discussion prepares the ground for the in-depth examination of these three dimensions in Chapters 6–8 respectively.

In Chapter 6, I begin to analyse empirical evidence from my fieldwork in Abuja, Nigeria. Field observations of IOM–NIS interactions reveal that Nigerian state actors actively shaped and reappropriated the IOM's practices in Nigeria, and that federal officials utilized MIDAS performatively in pursuit of their domestic and international political goals. The outsourcing of legal drafting and the development of biometric border control technologies gave credence to the Nigerian state's performances of 'biometric statehood'—the dominant norm of sovereign authority—vis-à-vis both domestic and international actors. Domestically, affiliation with the IOM reinforced the authority of federal agencies over state officials and non-state actors; internationally, the deployment of MIDAS and the development of new crimmigration law frameworks legitimized the Nigerian federal state's membership in an international society of biometric states.

Chapter 7 turns to an analysis of the development and deployment of MIDAS primarily from the perspective of the IOM. Based on field observations in Nigeria, this chapter builds on the conceptualization of the IOM's border control interventions in the Global South as a set of 'pedagogical performances', which serve to reaffirm the IOM's political neutrality and technical expertise. In contrast to the organization's claims to neutrality, I argue that its practices serve to reaffirm dominant Northern norms of territorial sovereignty and migration control, and in this way contribute to the reification of postcolonial global hierarchies. The organization's pedagogical performances pre-empted and neutralized potential criticisms by linking the deployment of MIDAS to 'global standards' and 'best practices' relating to human rights and the digitalization of border controls. Yet, the IOM's focus on the promotion of interagency cooperation between migration control and criminal justice authorities resulted in the unprecedented emergence of crimmigration control practices in Nigeria.

The final empirical chapter, Chapter 8, consists of an in-depth analysis of the technical components of MIDAS itself. I discuss how the technologies themselves shaped border control practices, often independently of the intentions of the human designers and operators of the system. Nonetheless, I also highlight how normative deliberation regarding competing conceptions of border control practices, and the future expansion of crimmigration control in Nigeria, was a uniquely human activity. I draw on insights from performativity and pragmatism to mediate between technological instrumentalism and material determinism, in order to highlight the importance of technologies in shaping human practices while simultaneously avoiding the depoliticizing tendencies of 'assemblage' perspectives that seek to level ontological distinctions between humans and non-humans.

Chapter 9 summarizes the key findings of this book and discusses the empirical and theoretical contributions of this research to the field of border criminology. The final chapter also maps out potential directions for future research, given the ongoing developments related to the global digitalization of border control and the recent proliferation of automated security technologies.

2
Sovereign Power, Postcolonial Hierarchy, and Global Crimmigration Control

> *Non-citizens, it would seem, call into question the 'limits of the sovereign state'. [. . .] The border cannot, in other words, and despite the best-laid plans of the state, protect us, nor differentiate 'us' from 'them'.*
>
> —Mary Bosworth (2008: 210)

The expanding field of border criminology

Currently operational in 29 states in Africa, Latin America, and Southeast Asia, the Migration Information and Data Analysis System (MIDAS) is the flagship 'border management information system' of the International Organization for Migration (IOM, 2018b). The IOM promotes MIDAS as a 'fully customizable [. . .] cost-effective and comprehensive' border management system to states in the Global South (IOM, 2018: 2). The system allows border control agencies to collect and store biometric information, verify travel documents, exchange data between other transnational biometric databases, and predict mobility patterns. MIDAS appears to live up to its name by providing a golden touch to recipient states, in the form of a one-size-fits all solution to the complex problems relating to migration management. Yet, just as the mythical King Midas failed to foresee the negative consequences of his golden touch, the lofty promises attached to MIDAS raise difficult questions regarding its impacts on migrants, states, and migration control agencies in the Global South, as well as the IOM's role in global migration management.

As I demonstrate in later chapters, contemporary global standards regarding the collection of digital biometric data in border control contexts

Outsourcing Crimmigration Control. Samuel Singler, Oxford University Press.
DOI: 10.1093/9780198927525.003.0002

create pressures for Southern states to 'modernize' their borders and perform their 'biometric statehood' to Global North states and international organizations. Northern states and Northern-funded organizations such as the IOM, in turn, are engaged in 'teaching' Southern states how to operationalize biometric border control systems, often drawing on universalizing discourses regarding human rights and modernization, which are similar to earlier civilizational rhetoric in colonial contexts. Finally, these new digital border control systems create technical and infrastructural path dependencies tending towards increased interoperability and data sharing between immigration control and law enforcement authorities. By blurring the boundaries between criminal justice and border control, systems such as MIDAS prompt political and normative questions regarding the proper scope of penal power, as well as practical concerns relating to the misuse of state power and deteriorating the rights and protections afforded to individuals at the border.

These questions have broader implications for the global criminalization of migration due to the extent to which novel border control technologies, particularly biometric identification systems and interoperable centralized databases, reflect a 'technologization of contemporary border security' (Muller, 2009: 75). As critical researchers have noted, 'the idea of borders cannot easily be separated from the border control technologies used to defend them; [. . .] borders are, in fact, largely constituted and defined through border protection technologies' (Pickering and Weber, 2006b: 209). In spite of this importance, such technologies in the Global South remain a relatively underexplored topic within criminology.

This chapter sets the scene for the theoretical and empirical investigation of MIDAS in later chapters. Before turning to that analysis, I want to explain in more detail why thinking about border control is relevant to criminology, and why the empirical examination of new digital border technologies is an analytically and politically constructive avenue into discussions about the nature of borders and criminal justice. I first briefly outline the historical relationship between penal power and border control, both of which are key pillars of the sovereign authority of modern states. I then describe how globalization—spurred by technological developments in transportation and communications—has challenged territorial conceptions of politics and society. Against the backdrop of globalization and the changing nature of territorial sovereignty, I highlight three key dynamics that underpin the global expansion of digital crimmigration control practices: continuing postcolonial hierarchies that result in unequal epistemic, economic, and political influence on a global level; the expansion of border 'externalization' practices by Global North states; and the global diffusion of digital biometric border control technologies, along with the technical standards, standard operating procedures, and technological imaginaries that support the expansion of these systems.

This chapter situates this book within the rapidly expanding criminological scholarship on borders and mobility, now characterized as its own subfield: the 'criminology of mobility' or 'border criminology' (Bowling, 2013; Franko Aas and Bosworth, 2013; Pickering et al., 2015). Border criminologists have produced invaluable insights into how globalization has impacted sovereign power, reflected in the legal and territorial disassembling of sovereignty and blurred boundaries between criminal justice and migration control. Authors such as Katja Franko (2020: 10) have illuminated the political functions of constructing migrants as 'crimmigrant others', suspicious outsiders whose claims to membership are 'tenuous and can be revoked through penal power'. Criminologists more broadly have highlighted the function of security practices and technologies in shaping and enacting boundaries of social exclusion, and border criminologists have illuminated the centrality of citizenship in justifying these political and technical mechanisms of exclusion (D Wilson, 2015; Zedner, 2010).

Despite the importance of globalization to border criminology, the concept of globalization itself is rarely problematized in terms of its ideational and political impacts (Larner and Walters, 2004). Instead, scholars have understood globalization mainly as a set of external transformations to which states have responded, overlooking its social and historical specificity as a 'social imaginary' that constructs and legitimizes a particular way of politically ordering and acting upon the world (Steger and James, 2013). For this reason, border criminologists have left underexamined the deterritorialization of sovereign power, particularly as it manifests outside the Global North. There are some important exceptions that have examined outsourced border controls and the agency of Southern actors in reshaping Northern policy initiatives (see, e.g., Bosworth, 2017b; Infantino, 2019; Lee, 2022; Mehta, 2016; Vigneswaran, 2013; Walsh, 2020). Nonetheless, a research gap remains for examining how deterritorialized sovereign power—put into practice by a range of actors including states, private companies, non-governmental organizations, and interstate organizations such as the IOM—reifies and justifies postcolonial dynamics of global hierarchy in border control contexts.

Criminology, mobility, and the limits of sovereign power

The historical and disciplinary roots of criminology are sufficiently complex to warrant Tim Newburn's (2017: 4) assertion that criminology 'is a strange beast'. This complexity has periodically resulted in attempts to define 'the basis and scope of this field given the infinite activities carried out in its name' (J Wilson, 2015: 61). Traditionally, definitions of the discipline centred on a focus on crime, criminals, criminality, criminal law, and the body of scientific knowledge about these topics (see, e.g., Garland, 2002; Garland and Sparks, 2000; Sutherland, 1939). However, the boundaries of the field and its proper focus have recently become so contested that it is now pertinent to ask whether 'criminology may be fragmenting at the precise moment that, as a discipline, it is so vibrant and successful' (Bosworth and Hoyle, 2011: 3). In this context of fragmentation—and, concurrently, theoretical and empirical exploration and innovation—one issue with which criminologists have become increasingly concerned is that of human mobility, including topics such as international migration and border security (Franko Aas and Bosworth, 2013; Pickering et al., 2015; Pickering and Weber, 2006a).

The roots of analysing geographical space and human mobility from a criminological perspective stretch back long before the dawn of the twenty-first century. A prominent example from the early twentieth century is the Chicago School, which focused on the impact of human ecology and rural–urban migration on criminality (Hardyns and Pauwels, 2018: 131). The pre-eminence of the Chicago School sometimes obscures even earlier ecologically focused criminological work. For instance, in the late nineteenth century, WEB DuBois argued that 'if men [*sic*] are suddenly transported from one environment to another; the result is lack of harmony with the new conditions [. . .] lack of harmony with social surroundings leading to crime' (quoted in Gabbidon, 1996: 107). Another important example is the European 'Cartographic School', originating in the pioneering work of André-Michel Guerry and Adolphe Quetelet, who in the 1830s utilized mapmaking techniques to visualize and analyse the spatial distribution of criminality in France (Hanson, 2015: 38–43).

More recently, criminologists have highlighted how 'the present scale of global movements of people, goods, and capital is introducing new dimensions that are radically transforming the contours of society' (Franko Aas and Bosworth, 2013: viii). The growing body of criminological scholarship on international migration, border control, and citizenship is now referred to as 'the criminology of mobility' or 'border criminology' (Bowling, 2013; Pickering et al., 2015). Border criminologists have shown that understanding issues relating to human mobility is crucial to contemporary criminology for two reasons. First, the use of 'criminal-justice-like powers' is no longer confined to the criminal justice system itself (Weber, 2002: 24). Second, it is no longer possible to fully understand classic criminological themes relating to social exclusion and penal power without asking how they intertwine with migration and border control (Bosworth et al., 2018b).

Migration control has become increasingly characterized by legal and practical elements traditionally associated with criminal justice. The merger of criminal law and migration law—into what Juliet Stumpf (2006) influentially termed 'crimmigration law'—has been extensively documented and critically assessed by academics focused on legal theory and practice (see, inter alia, Hernández, 2018; Armenta, 2017; Vazquez, 2015; van der Woude et al., 2014; Fan, 2013). Critical authors have highlighted three main ways in which migration has become criminalized in past decades:

> the increasingly harsh consequences attached to violations of laws regulating migration, the use of removal as an adjunct to criminal punishment in cases involving noncitizens, and the rising reliance on criminal law enforcement actors and mechanisms in civil immigration proceedings. (Chacón, 2009: 135–136; see also Hernández, 2017: 22)

Too often, however, crimmigration is understood simply as 'the criminalization of migration' (Kubal, 2014; Morales, 2014), as authors have found 'criminal law mechanisms and imagery being heavily resorted to as part of a general strategy for managing migration flows' and 'the growing use of criminal law to sanction migration law violations' (Marin and Spena, 2016: 147–148). These developments are a crucial component of crimmigration law, yet they represent only one half of crimmigration policies.

In addition to newly established 'crimes of migration' (Morales, 2014), criminal justice is, *de facto*, being carried out via the *de jure* administrative frameworks of migration law. As Mary Bosworth (2017: 42) has argued: 'Practices outside the criminal justice system not only feel punitive to those subject to them, but they have similar justification and effects.' In the UK, well before Stumpf's influential article on crimmigration law, Leanne Weber and Loraine Gelsthorpe noted how the legal and practical apparatuses of migration control appeared and were experienced as 'criminalizing', without the protections and due process of criminal law (Weber, 2002: 14; Weber and Gelsthorpe, 2000). In this context, Katja Franko (Franko Aas, 2006: 150) also argued that novel border control and identification technologies in particular, which were presented as neutral administrative tools for 'managing the growing global flows of people', were transforming practices of social exclusion and perceptions of deviance from outside the formal criminal justice system.

Ultimately, border criminologists have shown that answering classic criminological questions relating to social control, membership, and sovereign power in the twenty-first century requires analytical engagement with issues of mobility, borders, and territoriality. Traditionally, 'the natural unit of criminological inquiry' was the nation-state, and what happened outside its boundaries was viewed as beyond the purview of criminological analysis (Franko Aas, 2007: 286). There are good reasons for the traditional attachment of criminology to a nation-state framework. Modern states have been crucial to the development of criminology as a discipline, acting as the main funders and consumers of criminological research (Christie, 1997: 18). Criminal justice itself is politically and legally tied to a Westphalian notion of sovereignty based on exclusive territorial authority (Fitzpatrick, 2002; Kaufman, 2022). Nonetheless, in the age of globalization, it has become clearer than ever that many of the key findings of contemporary criminology can no longer be understood as problems internal to territorially bounded sovereign states (Pickering and Weber, 2006a). Of particular importance here is the criminological discussion relating to sovereign power and its limits.

One of the most influential theses in contemporary criminology is David Garland's (2001: 53) assertion that in the course of the twentieth century, the previously dominant 'penal-welfare framework' collapsed in the face of 'the crisis of penal modernism' within the broader social context of the market-oriented politics of neoliberalism in late modern societies. These developments, he argued, resulted in the perception of crime as an inescapable reality of everyday life. This perception was combined with 'a more limited sense of the state's powers to regulate conduct and prohibit deviance', in turn eroding 'one of the foundational myths of modern societies: namely, the myth that the sovereign state is capable of providing security, law and order, and crime control within its boundaries' (Garland, 1996: 447–448). The late modern state responded to this predicament through both 'adaptive' and 'punitive' strategies. Adaptive strategies, on one hand, focused on the 'rationalization and commercialization of criminal justice functions' through public–private partnerships (Hughes and McLaughlin, 2003: 3). On the other hand, punitive strategies focused on dispensing harsh punishments, which 'magically compensates a failure to deliver security for the population at large' (Garland, 1996: 460).

Garland's analysis left underexamined the extent to which the crisis of sovereign power was interlinked with the forces of globalization, and the fact that border control had become one of the most politically salient policy areas within which states have attempted to reassert their waning authority (Bosworth, 2008; Brown, 2017b). In the words of Leanne Weber (2002: 10), 'no other area of policy so clearly unites the late modern themes of the threatened state and the impetus toward social exclusion as immigration policy'. According to Mary Bosworth (2008: 210), 'non-citizens, it would seem, call into question the "limits of the sovereign state"' just as the continued prevalence of crime called into question the state's power to police law and order within its borders. Indeed, Garland's (1996: 461, original emphasis) distinction between adaptive strategies as a '*criminology of the self*, that characterizes offenders as rational consumers' and punitive strategies as a '*criminology of the other*, of the threatening outcast, the fearsome stranger, the excluded and the embittered' is now most apparent in the inside/outside distinctions drawn at national borders.

Criminology is uniquely attuned to problems of order, social exclusion, and the boundaries of political membership. The control of human mobility has long been a key factor in the enactment of disciplinary power and the production of order in society; Michel Foucault (1995: 141) noted that 'discipline proceeds from the distribution of individuals in space'. Leanne Weber and Ben Bowling (2004) have shown that the control of mobile 'suspect individuals' constituted a central component of the broader problem of 'maintaining public order' from feudal societies onwards. Furthermore, the spatial scale of strategies to control mobility shifted upward in time, first from the parish to the county level during the transition from feudal to industrial society, before being consolidated at the territorial borders of the nation by modern states (Weber and Bowling, 2008: 358–359). Weber and Bowling's notion of suspect mobile populations has affinities with Georg Simmel's (1950: 402) earlier discussion of 'the stranger [. . .] the person who comes today and stays tomorrow', as well as Stanley Cohen's (2011: 2) conception of 'folk devils: visible reminders of what we should not be'. All these notions refer to populations who are viewed as suspect due to their uncertain membership status within society. Previously, the control of internally mobile populations took place in the context of relatively static and nationalistic understandings of 'society', but the spatial scale for conceptualizing 'society' today is more global and dynamic (Aas, 2007: 7). This dynamism becomes particularly apparent when keeping in mind Weber and Bowling's (2008: 359) insight that

> [t]he strategies adopted at any point in time to produce order in the face of suspect mobility have been contingent on specific material and political conditions, and their form and social meaning can only be fully understood in the context of a particular historical milieu.

The present 'historical milieu' is that of a globalized economy and society. Analysing society from a global perspective attunes us to how criminological insights that have been formerly applied mainly to the domestic maintenance of social order can be applied to the processes and institutions of border control.

However, criminological questions and frameworks cannot simply be transplanted into the field of migration control. As Emma Kaufman (2015: 19) has argued, despite recognition of the transformative significance of globalization, 'academic paradigms for understanding punishment and state power have often struggled to follow suit'. Similarly, Tugba Basaran and Elspeth Guild (2017: 275) have noted how even scholarship that critiques distinctions between inside/outside, domestic/international, and citizen/foreigner often 'reaffirms the statist categories by leaving in place their boundaries, but providing them with different labels so as to change their normative association'. These arguments suggest that some conceptual translation and interdisciplinary theorizing is required when approaching border control from a criminological perspective. Problematizing the traditionally statist focus of criminology is a crucial first step in this analytical process.

Moving beyond the territorial trap

The idea that statist frameworks—perspectives which privilege territorial nation-states as the primary and legitimate political actors on a global scale (Cole, 2017)—empirically and politically limit social science scholarship is by no means new. The 'territorial trap' and the 'methodological nationalism' of modern social science have been critiqued extensively in a variety of fields, including International Relations, international political economy, migration and border studies, geography, sociology, cultural studies, and anthropology (see, inter alia, Walker, 1993; Agnew, 1994; Wimmer and Schiller, 2003; Newman, 2010; Brenner and Elden, 2009; Chernilo, 2006; Tawil-Souri, 2014; Malkki, 1992). The concepts of the territorial trap and methodological nationalism refer to three main shortcomings linked to the dominant statist frameworks of modern social sciences: the assumption that state sovereignty maps neatly onto its territorial boundaries; analytically privileging the territorial state vis-à-vis other actors in world politics; and equating the state with society, therefore assuming that the natural unit of scholarly analysis for any social science is the modern territorial state (Agnew, 1994, 2015; Wimmer and Schiller, 2003). Some disagreement persists over whether such assumptions have ever been empirically sound (compare Agnew, 1994 and Ruggie, 1993). Nonetheless, critics broadly agree that at least today, these assumptions prevent 'social science from getting at the heart of the dynamics of modernization and globalization' (Beck, 2007: 287).

The point of these critiques is not to throw out previous scholarship and start anew, but rather to ask how, and with what social and political effects, our assumptions about territoriality have been constructed. As Stuart Elden (2010: 757, emphasis added) has argued, '[w]e need to investigate not simply the implications of thinking within this trap—how it constrains our thinking, and hamstrings our potential for critique—but how it is *produced*'. Critiques of methodological nationalism have shown that: *(i)* the concurrence of sovereign power and territorial boundaries is highly contestable on empirical grounds; *(ii)* states are not the only important actors in world politics, though they do exert significant power and authority; *(iii)* territoriality need not be linked to the modern state, but rather can be useful in conceptualizing all forms of the social construction of space; and *(iv)* all politics need not be territorial, particularly in the context of the dynamic networked associations of a globalized world (Adamson, 2016; Braidotti, 2010; Sager, 2016; Shah, 2012).

The very expansion of the criminological agenda to include questions of border control already challenges previously dominant understandings of state and society within criminological scholarship. However, this development is not enough to overcome methodological nationalism without a deeper recognition of the epistemological and ontological distinctions between national and global notions of society (Franko Aas, 2011b). Falling short of this analytical move risks reifying notions of the state as a container of society, and the territorial border as a clear site of distinction between inside and outside. For instance, much literature on crimmigration law retains a focus on the legal frameworks of particular countries, most prominently the US, UK, individual EU Member States, and Australia (e.g., Hernández, 2018; Stumpf, 2010; Koh, 2016; Beckett and Evans, 2015; Hartry, 2012; Waasdorp and Pahladsingh, 2017; Woude and Leun, 2017; van Berlo, 2015; Gerard and Pickering, 2013). Analyses of the practical dimensions of penal power within the field of migration control—including the imprisonment of non-citizens, migrant detention, and the policing of migrants—mostly focus on particular states in the Global North as well (Kaufman, 2015; Ugelvik, 2014; Barker, 2018; Parmar, 2018; Bosworth, 2011; although see Mehta, 2020; Milivojevic, 2019a; Baird, 2019; Vigneswaran, 2013).

Noting that much border criminology scholarship focuses on individual states, usually in the Global North, is by no means meant to undermine the critical value of this scholarship. As Sharon Pickering and Leanne Weber (2006a: 10–11) have argued, state-centric border criminology research has expanded our critical understanding of 'what actions states are entitled to take' to defend their borders through crimmigration control measures. However, the question of *where* these actions are taken has received less scholarly attention. Furthermore, when this latter question has been addressed, the analysis has often moved even further into domestic spaces by highlighting how borders have diffused deeper inwards into societies in the Global North (Bowling and Westenra, 2018; Leerkes et al., 2013). In addition to these important avenues of inquiry, this question should also be directed outwards to contextualize crimmigration policies within a global society and transnational dynamics of power and inequality.

Taking seriously the shortcomings of the territorial trap and methodological nationalism suggests that a global framing is needed to understand the contemporary merger of criminal justice and border control. Some crucial contributions in this direction have already been made by scholars examining crimmigration control in the Global South (see, e.g., Badalič, 2019; Campos-Delgado, 2021; Lee, 2013; Mehta, 2016; Ramachandran, 2019; Vigneswaran, 2013). Such contributions, to which this book is indebted and upon which it builds, have highlighted how the reification of statist categories can be counterproductive by obscuring from view other important locations, actors, and practices underpinning global crimmigration control. In the context of globalization, 'we need to turn our attention to the underlying social transformations, caused by the emerging, deeply stratifying global ordering' (Franko Aas, 2007: 284).

Before turning to the question of global hierarchy, it is important at this point to unravel the notion of globalization to avoid some of the main pitfalls that arise from a lack of analytical clarity regarding this concept. Globalization usually refers to a range of economic, political, and social processes through which the world is becoming increasingly interconnected (Aas, 2007: 3–6). Political reactions against globalization have often followed in the wake of severe shocks, which appear to have revealed the 'sinister underbelly of globalization that threatens the security of all countries' (Flanagan et al., 2001: 7). Such shocks have included transnational terrorist attacks, global economic crises, and, as seen during the coronavirus pandemic from 2019 onward, the transnational spread of infectious diseases. Whether globalization is viewed as broadly positive or negative, increased transnational interdependence is often understood to herald the 'waning', 'diminishing', or even 'eclipse' of territorial state sovereignty (Brown, 2017b; Cable, 1995; Evans, 1997). However, such perspectives overstate the extent to which state power has been undermined by external transformations, whether they are economic, technological, or environmental.

Transnational modes of governance and public–private partnerships do not necessarily cause or reflect a decline of sovereign power. Although it might be fair to refer to a 'disassembling' of sovereignty (Sassen, 2007), how exactly and to what extent this disassembling affects the state's capacity to govern is a question for empirical analysis. In other words, globalization can be understood as 'the transformation of the state as it responds to pressures from domestic as well as international sources', where 'transformation' need not necessarily refer to a decline (Devetak and True, 2006: 242). For instance, non-state actors—such as for-profit companies and non-governmental organizations—in the fields of migration and security governance can strengthen rather than erode state power, both within and beyond the territorial bounds of the state. Rita Abrahamsen and Mike Williams (2009: 14) have shown in their study of public security agencies and private security corporations in Sierra Leone and Nigeria that, particularly 'in states with weak administrative or governing capacities', the outsourcing of security governance to private companies and international organizations can in fact be crucial to the 'continued functioning of state authority'. Federica Infantino (2019) has demonstrated how the outsourcing of border control functions in EU visa application centres in Morocco allowed states with already strong governing capacities to further strengthen their ability to govern.

The physical and legal distance created by outsourced border controls does not diminish sovereign power; rather, 'the distance with the governed emerges as the most valuable outcome' as states govern '*through* the distance' (Infantino, 2016: 4, original emphasis). Novel border security technologies such as the IOM's MIDAS have played a crucial part in the extension of governing capacity through a disassembling of sovereign power. The apparent objectivity and efficiency of automated border control systems has justified an expansion of states' border control capacities across a variety of geographical locations (Dekkers et al., 2018), demonstrating the importance of novel technical tools in allowing the concurrence of the disassembling of sovereign power with the expansion of states' capacity to govern. In short, novel border security technologies can allow states to increase their governing capacity, not in spite of the disassembling of *de jure* sovereign authority but because of it.

Considering globalization as a context for enacting new forms of governance, rather than a zero-sum trade-off between state and non-state power, allows us to reconceptualize it as a historically specific way of socially constructing and politically ordering the world (Kaufman, 2015: 20; Muncie, 2005: 36). The 'rather crude technological determinism' according to which external economic and technological pressures have prompted a straightforward 'response' from states should therefore be discarded (Wimmer and Schiller, 2003: 596). Such material determinism can be avoided by conceptualizing globalization as a new 'social imaginary' (Steger and James, 2013). This term refers to 'the dominant commonsense' that provides 'largely pre-reflexive parameters within which people imagine their social existence' (Steger and James, 2013: 23).

In the context of the social imaginary of globalization, migration has emerged as a 'problem' to be 'managed' on a global scale. It is a problem due to the threat it poses to the territorial sovereignty of states, and one which must be dealt with not only by states themselves but by a range of actors across the globe (Longo, 2018). Migration 'management' involves promoting mobilities that are necessary and beneficial to the globalized economy while simultaneously excluding mobilities that are deemed dangerous or suspicious. As Mark Salter (2013: 12) has argued, 'the bordering function is much more dispersed in world society', and this dispersal allows for the management of 'circulation through the security techniques of inclusion, facilitation, and acceleration as well as exclusion, detention, and imprisonment'.

Border security technologies have been crucial to the promotion and legitimization of this new social imaginary. It is not simply that technologies allow for the operationalization of a pre-formulated social imaginary; these tools also shape understandings of migration as a particular type of issue to be managed through technical and supposedly neutral means. In the words of Corey Robinson (2018: 421, original emphasis), novel border security technologies can be conceptualized as 'governing technologies', which 'bring migration into being as an object of global governance and perform it as a *global reality* to manage in technical and pragmatic ways'.

Viewing globalization as a social imaginary illuminates the political nature of socially and technically constructing border control as an issue to be addressed on a global scale. This insight suggests a need to move beyond a focus on policies and practices within states in the Global North, while problematizing the relationship between Northern and Southern states and the various forms of economic, political, epistemic, and technical influence between them. States have not simply become more attuned to the 'realities' of the global nature of migration control. Rather, the construction of migration as a problem to be addressed through global crimmigration policies, characterized by the deterritorialization of sovereign power, is historically specific and politically contingent.

The postcolonial legacies of global crimmigration control

The contingent social and historical context underpinning contemporary crimmigration control is characterized by global socioeconomic inequality, rooted in experiences of colonial rule and postcolonial power dynamics. Criminologists have already shown that the control of mobility has historically been driven by socioeconomic goals relating to the production of order and the safeguarding of privilege (Weber and Bowling, 2008). This general insight suggests that notions of migrant 'illegality' on a global scale can be understood in terms of inequality and privilege as well (Dauvergne, 2008). In other words, crimmigration policies cannot be fully grasped by looking only at their domestic legal, social, and political dimensions within states in the Global North. Instead, this book addresses the 'productive effects' of the global merger of criminal justice and border control, in particular 'the daily reinstatement of an unequal global order and its hierarchies of citizenship' (Franko, 2020: 83–84).

These hierarchies are rooted in centuries of colonial domination and exploitation. Nandita Sharma (2020) has highlighted how the 'postcolonial new world order of nationally sovereign states' is marked by the continuity of colonial forms of political, economic, and epistemic hierarchies despite formal decolonization. Contemporary inequalities are the product of 'a world economic system that was designed over hundreds of years to enrich a small portion of humanity at the expense of the vast majority' (Hickel, 2017: 101). Longitudinal economic analysis has shown that these inequalities are rooted in colonial-era circuits of economic extraction by imperial powers, and that even after decolonization global income growth has continued to be disproportionately captured by the Global North (Aguilera, 2020: 180–189). Moreover, financial institutions such as the World Bank and the International Monetary Fund, international political bodies such as the United Nations Security Council, and many influential international organizations including the UN-affiliated IOM are disproportionately funded and controlled by Western states (Abboud and Muller, 2013; Fine, 2018; Mamdani, 2010; Shaffer, 2005). Outsized Western influence has acted to the detriment of countries in the Global South which, for instance, have been forced to accept strict neoliberal conditionalities on international aid, often with disastrous consequences for domestic economies (Abrahamsen, 2000, 2004).

In spite of these insights, references to 'historical patterns of subordination of peoples and nations' within border criminology are often made only in passing, as a static background condition for analyses which focus more substantively on crimmigration experiences within the Global North (Provine and Zatz, 2015: 354; see Bosworth and Flavin, 2007). Some criminologists have, however, suggested that the continued effects of imperial domination are both material and ideational. For instance, indigenous populations still face political and legal marginalization based on colonial-era distinctions (Cunneen, 2011). Criminal justice systems as well as understandings of the relationship between politics and law in 'the postcolony' are heavily based on the ideas and practices carried over from colonial administrations (Comaroff and Comaroff, 2006). Moreover, comparative criminologists have shown that local social contexts impact the prevalence of crime and the character of criminal justice systems, and that economic inequality and absolute deprivation are consistently associated with higher levels of social disorganization (Hardie-Bick et al., 2005; Schaible, 2012).

Deprivation and notions of disorder in the Global South—and, importantly, concurrent notions of immigrant criminality in the Global

North—are based on continued postcolonial power relations. However, much political discourse relating to migration and development presents these inequalities either as a result of moral and political failings in the Global South, including a lack of 'good governance' practices or an inability to democratize (Abrahamsen, 2000; Autesserre, 2010), or as the result of 'natural' economic attributes such as technological development and comparative advantage (IMF, 2023; UNDP, 2024b). The result of such discourse is to 'depoliticize our understandings of global inequality and cultural difference', by 'localizing responsibility' for the legacies of colonial domination (Ferguson, 2006: 51).

Such depoliticization legitimizes the construction of popular images of the 'crimmigrant other', naturally inclined toward crime and disorder and identified through their lack of citizenship. The image of the 'crimmigrant other', Katja Franko (2020: 180) has argued,

> makes social exclusion—which might otherwise appear to be based on race, poverty, and religion—seem reasonable and legitimate. The exclusionary nature of nationalism is founded not only on the view that migrants represent a drain on the resources of the welfare state, but also on the notion of their otherness in terms of values and morality.

Existing scholarship based on a 'provincialization' of European ideas (Chakrabarty, 2008) has already uncovered important continuities and legacies between present-day political practices and discourses and those of European empires. In the field of crimmigration control, colonial-era 'raciological thinking' has been denounced yet replaced by elements of 'xeno-racism', whereby nationalistic social exclusion in the form of border control is given 'the respectable name of xenophobia. It may be xeno, in that it is directed at aliens, strangers, but it is racism in the way it operates against them' (Sivandan, 2002). This is not to say that categories of citizenship, deviance, and socioeconomic status have entirely excised differences of complexion as determinants of social exclusion.

The supposed moral neutrality of the category of citizenship as a basis for migration control is called into question by recognizing how contemporary notions of sovereignty and territoriality themselves were shaped by the colonial encounter. According to traditional accounts, the norm of territorial sovereignty was established at the Peace of Westphalia in 1648 and subsequently spread across the globe, culminating in the post-Second World War decolonization movements (Holsti, 2018). This story is one of

European ideational and normative innovation, in which 'the remarkable globalization of sovereign statehood' is presented as a natural process of diffusion (Jackson, 2007: 13). What is missing from these accounts is not only the role of imperialism in spreading European ideas about political governance, but also the substantive impact that the colonial encounter had in shaping the character of the sovereignty norm itself. The main tenets of contemporary sovereignty—namely exclusive internal authority, territorial control, and the conferral of membership within international society—were developed as solutions to legal contradictions that arose between notions of universal humanity and the colonial domination of non-Western peoples by European imperialists (Anghie, 1999, 2004). Similarly, the practice of demarcating linear territorial boundaries originated as a solution to dividing up what was characterized as *terra nullius* in the New World by imperial powers (Branch, 2014; Goettlich, 2019).

This last example demonstrates the significant impact that novel technologies can have in shaping practices of political ordering and social exclusion. The problem of dividing up North American *terra nullius* arose contemporaneously with the development of novel linear mapmaking techniques, and the concurrent commercial popularity of the new maps. This popularity was largely due to their aesthetic appeal and economic function in inventorying private property rather than their accuracy in representing political boundaries (Pickles, 2004: 100). European politics at the time was still characterized by ambiguous configurations of overlapping political authority between civil societies, monarchies, and ecclesiastical authorities rather than territorially exclusive state sovereignty (Beaulac, 2000). In short, novel technical tools played a crucial role in shaping responses to problems of political order in the context of early modern colonial globalization. The mapmaking technologies shaped responses to newfound problems of political authority, not vice versa: 'Any argument that maps depicted territorial authority because rulers wished to promote that idea is undercut by the chronology and character of early modern mapping' (Branch, 2014: 95). The role of mapmaking techniques in shaping and legitimizing colonial-era global hierarchy and social exclusion raises questions regarding the role of contemporary border control technologies in legitimizing global inequalities and crimmigration control in the postcolonial present.

At this point it is important to clarify what an examination of postcolonial power dynamics is not, namely a simple shift in the geographical focus of criminological research. It is not that criminology has exhausted the Global North as an object of study, and that therefore it would be interesting to examine the Global South 'in turn' as part of an 'exploration' of the unknown; the resemblance here with the pre-colonial age of discovery should already ring alarm bells. The point is rather that a proper understanding of global hierarchy, and therefore the global system of borders and migration control, requires a sustained analysis of continuities between colonial and postcolonial power as well as the connections and interdependence between former imperial powers and the postcolonies. It is in this sense that a global border criminology can explicate the political and normative dimensions of the visions of 'society'—and their concurrent lines of inclusion and exclusion—that are being played out in the form of global crimmigration control. Such limits are not enacted only at the territorial borders of Northern states. Inclusion within 'international society' is being policed at the level of both states and individuals through the daily reification and enactment of global hierarchy, based on socio-economic and racial distinctions (Franko Aas, 2007: 286; Jackson and Rosberg, 1986). Norms and practices that either originated in or were substantively shaped by the colonial encounter continue to discipline peoples in the Global South into accepting and adopting Western-centric modes of governance. This disciplining in turn legitimizes the exclusion of the Global South from the privileges that have accrued in the Global North following centuries of colonial and postcolonial subjugation, an exclusion 'most vividly expressed in the increasing visibility of the border' (Nisancioglu, 2020: 20).

Critical scholars have highlighted the historical role of the social and human sciences in enabling and legitimizing colonial rule by 'gathering colonial knowledge linked to governance' (Bush, 2013: 453; Said, 1979). After decolonization, linkages between academic knowledge production and global hierarchy have endured as a set of dominant Eurocentric and ahistorical assumptions (Acharya, 2014; Agozino, 2004). Critical reflexivity is required when applying criminological analysis to questions of global hierarchy, so as not to reify or naturalize global inequality, but instead to problematize postcolonial power relations as well as the historical role of the social sciences in their legitimation. Such reflexivity would include overcoming 'Northern epistemic hegemony' in the social sciences, which is constituted by four main components: '(a) the claim of universality; (b) reading from the center; (c) gestures of exclusion; and (d) grand erasure' (Franko Aas, 2012b: 7). Overcoming these epistemic issues is desirable for normative reasons as well as the development of criminology as a discipline: 'Developing more democratic epistemologies is not only a question of epistemological justice, but increasingly also an analytical imperative and an opportunity for theoretical innovation' (Franko Aas, 2012b: 16).

To better understand the dynamics of social exclusion that underpin the global criminalization of migration, my research includes in its analysis actors and practices in the Global South. This does not mean simply including marginalized or silenced voices, although such inclusion constitutes a significant normative rationale. Moreover, this view does not excise Northern actors from the analysis, but rather situates their actions within global hierarchies of power and inequality. The point of this analysis is to better understand contemporary dynamics of postcolonial power and hierarchy, which are crucial to understanding crimmigration control as a global phenomenon.

Border externalization and agency in the Global South

Much of the existing criminological and legal scholarship on borders in the Global South has focused on the externalization of border controls by states in the Global North. Such research has made important contributions by highlighting how outsourced border controls have given rise to a complex public–private 'migration industry', which operates as a 'mechanism to trade political and legal obligations toward refugees and migrants both among states and with non-state actors in an attempt to realize legal obligations at the lowest possible cost' (Sørensen and Gammeltoft-Hansen, 2012: 14). These measures have direct human costs. One disquieting example is the correlation of tighter migration enforcement practices with a higher number of migrant deaths at sea (Williams and Mountz, 2016). Moreover, externalization has the political effect of weakening political and legal frameworks that protect migrant rights. For instance, it has contributed to the 'death of asylum' by simultaneously making asylum claims more difficult to lodge as well as hiding from view asylum-seekers themselves, who often represent the most vulnerable of globally mobile populations (Gammeltoft-Hansen, 2011; Mountz, 2020). Externalization does not impact only asylum-seekers but all border crossers, as a range of border control mechanisms including border checkpoints, visa application centres, detention centres, forced returns, and the deployment of border security technologies have been externalized to a variety of public and private actors (Flynn and Cannon, 2009; Franko Aas, 2006; Infantino, 2019; Lemberg-Pedersen, 2012).

The role of Southern states within the global crimmigration control system is often conceptualized in terms of their involvement in externalization agreements with Northern states. Border control practices in Indonesia have been analysed to make sense of Australian externalization efforts (Menjívar et al., 2018: 5), Tunisia's crimmigration control measures have been viewed as part of the EU's 'external migration policy' (Badalič, 2019), and bordering practices in West Africa have been conceptualized as enacting 'penal neo-colonialism' by the EU (Stambøl, 2021b). International organizations, in particular the IOM, have been presented as key partners operationalizing Northern policy influence on the ground (Bartels, 2018; Dini, 2018; Fine, 2018). Such analyses are pertinent given the extensive policy focus and economic resources that Northern states have devoted to influencing practices in the Global South (Bøås, 2021), but nonetheless Southern crimmigration control practices are unlikely to be reducible to Northern policy interests.

Although research into border externalization is important, it often remains focused on the rationalities and policy goals of Northern states. Focusing on a Northern perspective has resulted in arguments that migrants, by being excluded from Northern societies, are excised from the law itself, drawing on Giorgio Agamben's notion of *homo sacer*, 'bare life' (Agamben, 1998; see, e.g., Pope and Garrett, 2012). Despite the affective potency of depicting some migrants' lives as 'characterized by misery, lack of self-determination, and irrelevance', *homo sacer* as a conceptual tool 'oversimplifies people's experiences' (Bhui, 2013: 11). For instance, this notion ultimately overlooks the ambiguity and complexity of migrant detention and expulsion within Northern states as well as migrants' own agency in responding to these practices and environments (Johansen, 2013). More broadly, the notion of 'bare life' misses the active construction of mobile individuals as particular kinds of subjects, that is, as 'migrants'. They are not excised from the law, but rather 'illegalized and criminalized through the sustained and targeted use of the state's legal apparatus' (Franko, 2020: 9). Digital border control technologies play a significant role in the political construction of the 'crimmigrant other', by not only identifying individuals but 'creating identities' by forcing people 'into patterns of identification, conditioning who they can be according to the state-imposed norm' (Longo, 2018: 164).

While a focus only on Northern goals of exclusion can result in the conceptualization of migrants as *homo sacer*, analysing ground-level practices and the deployment of novel border control technologies in the Global South can re-politicize crimmigration control. Analysing what Ben Bowling (2013: 293) refers to as the 'processes of criminalization' highlights the active nature of constructing the category of 'the migrant' and giving it particular political, legal, and social significance. Doing so brings into view the agency and subjectivity of local actors in responding to, resisting, and reshaping these practices in the Global South.

Too often are Southern public and private actors, as well as migrants themselves, viewed as 'passive recipients' of externalized border control practices (Bartels, 2018: 64; Rother, 2013). In contrast to such erasure, border criminologists focused on actors in the Global South have already demonstrated the value of incorporating these voices into the analysis. At the interstate level, Mary Bosworth (2017b) has shown how governments such as those of Nigeria and Jamaica have actively reshaped Northern states' efforts to externalize border control. Focusing on local public agencies, Darshan Vigneswaran (2013) found that South African law enforcement officials reappropriated discourses and practices of mobility control promoted by actors such as the IOM. Vigneswaran (2013: 123) has therefore argued that 'criminalizing mobility is not simply taught or imposed in a top-down fashion by global agencies concerned with migration dynamics and problems'. Focusing on the agency of migrants themselves, Sanja Milivojevic (2019b: 217) has argued that migrants have used digital technologies to respond to changes in border control efforts, in addition to creating 'active sites of resistance, by documenting abusive bordering practices in countries of transit and posting them on the digital knowledge commons'. Highlighting the theoretical value of including marginalized voices in border criminology research, Rimple Mehta's (2016: 296) study of the experiences and views of Bangladeshi women detained in India uncovered 'multiple meanings and interpretations [. . .] thereby giving us insight into the fractures that exist within the apparatuses of state security'.

To stress the importance of including voices from the Global South in border criminology research is not to claim that we should discard Northern actors or discourses from the analysis. Examining the official rationales used by Northern states to justify and legitimize the externalization of migration control provides a valuable foundation for critically interrogating the global merger of border control and criminal justice. It is crucial to understand and trace these discourses for several reasons: uncovering their relationship to actual practices on the ground; identifying which actors—Northern and Southern, state and non-state, domestic and transnational—are involved in the enactment of these practices; examining with what kinds of responses these practices have been met in the Global South; and, in turn, analysing how these responses have contributed to the reshaping of crimmigration agendas in the Global North.

The rationales of border control: Security, development, humanitarianism

Existing scholarship has already highlighted some of the main discourses and policy rationales used to legitimize border control policies, practices, and technologies. Security has a long history of being used to justify otherwise exceptional political and legal measures relating to migration control (Bourbeau, 2011; Huysmans, 2004, 2006). At the border, exceptional measures including profiling and the curtailment of rights have been 'legitimized by the prioritization of security demands' (Provine and Zatz, 2015: 355). Lucia Zedner (2019: 321) has argued that 'behind the phenomenon of crimmigration lies the driver of security', which has in turn transformed the border into 'a gray zone of eroded rights protections' that 'has allowed incursions on individual liberty that would not be tolerated elsewhere'.

Another policy discourse, distinct yet often interlinked with security concerns, is that of development. Northern states as well as international organizations have long justified economic and policy interventions in the Global South in the name of international development. These measures have included bilateral development aid, structural adjustment programmes, and 'good governance' initiatives (Abrahamsen, 2000; Ferguson, 1994; Williams, 2010). A more recent manifestation of development practice has been what Philippe Frowd (2018: 1657) terms 'developmental borderwork', that is, transnational interventions in the Global South aimed at managing local borders, which 'draw on the discourse of development but also its financial resources, forms of organization, and implicit understandings about the world'. The IOM, and its border management practices and tools such as MIDAS, have been central to developmental borderwork in the Global South (Frowd, 2018, 2024). Security and development rationales often combine to form a 'security-development nexus' (Chandler, 2007; Duffield, 2001), yet there is some tension between these aims: increased migration is simultaneously seen as both an 'engine for development' and a source of transnational security threats (Sørensen, 2012).

To further complicate this picture, security and development in the context of border control have become increasingly intertwined with humanitarianism, resulting in what Katja Franko and Helene Gundhus refer to as 'humanitarian borderlands' (Aas and Gundhus, 2015). Humanitarian discourse has been used to shift political focus from both sending and receiving states onto the migrants themselves, by demonstrating that 'border control and security practices may be the *sources* of humanitarian suffering' (Lohne and Sandvik, 2017: 7, original emphasis). These three discourses stand in uneasy relation to one another, often offering contradictory policy prescriptions. However, in the context of migration control, stricter border control measures in the name of security often prevail. Furthermore, as Mary Bosworth (2017b: 43) has pointed out, the discourses of development and humanitarianism can also be utilized to justify exclusionary measures:

> In 'bordering' and 'reordering', the state cannot rely solely on rhetoric and practices of security or punishment. Instead, they persuade countries to accept their returning citizens through investment and policy exchange. As border control and punishment merge, penal power and humanitarianism increasingly work together.

In this context, Polly Pallister-Wilkins (2022a) has argued that the merger of developmental and humanitarian rationales have given rise to 'humanitarian borderwork', which seeks to ameliorate the suffering caused by borders but without challenging the fundamental legitimacy of security-oriented border control practices.

All three discursive framings have, historically, had a depoliticizing function in justifying international interventions with reference to supposedly neutral technical expertise (Death, 2014). At the intersection of security, development, and humanitarianism, transnational interventions 'are predominantly legitimated by non-democratic claims to efficiency, economics, rationality—and humanitarianism, rather than articulated claims to "order" and "governance"' (Lohne, 2020: 156–157). Highlighting the tensions between the dominant discourses at work in justifying Northern crimmigration control practices raises a set of questions that demand engagement with and research in the Global South: what exactly do global crimmigration practices look like, if they are carried out in the name of contradictory policy discourses? Which actors enact these policies on the ground, and what kinds of frameworks of hierarchy, partnership, responsibility, and entrepreneurialism underpin their actions? How do these actors respond to, resist, and reshape these policies in practice? Crucially, as highlighted above, these practices of global crimmigration control are highly technologized (Franko, 2020; Pickering and Weber, 2006a). For this reason, understanding the contemporary global crimmigration control system requires a critical examination of its 'constitutive governing technologies' (Robinson, 2018: 419), that is, border security tools such as the IOM's MIDAS.

Digital border control: Suspect identities and suspect mobilities

Existing technology-oriented criminological research has often focused on particular security and surveillance technologies, while avoiding grand narratives and macro-level analysis. Grand theorizing in the context of technological innovation and technical practices is problematic, according to Lucia Zedner (2009: 258): 'Relying upon its distance from the details of everyday usage it ignores the fine distinctions and significant divergences, and so licenses sweeping generalizations.' In contrast, criminologists have sought to highlight 'how the classic theme of exclusion of otherness dominates everyday surveillance practices' (Franko Aas et al., 2009a: 9). Researchers have demonstrated how the diffusion of surveillance technologies along with new legal frameworks undermining previous standards of due process have resulted in 'surveillant assemblages' (Haggerty and Ericson, 2000). Surveillant assemblages 'not only counteract democratic legal institutions but also substitute a new basis for governing that is patently undemocratic in its mobilization of categorical suspicion, suspicion by association, discrimination, decreased privacy, and exclusion' (Ericson, 2007: 71).

Similarly, border criminologists have argued that 'the surveillance practices directed at crimmigrant bodies also demonstrate that the crimmigrant other's identity is strongly marked by distrust and suspicion' (Franko, 2020: 30). In other words, surveillance technologies at the border are based on an assumption of suspect identities, presenting transnational mobilities as suspect as well. In this way, border control technologies such as biometric identification systems—a central component of the IOM's MIDAS—operationalize a 'logic of inclusive exclusion', that is, justifying and enacting the exclusion of mobile populations by enrolling them into the biometric database and categorizing them as suspicious (Ajana, 2013: 590). The highly complex technical nature of novel identification technologies legitimizes their proliferation through claims to objectivity, efficiency, and reliability. As Katja Franko (Franko Aas, 2006: 151) has noted, however,

> the implementation of these technologies, as any other, is not unproblematic as they are open to inaccuracy, misuse and privacy violations [...]. Not only do they minimize the need for verbal communication, they almost completely eliminate the possibilities for doubt and negotiation.

Criminologists have also argued that policing tools such as predictive crime modelling algorithms can create 'a pernicious feedback loop' by justifying and intensifying the disproportionate policing of marginalized communities, as 'policing itself spawns new data, which justifies more policing' (O'Neil, 2016: 86). Even technologies not directly intended for criminal justice purposes, such as automated algorithms used to allocate welfare benefits and housing, have contributed to the disproportionate policing and punishment of poor, non-white populations (Eubanks, 2018).

In all these cases, the significant political and social impacts of new technologies stand in stark contrast to the neutral, depoliticized discourse that marks their adoption. Their technical nature itself seems to afford them a veneer of objectivity, as 'technology emerges as a source of symbolic and practical capital internally, with its worth being assessed upon its use-value within the assemblage, rather than upon broader ethical or moral questions about whether it should be engaged at all' (D Wilson, 2015: 142). These insights are relevant to critically interrogating border control technologies such as MIDAS as well, as 'systems like MIDAS are a key part of the IOM's positioning as a neutral, technical provider of border management solutions for states who may not be able to afford them' (Frowd, 2018: 1667).

The critical potential of focusing on specific technologies is particularly substantial in the field of crimmigration practices, due to the extent to which contemporary border control is marked by the deployment of a wide range of digital security technologies. According to Katja Franko (2020: 25):

> The crimmigrant body is mediated by technology. Today, the exercise of power, including in the penal domain, is essentially technological. Contemporary border control systems aim to create bodies which are fused with technology.

In this context, some border criminologists have justified a focus on digital technologies simply by highlighting that 'state responses to uncontrolled mobility continue to become more sophisticated and far reaching, employing highly technical, increasingly punitive and innovative methods of border control' (Pickering and Weber, 2006a: 9).

Borders and borderlands are not only sites where pre-existing security technologies are deployed, but also political and legal grey areas where new security technologies are developed and pioneered. Borders are now often described as 'laboratories' by private security companies and border control officials, 'as if migrants in those borderlands [. . .] were not only threats but also specimens under a large security microscope' (Miller, 2019: 76). Particularly prominent among novel border control technologies have been biometric identification systems and large-scale migration databases (Franko Aas, 2006; Muller, 2010). MIDAS, too, captures and stores biometric information in a centralized database that is interoperable with other transnational biometric databases such as those maintained by Interpol and the US Department of State (Privacy International, 2024; Zandonini, 2019).

Such technologies are highly promising as objects of border criminology research, not only due to their current prevalence at borders across the globe, but also given how they relate to the key themes of contemporary global crimmigration control identified above, namely deterritorialized sovereign power as well as the justification and reification of global hierarchy. Dean Wilson (2006) has argued that the recent popularity of biometric technologies is not simply a result of their technical capacities. Instead, the 'symbolism of biometrics, which is engaged by nation-states as a signifier of the renewal of sovereign power', offers a solution to the problem of governance in a globalized world (Wilson, 2006: 89). This solution is based on the promise of biometrics to balance the porosity of borders for desirable individuals with the fortification of borders against those deemed undesirable (Salter, 2013). Biometric technologies have appeared as a 'technique for sorting through different forms of life according to their usefulness and legitimacy' (Ajana, 2013: 584).

Notwithstanding the novelties of contemporary automated biometric identification technologies and large-scale migration databases, it is also important to recognize continuities with older identification techniques and tools. The focus on the body itself has a long criminological history dating back to Francis Galton's attempts to identify biological markers of deviance on the human face and Alphonse Bertillon's quest of standardizing individual identification through the use of anthropometric measurements (Maguire, 2009: 11–13). Later, Foucault (1995) noted the importance of the body as the central object of surveillance and disciplinary power. Such precedents are important not simply out of historical curiosity, but because they demonstrate how, in what contexts, and with what political effects identification technologies focusing on the body have been developed and deployed in the past.

Most significantly, biometric identification techniques were frequently first tested on marginalized and racialized populations, often in colonial contexts. Fingerprinting, for instance, was first pioneered by William Herschel in colonial India to overcome perceived problems in distinguishing between Indian individuals due to their ethnic unfamiliarity (Cole, 2001; Sengoopta, 2003). Later, American immigration officials similarly based their use of fingerprinting at the border on racialized otherness, arguing that 'the Chinese were physically indistinguishable' (Cole, 2001: 124). The categorization of racialized populations in colonial contexts shaped the development of ID cards as well, as Belgian authorities in colonial Rwanda saw ID cards as a 'reliable means of distinguishing the one from the many', in particular distinguishing between different ethnic groups (Lyon, 2009: 43). These ID cards served to fix previously flexible social and ethnic distinctions, later used to select victims of genocide (Lyon, 2009). These precedents need not imply that present-day biometric border security technologies conceal genocidal motivations, yet they do indicate that, historically, biometric identification has been suffused with logics of racialized othering, social sorting, and the safeguarding of privilege (Lyon, 2003). It is pertinent to ask how the rationales enacted by novel border security technologies such as MIDAS are similar or dissimilar to these earlier cases of biometric identification and social categorization.

Some authors have argued that the proliferation of biometric technologies and complex networks of migration databases—which are often developed and managed jointly by public agencies, international organizations, and private companies—reflects a process of states 'ceding classic markers of sovereignty for the sake of security' (Longo, 2018: 5). However, as argued above, the deterritorialization and disassembling of sovereign power has often increased rather than undermined the capacity of states to govern. In the context of biometrics, Katja Franko (2020: 28, original emphasis) has argued that these technologies increase Northern states' capacities to police their borders and more effectively exclude 'crimmigrant others', by 'ascribing a system of standardized identification and seeking to create the *global intelligibility* of populations'. The global scale of this rationale is highly significant. It reflects the operation of globalization as a new dominant social imaginary through which 'the global' is constructed as the appropriate scale for crimmigration control.

In practical terms, using biometrics and centralized databases on a global scale has extended the capacity of Northern states to surveil, profile, and deport non-citizens by further intensifying already existing dynamics of 'inclusion through exclusion [. . .] premised upon protracted deportability' (De Genova, 2013: 1184–1185; Koch, 2014). These technologies have been particularly important in enacting processes of exclusion and expulsion due to their supposed neutrality, which has naturalized and depoliticized crimmigration control by obscuring dynamics of global inequality and privilege underneath a veneer of technical objectivity. Even when the neutrality of decisions to include and exclude might be contested, the increased complexity of decision-making and the dynamics of discretion—caused by humans and automated systems operating in tandem—can still undermine accountability. As Dekkers and colleagues (2018: 248) have argued, '[b]ecause it is difficult to establish whether [border officers'] actions were the result of a discretionary decision or an automated risk assessment, potential wrongful selection practices could be brushed aside'. Questions of accountability become increasingly tricky when global crimmigration control and forced return practices are not only highly technologized, but also outsourced to transnational actors such as the IOM and operationalized by various state agencies. It is for these reasons that biometric border control technologies such as MIDAS constitute a promising empirical foundation for critically interrogating the contemporary global crimmigration control system.

Conclusion

Debates about state power, postcolonial hierarchy, and border control technologies have illuminated the importance of globalization in shaping crimmigration law and policy, the significance of racialized otherness as part of a broader discourse about the 'crimmigrant other', and the role of novel technologies in shaping practices of political ordering and social exclusion. Building on these insights, this chapter has identified remaining research lacunae: critically examining and problematizing globalization and the deterritorialization of sovereign power, uncovering the postcolonial legacies of contemporary global hierarchy in the context of border control, and empirically interrogating the role of novel border security technologies in shaping and putting into practice crimmigration control on a global level. A critical examination of the IOM's MIDAS is a fruitful basis for addressing broader conceptual and political questions related to the global merger of border control and criminal justice.

Yet, as I have suggested above, criminological questions and frameworks cannot always be directly transplanted into the field of migration and border control. Some conceptual translation is required. Walter Benjamin's essay on translation is useful for conceptualizing this endeavour. For Benjamin (2002: 257), 'the task of the translator' is not simply to locate surface-level correspondences between 'the ways of meaning' of two separate languages, but to dig deeper and uncover 'what is meant'. When formerly domestic notions of order, social exclusion, and political membership are transmuted into processes and technologies of border control, it is likely that differences in the political and legal registers between domestic penal power and territorial border control—distinct 'ways of meaning'—obscure important similarities in 'what is meant'. This book addresses these deeper affinities while highlighting actual rather than superficial distinctions, moving beyond the statist framings that still often limit scholarship on migration and border control.

To successfully carry out this process of conceptual translation, the theoretical and empirical toolkits of criminology can be buttressed by incorporating insights from a number of other disciplines. Such interdisciplinarity is in line with existing scholarship on human mobility and borders (Basaran et al., 2017; Bigo, 2016). In recognition of the complex and multidimensional character of contemporary border control, such scholarship has sought to overcome traditional disciplinary boundaries in favour of 'transversal' modes of analysis (Huysmans and Nogueira, 2016). Against this background, the next chapter draws on interdisciplinary theoretical scholarship to construct a framework that will inform my empirical research into the IOM and MIDAS in Part II of the book.

3
Theorizing Crimmigration Control Technologies: Performativity, Pragmatism, and Humanism

> *Technology can be used to shape the world—rightly or wrongly, prudently or imprudently, in pursuit of valuable goals or detrimentally to such pursuits. We cannot rid ourselves of normative questions in the context of technology, any more than we can do so in any field of cultural experience.*
>
> —Sami Pihlström (2021: 160)[1]

The socio-technical foundations of border control

Digital technologies have transformed border control and criminal justice on a global level. Analysing digital crimmigration control practices globally requires answering the broader question of how to conceptualize the political agency and effects of Northern and Southern state and non-state actors, international organizations such as the International Organization for Migration (IOM), and border control technologies themselves. These topics could be analysed from a range of theoretical perspectives and by focusing on various kinds of empirical case studies. In this book, I have opted to approach these complex issues by focusing on a particular digital border control technology, the IOM's Migration Information and Data Analysis System (MIDAS). Digital technology is the empirical glue that holds together the theoretical and political issues discussed in the remaining chapters of the book. In this chapter, I outline how we can think about technology in order to make sense of the relationship between particular

[1] Author's translation from Finnish.

Outsourcing Crimmigration Control. Samuel Singler, Oxford University Press. © Samuel Singler 2025.
DOI: 10.1093/9780198927525.003.0003

technical tools and wider social problems relating to mobility, global hierarchy, and criminal justice.

'Technology', in everyday use, usually refers to material artefacts and objects that allow humans to carry out some activity or solve a particular problem. In our digital era, technology conjures up mental images of complicated digital devices such as smartphones and computers, as well as the codes and algorithms that make those devices work. Technological artefacts also include relatively 'low-tech' objects such as wheels, hammers, and pencils, which have allowed us to carry out productive tasks for centuries. This colloquial usage of technology to refer to material objects is not an exhaustive definition, as suggested by the Greek root of the word, *techne*, which refers more broadly to 'craft' or 'productive knowledge' (Johansen, 2021: 1). In this book, I draw on this broader understanding of technology. I use the term to refer not only to the materiality of the various components of MIDAS—passport scanners, fingerprint readers, servers, search algorithms, and so on—but also the set of practices and forms of knowledge that allowed this system to be developed and deployed. To highlight how digital technologies combine material artefacts, practices, and knowledges, scholars of technology have referred to them as 'sociotechnical systems' (Matthewman, 2011: 11).

Conceptualizing MIDAS as a socio-technical system points us to two key sets of analytical issues which help critically analyse its development and deployment in Nigeria. First, the term highlights the ideational and social nature of technology. New technological devices are not only material creations, but are also based on ideas and various forms of productive knowledge. Digital tools are often created to solve practical problems, but their impacts can be both material and ideational. Even when new technical systems don't 'work' in their intended fashion, they can nonetheless have symbolic and social effects. For instance, while writing this book in 2024, narrow Artificial Intelligence (AI) systems and large language models have already had immense social effects, even though the extent to which these systems truly represent a technological 'revolution' continues to be hotly debated (Perez, 2024). To fully unpack the social and political impacts of a system like MIDAS, we need theoretical tools to highlight its symbolic effects alongside its practical impacts.

A second set of analytical issues relevant to thinking about crimmigration control technologies relates to the fact that these systems include a network of objects, actors, and knowledges which come together to produce new technical tools and practices. Despite the traditional focus of criminology on the formal state institutions and agencies of criminal justice, researchers have recently highlighted how new criminal justice and surveillance technologies are often developed by a range of private technology companies, international organizations, and public–private partnerships (Hannah-Moffat, 2019; Joh, 2017).

In addition to these various human actors, critical researchers have pointed out the independent effects of technical tools themselves. For instance, Robert Werth (2019) has demonstrated that digital risk assessment technologies exert penal effects in a parole context, by triggering higher levels of supervision even when parole personnel disagree with these tools' assessments. Such analyses attribute varying levels of 'agency' to technical objects themselves. A theoretical framework for analysing a system like MIDAS must also consider the practices and aims of a variety of (human and non-human) agents who are involved in the development and deployment of the system. Each of the developers and users of a complex technology such as MIDAS has their own motivations and goals, which can include the solution of practical problems and the pursuit of symbolic or social capital. The technical objects themselves, in turn, can have effects that were predicted and desired by their developers and users, and can also produce unintended effects independently of human desires and beliefs.

To address these two sets of analytical issues, in this chapter I synthesize insights from the theory of performativity and the philosophical tradition of pragmatism. This theoretical synthesis provides an analytically and normatively useful basis for theorizing new border control technologies in the Global South. Pioneered by feminist philosopher Judith Butler (2007; 2010), the notion of performativity seeks to move away from essentialized and fixed understandings of social identities. In their analysis of gender, Butler argued that performances of gendered identities should not be viewed as a kind of 'role' played by pre-existing subjects, but rather that their identity is constituted through these performances: 'gender is always a doing, though not a doing by a subject who might be said to preexist the deed' (Butler, 2007: 34). Examining the deployment of novel border control technologies in the Global South through the lens of performativity is useful in calling attention to the kinds of roles that Southern state actors and the IOM perform through the adoption of a system such as MIDAS. What kinds of subjectivities are produced, and what social norms inform and structure these performances? Importantly, what are the symbolic and political effects of these performances in terms of social inclusion and exclusion within the broader context of global postcolonial hierarchies?

While the framework of performativity has been utilized by border criminologists (Fabini, 2019; Palmer, 2021; Stambøl and Solhjell, 2021; Wonders, 2006; Wonders and Jones, 2018), pragmatism is a rarer theoretical perspective within the criminological field (Wheeldon, 2015; Wheeldon and Heidt, 2007). The central assertion of pragmatism is that knowledge is always situational to specific actors engaged in practical efforts to solve particular social problems; the truth of epistemic claims is determined by their utility to solve those problems and cannot be evaluated against some external measure (Chang, 2022). By conceptualizing technologies as being produced within particular epistemic frameworks of justification, this view provides an alternative to instrumentalist views of technology as a neutral tool. The perspective highlights the specifically human capacity to deliberate upon what kinds of social or political 'problems' technical tools should even aim to address, even as material objects and technologies shape these discussions (Pihlström, 2021). Pragmatism can contribute to the broader criminological project of 'prizing open the black box of technology's ontology' in order to develop 'theories of technology-related harm that do not collapse the technological with the social and that avoid social determinism on the one hand and technological determinism on the other' (Wood, 2021: 627). What kinds of social problems were the developers and users of MIDAS trying to solve? What epistemic and social assumptions motivated their use of specific kinds of biometric technologies, and how was the success or failure of these tools evaluated? Which epistemic actors were successful in shaping the field of digital border control practices in the Global South?

I begin this chapter by situating the digitalization of criminal justice and border control practices within the broader context of the 'digital revolution' of the early twenty-first century (Balbi, 2023). Doing so helps explain why it is analytically productive and politically important to analyse digital technologies from a criminological perspective. In short, new tools have transformed law enforcement practices and collective perceptions of the proper limits and goals of criminal justice and border control. I then turn to the theoretical explication of the concept of performativity, demonstrating that systems like MIDAS can have symbolic and constitutive effects that allow their users and developers to perform particular social and political identities. Following the discussion of performativity, I examine popular accounts of the 'agency' of technical tools, arguing that pragmatist humanism provides a productive way to account for the independent effects of new digital tools while retaining the normative potency and critical edge of humanism. Viewing normative deliberation and intentional decision-making as uniquely human characteristics allows for more productive forms of critique, which hold up against commonplace arguments about the supposed neutrality or inevitability of technological development. This perspective also allows for a normative defence of decolonizing and democratizing criminology. Due to its 'rejection that there is any such thing as judgements or knowledge in general', which foregrounds the situatedness of knowledge claims within particular social and historical contexts (Hickman, 2007: 44), pragmatism promotes an open and democratic attitude toward theorizing border control. It provides a basis for viewing both Northern and Southern perspectives and practices 'as partial, as situated knowledges shaped by their social locations' (Mehta, 2016: 297). In so doing, it can broaden the range of voices partaking in contemporary discussions on borders, social exclusion, and criminal justice.

Why technology matters

Digital technologies are ubiquitous in our everyday lives. Public spaces are monitored and regulated by 'smart city' technologies, private homes have become enmeshed in the 'internet of things' through 'smart' appliances, and most of us carry around a smartphone on a daily basis (Greenfield, 2016). The functionality of digital tools seems to expand at a steady rate. Smartphones, for instance, have gone from fairly limited internet connectivity to multipurpose devices that are now used for secure payments, health tracking, listening to music, and secure digital identification. The future promises only more digitalization: AI, automated algorithms, robots, and futuristic climate-saving technologies are just some of the utopian digital tools we have been promised in the near future (Markelius et al., 2024; Milivojevic, 2021; Ribeiro and Soromenho-Marques, 2022). Technological hype has reached historically unmatched levels across various sectors of society, including the field of criminal justice and law enforcement (Fussey and Sandhu, 2022; Markelius et al., 2024).

Public law enforcement agencies and private security actors have enthusiastically embraced the digital revolution by adopting a range of digital technologies across the criminal justice system. Urban surveillance increasingly relies on automated surveillance tools and behavioural interventions (Pali and Schuilenburg, 2020); policing practices are shaped by predictive analysis software (Kaufmann et al., 2019); criminal sentencing is informed by algorithmic risk assessment tools (Villasenor and Foggo, 2020); and prisons are digitalized and 'smart' as well (McKay, 2022). Civil society organizations and researchers have repeatedly expressed concerns that expansive digital surveillance and policing technologies will have discriminatory effects, undermine individual rights, and weaken the legal protections enshrined in the criminal justice system (Achiume, 2020; Fussey et al., 2020; Tsui et al., 2023). Despite these criticisms, the normative value of digitalization in the criminal justice system seems like a foregone conclusion, in line with the dominant ideology of the 'digital revolution' which presents digital technologies as desirable and inevitable (Balbi, 2023).

Technology matters in criminal justice contexts because digitalization and technological experimentation are shaping the practices of law enforcement and social control, the boundaries and limits of criminal justice, and social perceptions of surveillance and punishment. More than a decade ago, Benjamin Goold, Ian Loader, and Angélica Thumala (2013) noted how the proliferation of CCTV cameras in public spaces rapidly normalized expansive surveillance practices in the UK. The sudden ubiquity of cameras, and their promotion as part of a generally desirable push to 'upgrade' surveillance practices through digitalization, quickly made these new devices appear banal. Crucially, this uncritical approach to the desirability of digitalization and the banality of CCTV cameras transformed public security practices in the absence of serious public discussion about the proper limits of surveillance:

> The spread of CCTV suggests that the myopic and colonizing properties of security can also assert themselves when people *stop* talking about crime-control practices and technologies, when they cease to notice or pay attention. Banality may, in other words, be another way in which security slips beyond the boundaries of democratic politics—not through speech-acts, or claim-making, but in their absence. (Goold et al., 2013: 988, original emphasis)

The ideological dominance of the 'digital revolution' has only increased in the intervening decade, and so too have technological innovation and experimentation in criminal justice and border control contexts.

Discourses of security, risk, and humanitarianism have been used to justify testing experimental technologies such as AI-powered live facial recognition, biometric registration, and portable drug detection devices (Degenhardt and Bourne, 2020; Fussey et al., 2020; Madianou, 2019).

Practices of technological innovation have also blurred the boundaries between criminal justice and border control as public–private partnerships aim to develop 'interoperable' systems for sharing data, risk assessments, and alert lists between immigration control and law enforcement authorities (Bigo, 2020; Leese, 2022). Such experiments are often carried out within Global North countries, and recent legislative frameworks like the European Union AI Act of 2024 have exempted law enforcement and security purposes from the general legal protections designed to ensure the compatibility of new digital tools with individual rights (Access Now, 2024).

New border control technologies are often even more experimental than digital law enforcement tools, due to lower levels of legislative oversight and regulation, and higher levels of militarization in border zones (Molnar, 2019, 2024). Law enforcement and border control practices in the Global South are characterized by extensive technological experimentation sponsored by Global North states, international organizations, and private technology companies. The global digitalization of border control—to which logics of security, risk, and crime control are central—is underpinned by hierarchies of epistemic, economic, and political influence. According to Petra Molnar (2021: 77), 'monopolies of knowledge and corporate consolidations of power and authority are allowed to exist because there is no unified global regulatory regime governing the use of new technologies, creating laboratories for high-risk experiments with profound impacts on people's lives'. New technological initiatives sponsored by Global North states and international organizations have proliferated in recent years, including digital tools such as the IOM's MIDAS, the UNHCR's Biometric Identity Management System (BIMS), and the UN Office of Counter-Terrorism's goTravel system.

Against this broader background of societal hype regarding digitalization, and the more specific practices of technological experimentation in criminal justice and border control contexts, it is important to inquire into the underlying assumptions, perceived social problems, and social and political aims that underpin the digitalization of crimmigration control globally. Critically assessing these systems requires deconstructing their ideational and symbolic dimensions from the perspective of both Northern and Southern states as well as the developers of these technical tools, while contextualizing these effects within global hierarchies of technical expertise, economic influence, and political authority. The concept of performativity provides useful analytical tools for doing so.

Performing statehood through border control

The term 'performativity' connotes theatrical performances, stages, scripts, and actors. In this view, individuals enrolled in drug treatment courts have been conceptualized as 'performers' acting out 'scripts of responsibilization' (Moore and Hirai, 2014: 15); activist campaigns exposing the bodily suffering of prisoners have been analysed as a form of 'protest theater' (Corcoran, 2020: 653); policing practices have been characterized as a 'dance' to the 'music' of the 'structure of policing' (Manning, 2008: 22); and borders have been understood as 'the performance of various state actors in an elaborate dance with ordinary people who seek freedom of movement and identification' (Wonders, 2006: 64). Importantly, this work reminds us that practices of policing, justice, control, and resistance should not always be taken at face value but should in addition be analysed in terms of their intended and unintended communicative effects. As Mackenzie and Green (2008: 150) have argued, in many cases criminal justice practices are 'primarily about performance rather than about substance, and [are] in this sense fake or superficial'.

Yet, by implying that practices are sometimes 'fake', the theatrical metaphor raises the question of what an 'authentic' practice looks like. Ontologically, performativity understood mainly as a theatrical metaphor assumes the existence of subjects with 'real' identities prior to and independent of their performances, who are then able to engage in either authentic practices or superficial performances. This assumption comes to the fore when scholars argue that the object of performances—such as migration as an object of 'citizenship performances'—should '*accurately* be reframed' in terms that diverge from dominant understandings (Wonders and Jones, 2018: 147, emphasis added). Similarly, calls for alternative immigration control policies are sometimes based on the claim that 'border constructions and enforcement should be more closely linked to the *actual dangers* posed by various kinds of border crossers' (Wonders, 2006: 65, emphasis added). Although the basis of claims about authenticity and accuracy remains unclear, some criminologists have expressed unease at embracing a more ontologically radical conception of performativity. Critics have argued that such an approach 'provides no grounds for contesting its knowledge claims' and so undermines the epistemic coherence of the criminological endeavour (Edwards and Hughes, 2008: 66).

In spite of such warnings, border criminologists and scholars of transnational criminal justice have demonstrated the full critical potential of performativity, based on Judith Butler's (2007, 2010) formulation of the concept in their *Gender Trouble* and later writings. In their analysis of gender, Butler (2007: 34) does not suggest simply that pre-existing subjects choose to perform either masculine or feminine gender 'roles', but more radically that there exists no gendered subject independent of these performances; they are constitutive of gendered identities. Deploying this framework in the context of border criminology, Giulia Fabini (2019: 177, original emphasis) has argued that '[t]alking about border *performativity* is tantamount to saying that borders do not exist before the individuals who cross them. Borders and migrants are mutually constitutive through border performances.' This conception of performativity is more radical than the theatrical metaphor in suggesting that there is no 'real' or 'accurate' conception of borders or migrants beneath these performances.

This is not to say that borders are performatively 'produced *ex nihilo* at every instant, but only that [their] apparently seamless regeneration brings about naturalized effects' (Butler, 2010: 149). In other words, performances are not singular acts free from external constraints, but are instead based on, constrained, and shaped by existing discourses, practices, and material objects. Performances are 'ongoing citational processes whereby "regular subjects" and "standards of normality" are discursively co-constituted to give the effect that both are natural rather than cultural constructs' (Weber, 1998: 81). Seen in this light, performativity provides an avenue for critically examining how—through what discourses, practices, and material interventions—statehood, global crimmigration control, and 'the migrant' as a political subject are constituted and naturalized. In other words, it can act as a framework for examining the interplay between the structures of global hierarchy on the one hand, and the political agency of Southern actors, the IOM, and new border control technologies on the other.

Although based on the speech act theory of JL Austin (1955), the lens of performativity brings into view more than just language and discourse. Butler's framework can also be used to highlight the performative effects of repeated embodied practices as well as techniques of calculation and governance. For instance, 'the autonomy of the market', according to Butler (2010: 150), is not performatively brought into being only through politicians' and economists' discursive utterances, but also through repeated practices of prediction and calculation by both humans and non-human technologies that 'enter into specific economic activities such as price-setting'. In their performative analysis of gender in the context of military conflict, Priscyll Anctil Avoine and Rachel Tillman (2015: 224) have argued that gender is performed through embodied practices of femininity by women combatants seeking to 'pass in social situations where male combatants could not'.

Performativity is not limited to an analysis of human subjects engaging in discursive and practical performances, as 'performativity is challenged by the heterogeneity of socio-technical assemblages and the proliferation of devices', calling for a performative 'analytics of devices' (Amicelle et al., 2015: 299). A performative analysis can complement existing critical research into criminal justice and border control technologies by asking not only how new technical systems shape crimmigration control practices, but also how the norms governing the use of these technologies have been 'created, assembled, displaced, or adopted' on a global level (Frowd, 2020: 61). Amicelle and colleagues (2015: 298) have outlined how security devices, such as biometric border control technologies, exert performative effects:

> they (re)configure social spaces, (re)draw boundaries and (re)distribute meanings. Therefore, security devices are performative in that they do not only enact or alter particular realities and categories depending on the successful stabilization of complex socio-technical configurations, but also draw legal, gender, race or class boundaries and lines of exclusion.

Applying the framework of performativity to new digital crimmigration control technologies highlights the ideational and symbolic effects of these tools. From this perspective, states, international organizations, and migrants are not viewed as pre-existing political subjects who then develop or use neutral technical tools to achieve some predefined goals. Instead, a performative analysis suggests that these actors' identities are constituted and shaped partly by their deployment of new and existing digital technologies and the discourses, practices, and forms of knowledge that underpin these systems. As I argue in later chapters, the development of MIDAS has been crucial to the IOM's identification as a 'technical expert' organization on a global level, because developing new digital tools is what technical experts do. The IOM's status as a technical expert and teacher of digital border management did not predate systems such as MIDAS; rather, these new technologies have performatively constituted this expert status.

In this vein, Eva Stambøl has analysed the performative dimensions of digital border checkpoints deployed by West African law enforcement and immigration control agencies. In the West African political context, state authority is 'expressed more as control over people rather than territory, meaning that networks of patronage, not territorial presence (as assumed by the Westphalian state model), are a more predominant method of social control' (Stambøl, 2021a: 487). However, deploying digital border control technologies has allowed state authorities to perform their territorial statehood to an international audience according to the accepted scripts and technical norms of border control, even in cases where the practical effects of new digital tools on the ground have been limited. Presuming the existence of, for instance, 'the Malian state' as a unitary actor would obscure from view divergences between Northern and local 'notions of territory, mobility, sovereignty and crime' as well as discrepancies between official discourses of state authority and realities on the ground (Stambøl, 2021a: 487).

Performativity provides a way to analyse the dynamic relationship between pre-existing discursive, practical, and material structures on the one hand and the constitutive performances by agents on the other. To illustrate this interplay between structure and agency underpinning the performative effects of digital border control tools, Eva Stambøl and Randi Solhjell (2021: 500) have argued that West African state agencies' border digitalization efforts—funded by Global North actors such as the EU—have been structured by 'dominant Global North problem formulations' and hierarchical relationships of uneven epistemic, economic, and political authority. Within these structures, however, West African state agencies' performances of territorial statehood and transnational criminal justice through digital border control technologies have been characterized by 'contestations and frictions, and sometimes outright resistance' (Stambøl and Solhjell, 2021: 506). In later chapters, I show that the deployment of MIDAS by Nigerian federal authorities has been profoundly influenced by Northern-produced technical standards and political norms regarding crimmigration control. Simultaneously, federal agencies such as the Nigerian Immigration Service (NIS) have shaped the deployment of MIDAS according to their own political goals to actively perform a particular kind of statehood to both domestic and international audiences. These examples illustrate that performativity can foreground Southern agency while situating these actors' performances within the broader context of existing sociopolitical and technical structures.

Extending the framework of performativity to include material devices and objects in addition to human actors calls for additional theoretical refinement, as a common criticism of performativity is that this framework supposedly focuses on discursive speech acts by humans while marginalizing materiality and embodied practices (Harrison, 2000). In the most extreme discourse-centred view, a performative analysis would conceptualize human actors as 'surrounded by material props' which do not affect the agency of these humans to any significant extent (Law and Singleton, 2000: 771). As I outlined above, however, the rapid digitalization of criminal justice and border controls has reshaped practices, expanded the boundaries of these fields, and transformed public perceptions of digital surveillance and control. As Sanja Milivojevic and Elizabeth Radulski (2020: 198) have argued, analysing the impact of new technologies 'on human agency and autonomy is just one of the many conundrums social scientists, including lawyers and criminologists will have to unpack in the near future'. A critical analysis of digital crimmigration control technologies such as MIDAS requires theorizing human–technology relations more clearly in order to account for the role of material devices in shaping human practices by exerting performative and practical effects of their own.

Levelling the playing field: Assemblages and the contested status of humanism

Highlighting the social impacts of new technologies has been invaluable for expanding our understanding of how digitalization can shape criminal justice and security practices. Expansive surveillance systems have been made possible by new tools for data collection and analysis, as well as increased capacity for real-time data sharing between law enforcement agencies within and across national borders (Aden, 2018). In the context of twenty-first-century globalization, security and border practitioners have argued that increased global interconnectivity and mobility has a dark side as well: 'organized crime, drug trafficking, and terrorism, aided by the latest information technology, are also growing, to the point where they already form a sinister underbelly of globalization that threatens the security of all countries' (Flanagan et al., 2001: 12). Consequently, 'a key aspect of the post-9/11 window of border enhancement hinged on risk management and data-sharing protocols, rather than tactical infrastructure' (Longo, 2018: 115).

A key insight of critical research into novel border control and security technologies is that these tools often produce unintended consequences, which shape social practices independently of the beliefs and intentions of their human designers and operators (Dekkers, 2020). One common way in which new surveillance systems can later contribute to increased monitoring and suspicion of previously untargeted populations is 'function creep' (Leese and Ugolini, 2024). This term refers to processes whereby technical devices initially created for a specific use-case are later used in a much broader context, such as when the European asylum database EURODAC was expanded to allow for law enforcement access years after its initial deployment (Dijstelbloem, 2021: 42). The EU Visa Information System has undergone a similar process of law enforcement function creep (Tzanou, 2010).

Digital technologies can also shape their users' actions by influencing their decision-making and by making certain practices easier and likelier than others. For instance, Alpa Parmar (2019: 948) has demonstrated how the digitalization of information systems in British policy custody contexts resulted in 'increased levels of scrutiny for target groups such as foreign nationals or black and minority ethnic suspects' by prompting officers to view racialized individuals as more suspicious than others. These effects materialized despite the fact that 'technologically prompted procedures [. . .] were compelling in their capacity to give the illusion of sameness and color blindness', and that digitalization was initially intended to 'limit discriminatory practices' (Parmar, 2019: 945).

The ability of technologies themselves to have a social impact originally unintended by their designers and operators raises the analytical question of how to conceptualize this technological agency vis-à-vis human agency. Interdisciplinary scholarship on borders and the transnational diffusion of technologies has sought to move beyond instrumentalist views according to which 'technology is neutral, a tool that can be turned to whatever use a user desired' (McCarthy, 2018: 6). In contrast to such instrumentalism, scholars have argued for varying degrees of technological autonomy and ability to influence social relations independently from humans, arguing that the 'instrumental conception of technology [. . .] provides no latitude for examining the impact that technologies have on their human "users"' (Wood, 2021: 629).

At the turn of the century, Kevin Haggerty and Richard Ericson (2000) referred to the emerging network of digital surveillance devices in a criminal justice and policing context as a 'surveillant assemblage'. Since then, these technologies have become much more expansive and complex. Conceptualizing networks of digital devices, law enforcement agencies, and targets of surveillance as 'assemblages' has become a popular way to highlight the importance of non-human objects and technologies within networks of criminal justice and border control (Madianou, 2019; Sullivan, 2022; Vukov and Sheller, 2013). This concept, based on the philosophical work of Gilles Deleuze and Felix Guattari (1987), seeks to highlight the relational nature of social life, in which actors come together in heterogeneous formations to assert their agency within networks consisting of both humans and non-humans. Assemblage theories foreground the multidimensional nature of agency by seeking to dissolve 'the distinction between the technical and the social' to varying extents (McCarthy, 2018: 12). Border criminologists have argued that the concept of assemblage 'is particularly apt to capture the growing intertwining of the technological and the social, or better the novel forms of sociality where the digital is increasingly the social' (Franko Aas, 2012a: 241).

The assemblage approach levels ontological distinctions between humans and material objects to avoid both material determinism and constructivist or discursive approaches that overlook the importance of the material world in shaping social practices (Brown, 2006). In other words, this notion widens 'the scope of agencies to be included in sociological inquiry' such that socio-technical 'networks are composed of people, beings and objects' in which 'associations between human agents cannot be assumed to have ontological precedence' (Jeandesboz, 2016: 295). In the context of border control, this analytical symmetry of human and non-human actors 'entails unpacking the institutional structures, technological and material assemblages, and emerging migrant configurations simultaneously' (Dijstelbloem, 2021: 137).

Levelling the ontological playing field between humans and non-humans results in a view of socio-technical networks as being composed of 'actants' with varying degrees of agency (Sayes, 2014). Such perspectives can be characterized as 'posthumanist', although criminological scholarship on digital technologies rarely explicitly mentions this term (Berg, 2021: 27). Recognizing the growing importance of novel technologies and environmental changes to human societies in the twenty-first century (Milivojevic, 2021), the framework of posthumanism espouses a decentring of the traditional human subject of Western philosophy and social theory (Badmington, 2003; Braidotti, 2006; Hayles, 1999). Decentring the human in social analysis is based on the recognition of the normative and analytical limits of traditional Enlightenment humanism. Normatively, critical authors such as Rosi Braidotti (2013: 68) have demonstrated how humanist values have historically underpinned categorization of some people as less than human in various ways, for instance by differentiating between 'savages' and 'developed' peoples according to a teleological understanding of 'aesthetic and moral ideals based on white, masculine, heterosexual European civilization'.

Analytically, humanist frameworks have been presented as ill-equipped to deal with the increasingly complicated relationships between humans and digital technology (Rose, 2017), or with the global climate disaster (Cielemęcka and Daigle, 2019). In this view, climate change 'mandates a recognition that what was once quaintly called "external nature" does not simply exist as our resource to plunder and that we must rapidly and dramatically accommodate our ways of life *and* problem-solving to this truth' (Brown, 2017a: 26, original emphasis). This focus on non-human objects and the environment at the expense of human agency is a deliberate move meant to question traditional assumptions about the relationship between human actors and the material world. For instance, in the context of climate change, 'posthumanism presents our over-reliance on anthropocentric justifications and on human social, political and economic institutions as primarily responsible for environmental losses' (Holden, 2020: 195).

Posthumanist approaches have been productively utilized by critical border scholars to analyse the digitalization of border controls globally while highlighting that these new digital technologies can have unintended and performative effects that have shaped human practices and perceptions of migration control (Jeandesboz, 2016; Pallister-Wilkins, 2022b; Squire, 2014; Sundberg, 2011). For instance, Philippe Frowd (2020: 10) has argued that digital technologies have directly shaped how state capacity in the Global South is perceived both locally and by IOs: 'the ability of states to enact sovereignty' is now measured in terms of 'the technological ability, willingness, and sensory capability of a state'. Similarly, Corey Robinson (2018: 421, original emphasis) has argued that digital technologies 'bring migration into being as an object of governance and perform it as a *global reality* to manage in technical and pragmatic ways'.

Although posthumanism has proven a useful framework to amend a lack of focus on materiality, it comes with the risk of over-emphasizing the agentic importance of non-humans within 'actant-networks' (Brown, 2006: 235). In seeking to rectify an earlier marginalization of materiality within social science scholarship, posthumanist literature often explicitly ignores questions of human subjectivity: 'the important topic of subjectivity thus gets short shrift so that I may focus on [. . .] the active powers issuing from nonsubjects' (Bennett, 2010: ix). Unfortunately, in the context of the 'digital revolution' and the contemporary popularity of uncritical attitudes toward digitalization, posthumanist perspectives risk reifying technicist arguments about the inevitability and neutrality of technological development. Focusing too much on the independent agency of technological devices can obscure the social perceptions, values, and political decisions that underpin the process of technological innovation. As Thomas Lemke (2018: 33) has argued in his critical analysis of Jane Bennett's (2010) posthumanist theory of the 'vitality of matter', focusing too much on non-human agency can result in a 'systematic blindness concerning the inequalities, asymmetries and hierarchies' that underpin the development of new digital technologies.

Contemporary discussions of digital technologies are replete with claims about the teleological and value-neutral nature of technological development. Private industry representatives have presented digitalization as 'an unstoppable mega trend' (Gillior, 2018) while public institutions have also argued that the 'march of technology' is 'unstoppable' (UK Government, 2024: 5). Such arguments are, ironically, compatible with the critical analytical project of posthumanism insofar as they also present humans as not entirely in control of digitalization processes. This compatibility is worrying in terms of our ability to develop normatively convincing critiques of digital crimmigration control systems. Attempts to highlight the political responsibility and accountability of the developers and users of these digital tools can be deflected through claims about the autonomy and inevitability of technological development. Autonomous border control technologies present only the starkest example of how technological innovation can obscure political responsibility: 'Tracking and untangling responsibility for any bias or trend in decision-making (is it the human or the machine determining the outcome?) will become an even more central component of litigation and public accountability' (Forster, 2022: 12). As I demonstrate in later chapters, similar accountability problems arise in the context of non-autonomous digital technologies as well, as the political and ethical decision to develop and deploy security- and crime-control oriented biometric technologies at the border has been presented by their proponents as a result of inevitable and neutral processes of technological development and modernization.

This discussion of the utility and limits of posthuman theorizing demonstrates that the agential status of humans vis-à-vis technological objects is a key normative stake in contemporary analyses of digital technology within the context of criminal justice and border control. When analysing the deployment of novel border control technologies in the Global South from the perspective of the performative effects of these technologies, the insights of posthumanism need to be tempered by an attentiveness to the specifically human capacity for moral intentionality and normative deliberation, which are the basis of humans' political responsibility. A humanist perspective that accounts for the independent and unintended effects of new technologies, while holding humans uniquely accountable for their development and deployment, can ground critiques of digital crimmigration control while guarding against popular ideological claims regarding the inevitability and neutrality of the 'digital revolution'. To this end, the philosophical tradition of pragmatism provides useful analytical tools for normatively and politically evaluating technologized border controls.

Pragmatism, political responsibility, and technological development

The central insight of pragmatism is that knowledge and truth claims can only be evaluated with reference to their practical effects. Rather than viewing the material world as external to humans and in some way objectively knowable, pragmatism instead views epistemic activities—including the application of productive knowledge through the technological innovation—as situated within systems of practice that specify 'some particular *problems* deemed worth addressing, the right *methods* of tackling those problems, and the *criteria* by which the solutions to the problems are assessed' (Chang, 2022: 14, original emphasis). In short, a 'truth claim is to be judged in light of its practical consequences' (Bohman, 2002: 499).

Unfortunately, within criminology the pragmatist position has often been misconstrued as a cynical or even relativist perspective that allows epistemic claims to be self-interestedly and uncritically used to pursue 'pragmatic' crime-control efforts to the detriment of more critical legal and philosophical reflection (Gundhus, 2021). In fact, pragmatism provides several analytical insights that are useful for analysing human–technology relationships in criminal justice contexts. This perspective is also normatively oriented towards challenging epistemic and political hierarchies that underpin processes of digitalization, by expanding the range of voices represented in epistemic activities.

In line with the framework of performativity, pragmatism asserts that 'there is no such thing as the way the thing is in itself, under no description, apart from any use to which human beings might want to put it' (Rorty, 1991: 4). This view is compatible with viewing identities as constituted through discursive and practical performances. We have seen above that the notion of performativity implies that subjects are not able to entirely determine the nature and effects of these performances independently of any structuring effects of the surrounding material and social world. Similarly, pragmatism does not claim that the external material world is not ontologically 'real', but rather that the particular meaning and value of all claims about that external world are always already framed by the human knower. Hasok Chang (2022: 71) has helpfully distinguished between ontologically relativist perspectives that view the external world as 'mind-controlled' and the more moderate pragmatist position that the external world is always 'mind-framed'.

This position is useful for analysing human–technology relations as it provides a middle ground between instrumentalist and determinist perspectives of technology. The former presents humans as entirely in control of their technological development, while the latter views human actions as entirely shaped by our material environment. The pragmatist conception of 'mind-framing' highlights that technical knowledge is always 'active knowledge', in the sense that it is always based on some practical activity and guided by the pursuit of particular social goals (Chang, 2022: 18). This aim-oriented conception of epistemic activities points to the importance of asking what kinds of perceived social problems these activities were meant to solve. The political and contingent nature of particular technological solutions is foregrounded through the recognition that '[t]o establish a truth pragmatically is to settle a controversial or complex issue for the time being, until something comes along to dislodge the comfort and reassurance that has thereby been achieved, forcing inquiry to begin again' (Cochran, 2002: 527).

In this way, pragmatism can incorporate the insights of posthumanist assemblage approaches, by viewing material objects and technological devices as both products of humans' aim-oriented epistemic activities and part of the material structures that shape later activities. Pragmatists conceptualize technology as 'the invention, development, and cognitive deployment of tools and other artifacts, brought to bear on raw materials and intermediate stock parts, with a view to the resolution of perceived problems' (Hickman, 2001: 12). These technological solutions, once adopted to solve some particular social problem, then continue to structure practices and shape social perceptions in the future. In other words, the practical success or failure of attempts to resolve social problems can later reshape our conceptions of what is normatively desirable or valuable in the first place. Eventually, technologies can become part of the 'habitualized tools, artifacts, and skills' (Hickman, 2001: 12) that shape what kinds of problems we deem worth addressing, what kinds of methods are used to address those issues, and how the success and failure of these solutions is evaluated. As new technologies recede into the mundane background of everyday practices, they increasingly shape human practices precisely because of their perceived mundanity. Technological devices that were initially controversial can become perceived as banal—as we have seen above with the case of CCTV cameras in the UK (Goold et al., 2013)—which can make it difficult to critique and challenge these systems.

Despite their similarities in terms of highlighting the independent effects of both humans and non-humans within socio-technical systems, pragmatism and assemblage theories differ in terms of their analytical and normative orientations. Assemblage approaches foreground their 'relational ontology' that dissolves distinctions between humans and material objects, and the focus of analysis is usually the relationship between these 'actants' as well as the 'emergent effects' of these networks (Dewsbury, 2011). The status of humans in such analyses is slightly ambiguous, as authors concede that humans' intentionality sets them aside from most non-human objects yet maintain that 'it would be a mistake to see this as a *fundamental* difference' (Dittmer, 2014: 389, original emphasis).

In contrast, pragmatism foregrounds the intentional, aim-oriented nature of human practices, which are mediated to varying extents by the material environment and technological objects. While accounting for the independent effects of new technologies on human actions, these tools are themselves viewed as results of prior epistemic activities and normative decisions taken by human epistemic agents. According to Chang (2022: 27):

> Epistemic agents do not simply possess beliefs and desires [. . .] They are beings also endowed with certain physical and mental capacities, who engage in purposive actions, and make genuine choices and judgements. Epistemic agents are embedded in social communities that embody and enforce certain normative standards.

In addition to social communities and norms, epistemic agents are embedded within historically contingent material environments composed of non-human objects and technologies. Productive knowledge—including new technologies in which such knowledge is embedded and through which it is enacted—consists of a system of socio-technical practices through which humans aim to solve social problems (Sullivan, 2001).

Conceptualizing human developers of new technologies as epistemic agents who are capable of normative deliberation is politically important. For instance, the European Union developed a host of digital border control systems in 2010s under the 'smart borders' initiative (Jeandesboz, 2016). These databases were initially designed for relatively clear and discrete use-cases, such as processing visa applications (VIS) and recording the biometric data of asylum seekers (EURODAC). Initially, each system was a technological response to a relatively clear perceived social problem such as visa overstaying or managing refugee registration across the union. Once these digital systems were rolled out, however, they began to shape perceptions about what are the important problems relating to border control in the EU, and how these issues should be addressed. The limited scope of each system, and the inability to exchange data between them, later became reframed as a serious problem giving rise to 'information gaps' that needed to be addressed through new technical infrastructures ensuring interoperability between these various digital databases (Leese, 2022; Tomaszycki, 2018). By 2024, the desirability of interoperability and expansive digital surveillance at the border had become a baseline assumption shaping future digitalization initiatives, despite concerns among civil society organizations and the EU Agency for Fundamental Rights (2018; Tagliapietra, 2022)

An assemblage analysis of these digital systems consists of an 'associational' inquiry in which humans are only one of many actors shaping EU border control politics. In this view, the interoperability agenda can be understood an emergent effect of socio-technical networks shaped by both humans and non-human digital databases; this perspective conceptualizes border security 'in terms of heterogeneous setups that have to be worked upon intensively in order to remain stable' (Jeandesboz, 2016: 305). As Julien Jeandesboz (2016: 306) has argued, this approach is useful for challenging uncritical views of border control technologies as a straightforward 'response' to 'insecurity'. However, the critical political potency of this analysis is undercut by the ambiguous status of human decisionmakers whose responsibility for border securitization is diffused across the many 'actants' involved in these socio-technical networks. The risk of such an analysis is that 'placing things and beings, human and non-human, within a particular relational straitjacket that does not allow for a remainder or constitutive outside. [. . .] This gesture risks precisely to off-stage the political' (Swyngedouw and Ernstson, 2018: 4).

A pragmatist conception of EU decisionmakers and technical experts as epistemic agents more positively focuses on how the current landscape of digitalized border controls in the EU is composed of technical devices created by human actors to solve perceived social problems. These human actors—including, prominently, individuals from the European Commission—have taken a series of normative and political decisions towards normalizing expansive surveillance and suspicion of migrants despite repeated criticisms and calls to do otherwise from civil society actors. Ultimately, these decisions have led to the creation of digital technologies that privilege logics of crime control and national security over more progressive political alternatives. These tools, later on, have begun structuring social perceptions of migration as a particular kind of social problem that can be 'solved' through the application of digital technology. This dynamic is exemplified by the reframing of scope limitations as 'information gaps', a term which now shapes social perceptions of border control as an issue of expansive data collection rather than political deliberation.

This example illustrates how pragmatism holds on to a 'self-critically humanist' normative orientation while recognizing the impact of non-human environments and technological devices on human practices and decision-making. As Finnish philosopher Sami Pihlström (2021: 53, original emphasis) has explained: 'Only humans can engage in the kind of *self-critical humanism* that can, for instance, seek to broaden the scope of moral responsibility' to include non-human technologies as well.[2] Holding on to this self-critical humanism is crucial for resisting the depoliticization of border control technologies through solutionist arguments about the neutrality and inevitability of technological development. It foregrounds the role of humans in making decisions about the future direction of technological innovation according to particular, contingent understandings of the kinds of social problems that are worth solving and what methods are suitable for doing so. Conceptualizing border control primarily as an issue of national security and crime control—rather than economic policy or human rights, for instance—privileges the development of particular kinds of border security technologies over alternative solutions. Although non-human material conditions and objects shape human deliberation regarding border

[2] Author's translation from Finnish.

control technologies, 'relative to other creatures, human beings are *under*-determined by nature, and the possibilities of action available to them that much greater in consequence' (Soper, 2012: 366, original emphasis).

In short, pragmatist humanism allows us to recognize posthumanist insights into the independent and structuring effects of non-human technologies upon human perceptions and practices. Nonetheless, the capacity to normatively deliberate and choose between several political alternatives remains a uniquely human activity, for which humans need to be held responsible and accountable. One helpful distinction for thinking about the differential levels of political responsibility we should attribute to humans and non-humans is between 'decisions taken *within* a structure and decisions taken *about* a structure' (Howarth, 2013: 185, original emphasis). Especially when epistemic agents are confronted by a 'problematic situation' which prompts them to begin the process of inquiry anew, humans must engage in a process of intentionally choosing what kinds of social problems to solve and which practical methods and technological tools should be used to pursue those new aims.

Contesting technological solutionism

This balance of humanism on one hand and the recognition of the symbolic and structuring effects of new technologies on the other can ground effective critiques of digital crimmigration control technologies within the Global South, while resisting the contemporary ideological dominance of the 'digital revolution' (Balbi, 2023). Contemporary discussions about digitalization have demonstrated that critiques based on claims about accuracy, efficiency, and the discriminatory effects of new surveillance tools have been ineffective against the solutionist claims of technology developers.

Proponents of digitalization dismiss these practical issues as temporary speed bumps on the road towards inevitable and desirable digitalization in the future. As prominent technology venture capitalist Marc Andreessen (2023) put it in his 'techno-optimist manifesto': 'give us a real-world problem and we can invent a technology that will solve it.' In the context of border surveillance, private technology companies now welcome serious criticisms regarding biometric recognition technologies by positioning themselves as developing newer, better digital tools that will solve those issues in the near future. For instance, in a 2023 presentation at the ID4Africa conference, Slovakian technology company Innovatrics drew attention to several serious issues that still undermine the utility and legitimacy of digital biometric identification systems, such as 'precision', 'error rates', 'bias', and 'accuracy' (Innovatrics, 2023). In the same presentation, however, the company argued that all these issues would inevitably be solved through technological innovations in the future.

Contesting the deployment of novel border control technologies on the basis of their accuracy fails to mount a deeper criticism, which would be aimed not at the precision of calculations regarding the risks posed by particular border crossers but the very calculability of such risks in the first place. As Louise Amoore (2014: 434) has argued:

> In contemporary security calculations, everything is rendered amendable to the formulation of a decision procedure [. . .] The procedures and rules are written as algorithmic code, in such a way that two things are forgotten: first, that these are problems for which it is possible that no definitive decision procedure can be arrived at; and second, that the ingenuity of the algorithm was written in large part intuitively.

In other words, the political nature of claiming calculability of the 'riskiness' of migrants is forgotten underneath the veneer of scientific objectivity attached to these technical procedures and justified with reference to the 'accuracy' of knowledge of the 'real' world. This is what Martin Heidegger (1993: 129), in his philosophical work on the nature of technology, described as a process in which 'technical mastery over things' covers over their historical and social contingency such that the latter is 'simply forgotten'.

Digital crimmigration control practices are embedded within the broader 'digital revolution' and a technicist framing of 'migration management' as a 'technical, pragmatic and, in short, nonpolitical' issue (Robinson, 2018: 431). Solutionist and technicist framings have become mainstreamed through publicly backed initiatives that conceptualize expansive digitalization as a necessary condition for promoting human rights and equality on a global level. For instance, the UN Legal Identity Agenda has presented universal digital identity as a solution to conditions in which populations across the globe are 'exposed to extreme vulnerabilities and have limited access to public goods and services as well as private services' (UNDP, 2024a). Private developers of biometric surveillance technologies have latched on to these techno-optimistic views to argue that expansive border surveillance could provide a basis for the universalization of digital ID (see, e.g., iProov, 2024; Veridos, 2021). These border surveillance technologies, however, also reify securitized conceptions of migration and contribute to the merging of border control and criminal justice, as I demonstrate in later chapters.

Of course, contesting the accuracy, reliability, and fairness of new digital surveillance and crimmigration control technologies is politically invaluable (Fussey et al., 2020). However, such criticisms risk being reappropriated by proponents of expansive surveillance practices unless they are accompanied by broader normative and political critiques regarding the desirability of crimmigration control (Lisle, 2018). Challenging new digital technologies not only on technical grounds but also on a broader political basis can illuminate how 'policymaking is considerably broader than technical decision-making, which means that policymakers often compromise on critical issues and act on public perceptions or fears' (Beduschi, 2021: 584). Humanist pragmatism offers new, productive avenues for critiquing crimmigration control practices in two ways. First, it can sidestep tricky ontological debates about the agentic status of human and non-human 'actants' by focusing instead on the practical impacts of new technical systems in reshaping the boundaries of criminal justice and border control. Second, by focusing on the normative nature of humans' decisions to develop new digital technologies, humanist pragmatism foregrounds human accountability and responsibility for those practical effects. In so doing, this framework is normatively oriented towards expanding the boundaries of technical decision-making beyond the narrow epistemic communities of technical experts, to include a wider range of voices in the process of determining what kinds of social problems new tools should aim to solve.

Technical expertise, global hierarchy, and Southernizing criminology

Synthesizing performativity and pragmatism can help us remain attentive to the symbolic and practical effects of new technologies, while pointing to moments of normative deliberation, decision-making, and technological innovation by humans as key drivers of the expansion of digital crimmigration control in the Global South. Retaining this humanist orientation is useful for highlighting the contingency and contestability of technological developments. Resisting claims about certainty and epistemological closure was central to the work of the early American pragmatists such including John Dewey, who argued that productive knowledge and technology are 'what results from doing, from identifying problems of everyday experience which require resolution and intervening to determine the relationships of their occurrence in an effort to regulate them in ways fitting with the purposes of a community' (Cochran, 2002: 530).

The view that productive knowledge is always aim-oriented and shaped by perceived social problems is democratically oriented in that it implies the need to develop technological solutions based on the needs and views of communities themselves. Technical expertise, in this view, should not be the exclusive purview of a small group of highly educated, epistemically privileged individuals who tell the masses what kinds of technological developments are desirable and inevitable. Instead, pragmatism suggests:

> All affected parties [should] be heard from not only during the planning stages of significant public projects, but during the stages of their implementation as well [. . .] The role of the 'expert' within productive pragmatism is thus to draw on the energies and sources of information within affected publics and to formulate scenarios for action, but not to exercise ultimate decisions regarding the determination and execution of public policy. (Hickman, 2001: 61)

This understanding of the proper role of technical expertise can provide a normative basis for contemporary calls to democratize criminological research. As Joan McDermott (2002: 287) has demonstrated, pragmatism aligns with the progressive critical and feminist agendas in criminology thanks to its 'future-orientation in scholarship, the goal of liberation, a critique of dominant epistemology and methods, and an emphasis on social responsibility and the integration of theory and practice'. These foundations can be productively harnessed to pursue the closely related projects of decolonizing and Southernizing criminology, which constitute a key normative goal of this book.

Criminologists have recently argued that decolonizing the field requires shifting 'the criminological gaze away from the North, while also intending to utilize the lessons gained from such a perspectival shift to comprehensively challenge the foundations of this field of knowledge' (Aliverti et al., 2021: 299). Examining the performative nature of digital crimmigration control practices—by both Northern and Southern actors—can highlight how relations of global hierarchy are both continually reified and challenged through performances of particular kinds of subjectivities. Performances of digital crimmigration control are shaped by epistemic, economic, and political hierarchies embedded in the scripts and global norms of border control. As I demonstrate in later chapters, Southern state agencies exercised their agency by utilizing MIDAS to perform a particular kind of statehood to both domestic and international audiences according to global technical and political norms.

In turn, pragmatism problematizes arguments about digital crimmigration control tools as a neutral, desirable form of technological modernization by focusing on technological innovation as an aim-oriented activity carried out by epistemic agents in an attempt to solve particular kinds of perceived social problems. In Chapter 7, I examine what kinds of political rationales and technological assumptions underpinned the IOM's development of MIDAS. The crime-control and security-oriented logics of this system are contingent and contestable, yet they will become more difficult to challenge and increasingly influential in expanding crimmigration control as they continue to recede into the mundane background of everyday practice.

In short, performativity and pragmatism highlight how debates regarding the production of criminological knowledge are 'onto-political' in nature, in the sense that different theoretical 'accounts of specific situations arrive at their conclusions by injecting ontological presumptions into their claims of actuality without disclosing their complicity in the representational process' (Campbell, 2005: 128). Making evident this onto-political dimension of contemporary criminological debates, through the deployment of an analytical framework that centres on an openness to alternative worldviews, can directly contribute to the goals of decolonizing and democratizing criminology. This framework therefore provides a way to 'labor at the interface by incorporating a range of theoretical perspectives' when analysing the digitalization of crimmigration control (Weber and McCulloch, 2019: 508).

This wider range of theoretical and political perspectives must include experiences and voices from the Global South as well. Otherwise, criminological analyses of crimmigration control risk reproducing the kinds of technicist, non-democratic arguments that are reflected in contemporary debates about climate change and potential technological solutions to this issue. Recently, techno-solutionists of various political orientations have argued that climate change does not, in fact, represent an 'existential risk' to humanity. Accordingly, radical changes to our patterns of production and consumption should not take precedence over further technological innovation that might potentially 'solve' climate change in the near future (for a critical discussion, see McLaughlin, 2024). However, proponents of such views understand 'humanity' in quite limited terms. William MacAskill (2022: 136), for instance, has argued that climate change is not an existential risk because 'richer countries would be able to adapt, and temperate regions would emerge relatively unscathed', although billions of people in the Global South would face life-threatening conditions and see their agricultural livelihoods destroyed (Torres, 2024).

Just as debates regarding the negative social impacts of climate change must take into account the experiences of different populations globally—not just across Global North countries—so too should the digitalization and expansion of digital crimmigration control measures be analysed in terms of the experiences of states and populations in the Global South as well. By inquiring into the social structures within which states performatively deploy systems such as MIDAS, and foregrounding the role of technical expert organizations such as the IOM in developing these digital systems to solve particular social problems, the framework developed in this chapter provides theoretical tools for contributing to the democratization and decolonization of border criminology. These projects are a crucial part of criminology's broader pursuit of epistemic justice.

Conclusion

The analysis above has demonstrated the potential utility of the framework of performativity and the tradition of pragmatism for analysing contemporary technologized bordering practices in the Global South. This framework provides analytical tools to address the epistemic and analytical issues raised in the previous chapter. Focusing on the performative nature of MIDAS allows us to move beyond methodological nationalism by problematizing statehood as a set of performative practices aimed at enacting 'biometric statehood' to domestic and international audiences. Simultaneously, the IOM has deployed MIDAS to performatively enact its own technical expertise and present its capacity-building practices as politically neutral efforts to uphold 'global standards' relating to digital border control. Critically analysing these performances brings into view the interplay between the agency of Nigerian federal authorities and the IOM on one hand, and on the other hand the postcolonial global hierarchies that structured the performative deployment of MIDAS.

In addition to these performances by human actors, a focus on border control technologies can highlight 'transversal connections among material and symbolic, concrete and discursive entities or forces, which include non-human[s]' (Braidotti, 2013: 159). This insight calls for an examination of the performative impact of the technical tools associated with MIDAS, as well as the structuring effects of material environments on the roll-out of the system in Nigeria. Again, however, the 'agency' of these technologies can never fully determine human behaviour, therefore demanding a critical analysis of the 'co-production of science, technology and social order' (Martins and Jumbert, 2022: 14; Jasanoff, 2004b). Synthesizing performativity and pragmatism can provide a middle way between frameworks that overlook the importance of material objects in shaping crimmigration control practices and those that struggle to relocate political accountability when ontologically flattening all distinctions between humans and non-humans. Instead of dissolving these ontological distinctions entirely, pragmatism guards against depoliticization by highlighting the specifically human capacity for normative and political deliberation about the social world. As Pihlström (2021: 160) has argued: 'We cannot rid ourselves of normative questions in the context of technology, any more than we can do so in any field of cultural experience.'[3] Although non-human technologies shape social practices and can enact performative effects originally unintended by their human designers and operators, these effects only have normative and political significance for people, those 'reflexive and intentional agents who can create meaning' (Brinkmann, 2017: 127).

[3] Author's translation from Finnish.

4
From Unease to Critique: Pragmatism as a Research Paradigm

> *We have been taught to tidy our texts, not to reveal the struggle we have in getting somewhere.*
>
> —Sara Ahmed (2017: 13).

> *There is a familiar tale of a peasant who is stopped by a traveler in a large car and asked the way to the capital. 'Well,' she replies, after pondering the matter a while, 'if I were you, I wouldn't start from here.'*
>
> —Kwame Anthony Appiah (1992: 26).

Avoiding methodological lies

Pragmatism is useful for critically analysing the production of expert knowledge in the field of digital crimmigration control, and theorizing the political effects of novel technologies. Yet this philosophical framework also has implications for reflecting critically on the process of producing critical academic knowledge about these practices and digital tools. In this chapter, I outline these implications by reflexively conceptualizing pragmatism as a broader research paradigm within which this book is situated. Because pragmatism views truth and knowledge as the temporary and contingent product of epistemic activities carried out by human knowers—who interact with the material world in an attempt to solve particular social problems—this framework produces a methodological and political commitment to broadening the scope of voices that should be heard in the process of knowledge production. As Richard Rorty (2021) put it, pragmatism can, in this sense, be viewed as fundamentally

Outsourcing Crimmigration Control. Samuel Singler, Oxford University Press. © Samuel Singler 2025.
DOI: 10.1093/9780198927525.003.0004

'anti-authoritarian' in that it resists any claims to privileged knowledge positions that should be viewed as universally more valid than others. Pragmatism also reminds academic researchers of the inherent limitations of their claims to knowledge, promoting a stance of humility and openness as the basis for intellectual curiosity which drives us to research socially and politically contested topics such as criminal justice and border control.

Methodological discussions often begin by identifying a relatively clear research problem or question to be investigated, then situate the research in one of two broad methodological camps—quantitative or qualitative—before identifying the most appropriate (or most feasible) methods for answering the research question (see, e.g., Fabini, 2019; Franck and Vigneswaran, 2021; Franko, 2021; Martin-Mazé and Perret, 2021; Parmar, 2019; Stambøl, 2021). In criminology and social science more broadly, such discussions are useful in demonstrating the problem-oriented, rather than method-driven, attitude of researchers seeking the best tools for making sense of complex social issues. The 'appropriateness' and 'congruence' between method and research question are, rightly, presented as key determinants of methodological choice (Fossey et al., 2002: 724; Maxfield and Babbie, 2015: 17).

However, as Mary Bosworth and Carolyn Hoyle (2011: 5) have argued, this seemingly neat and linear relationship between research question, hypotheses, methods, and results has meant that 'criminologists rarely explicitly address the assumptions underpinning their favored research techniques'. The construction of a methodological narrative in which researchers begin with a clearly formed research question, which logically entails the deployment of a specific method to uncover data in predictable fashion, also risks contributing to a 'methodological lie': the *post hoc* presentation of the research process as an unproblematic and successful endeavour, and of the findings as logically and predictably following from the original identification of a research question (Bosworth and Hoyle, 2011: 5). A similar phenomenon was described by pragmatist John Dewey nearly a century ago (1929: 29) as 'the philosophic fallacy', in which 'an inquirer analyzes a complex situation into its constituent parts for the sake of resolving some perceived difficulty, but then insists that the parts secured by the means of inquiry were present all the while—*prior* to inquiry and in some absolute sense' (Hickman, 2001: 84–85, original emphasis). As Sara Ahmed (2017: 13) has highlighted, academics are often taught to 'tidy their texts' in order to demonstrate their expertise.

In academic research, this methodological lie relates to what postcolonial theorist Julietta Singh (2018) terms the pursuit of 'mastery' by researchers over their research subjects. By presenting the researcher as largely in control of a linear and predictable research process that uncovers unambiguous new knowledge, the methodological lie perpetuates a hierarchy between the authoritative researcher and their passive research subjects. In qualitative research, this hierarchy is established through a 'balancing act' between the researcher's position as both 'insider' and 'outsider' (Lie, 2013: 210). Social scientists often deploy Max Weber's notion of *verstehen* to describe 'an ideal of deep understanding' (Aitken, 2019: 108) that reflects an intimate knowledge of the research field. Despite this intimacy, the researcher's understanding is distinguished from those of other social actors. The former is able to occupy a position 'in the hinterland between objective reality and subjective lifeworlds. Here, we can see not only how things are but what they mean and why they matter' (Aitken, 2019: 108). This ability to move between objective reality and subjective views is not usually afforded to others in the field, establishing the researcher's authoritative position relative to the participants.

Highlighting the risk of slipping from methodological discussions to the implicit pursuit of mastery does not mean that there is not, or should not be, anything distinct about academic research relative to more everyday forms of knowledge creation. Criminologists experience specific pressures to establish their epistemological authority owing to the intensely contested and political nature of their research topics. In this context, it is understandable and indeed necessary for criminologists to explain 'how they know what they claim to know, and why their claims to expertise are to be trusted more than those advanced by journalists, politicians or members of the public' (Gadd et al., 2012: 1).

In this chapter, I too seek to explain how I know what I claim to know. My aim is to do so while remaining wary of the pursuit of mastery, instead advocating what Enrike van Wingerden (2022) has called 'unmastering research'. In other words, I avoid claims to authoritative expertise by contextualizing the knowledge claims put forth in this book and highlighting the unpredictability and subjectivity of the research process. This does not mean repudiating all claims to knowledge or methodological rigour whatsoever. Rather, my aim is to be transparent about the research process and my role in it, while simultaneously arguing that my research findings are rigorous, legitimate, and warranted based on the empirical evidence I have collected and analysed. As van Wingerden (2022: 5) has argued, 'acknowledging that we know what we know because of dynamic social and material relations that enable some paths of inquiry while foreclosing others is less an assault on truth than a reckoning with the empirical realities of truth-creation'. Recognizing that mastery over our research topics is impossible is akin to acknowledging that, in the short tale recounted by Kwame Anthony Appiah (1992: 26) in the epigraph to this chapter, the peasant's response to the traveller is absurd; we cannot *not* 'start from here', as we are always already shaped by our pre-existing beliefs regarding our research topics and practices, as well as our place in the world.

My view of knowledge as the product of a dynamic interplay between pre-existing beliefs and empirical realities is rooted in the philosophical tradition of pragmatism (Bohman, 2002; Kaushik and Walsh, 2019; Pihlström, 2021). As I outlined in the previous chapter, in this view 'truth' is only ever provisional. Knowledge consists of 'beliefs that have been established in inquiry and are presently not in question', which help us practically make sense of and navigate the world around us (Bacon, 2012: 20). In other words, to 'establish a truth pragmatically is to settle a controversial or complex issue for the time being, until something comes along to dislodge the comfort and reassurance that has thereby been achieved, forcing inquiry to begin again' (Cochran, 2002: 527). Rather than basing epistemological claims upon prior assumptions about the fundamental nature of reality, pragmatism instead asks what difference these new claims make to our social practices, that is, what contribution they can make to solving or better understanding particular social problems (Bacon, 2012: 53).

This philosophical basis affected the analysis of digital crimmigration control technologies in later chapters, and informed the research process itself. Pragmatism cannot be used to understand the development and deployment of new surveillance technologies as contingent, political epistemic activities while simultaneously claiming that the process of academic research somehow allows us to uncover the underlying objective realities of social practices. The production of knowledge through academic research is not 'about an abstract relationship between the knower and the known; there is an active process of inquiry that creates a continual back-and-forth movement between beliefs and actions' (Morgan, 2013: 1049). The goal of social inquiry understood in pragmatist terms is not 'truth' or 'knowledge' in some absolute sense, but rather what Dewey (1938: 9) termed 'warranted assertability'. Assertions are warranted if they are in accordance with empirical evidence and produce useful practical consequences. These assertions may later be called into question by changes in the empirical environment or in our worldviews, but until that time they can be held as 'truthful' to the extent that they are useful for our attempts to make sense of and solve a given social problem.

One key implication of this perspective is that—just like expert knowledge regarding digital surveillance technologies or any other field of epistemic activities—academic inquiry also aims at producing a kind of expert knowledge whose merits will be determined by the social and practical implications of that research. In other words, the products of academic research cannot and should not be abstracted from the attempt to better understand and solve whatever pressing social problems have motivated the research in the first place. This research was motivated by a feeling of unease regarding the contested politics of unequal mobility, racialized exclusion, and global hierarchy that underpin the development of new digital border control tools. In addition to producing traditional academic outputs such as articles and this book—which I hope will inform future critical research practices—I have been actively engaged in shaping policy discussions and civil society action through extra-academic forms of knowledge exchange and collaboration. Such activities were motivated by the pragmatist perspective, which views all forms of knowledge as unavoidably social and political.

In this chapter I present pragmatism as a broader 'research paradigm' within which this book is situated (Kaushik and Walsh, 2019; Morgan, 2013). Best known from Thomas Kuhn's (2012) pioneering work on the history of science, according to Kaushik and Walsh (2019: 1) the term 'paradigm' refers to the 'basic set of beliefs that guide the actions and define the worldview of the researcher. [. . .] Paradigms are conceptual and practical "tools" that are used to solve specific research problems; in other words, paradigms function as heuristics in social research.' Below, I demonstrate the benefits of pragmatism as a research paradigm, arguing that it is useful for avoiding uncritical statements on researcher reflexivity, which risk implicitly reifying both the pursuit of mastery over our research topics as well as the privileges and hierarchies that this research seeks to critique.

I begin the chapter by giving an account of the emotions and beliefs that motivated me to undertake this research. While the theoretical, methodological, and empirical dimensions of this book changed over the course of the research project, my motivations for conducting the project remained stable. This account of my motivations leads to a discussion of the role of pre-existing beliefs in knowledge production more generally, which allows me to unpack the pragmatist conception of academic research. I then utilize this pragmatist orientation to critically discuss what have now become common statements about the nature of qualitative inference, the 'positionality' of researchers in the field, and the importance of reflexivity in criminological research (see, e.g., Chan, 2000; Loader and Sparks, 2010; Lumsden and Goode, 2018; Lumsden and Winter, 2014). The final section describes the practicalities of the research process, including its unpredictability, obstacles to access, and the role of luck in facilitating the research. Highlighting the contingent and unpredictable nature of the academic research process provides a way to nuance the claims made in the remainder of the book by advocating reflexivity and centring intellectual humility, while aiming to produce socially and politically useful critical knowledge on digital crimmigration control technologies.

Starting 'from here': Unease and the politics of mobility

A welcome social development in many Global North countries in recent decades has been the critical public reckoning with past and present structural inequalities, forcing many to reflect on their positions of privilege based on their race, gender, class, and citizenship (Friedman, 2020; Gani and Khan, 2024; Hirsch, 2018; Kendall, 2021; Shukla, 2016). Having moved to the United Kingdom from Finland to attend university in 2014, I quickly became aware of how privileged my experience of migration had been compared to many others with whom I interacted in London. In that context, I experienced strong feelings of unease regarding the effortlessness of my move to the UK.

Like so many others across the globe, I had viewed migrating to another country as an opportunity to receive a world-class education and eventually to look for employment as well. For me, the main obstacles to moving to the UK were financial: how much would I need to work alongside my studies to afford to live in London? Would I be eligible for a student loan to cover tuition fees? Did it make sense financially and career-wise to pay for university education abroad? Once I decided to move to London, however, I did not spend much time worrying about how exactly I could make it across the English Channel, or whether I would be pulled aside by the UK Border Force at the airport. I did not even need to obtain a visa, thanks to the UK's membership in the European Union at that time. I did not interact with a single British immigration or border official at the airport. I simply walked through an automated biometric passport gate, which felt like a convenient and efficient tool that facilitated cross-border mobility.

Such convenience is not how migration is experienced by millions of people across the globe. Financial considerations relating to student loan eligibility are a moot point for those risking their lives on the perilous journey across the Mediterranean or the English Channel (United Nations, 2021). Given my interest in technology—particularly digital surveillance technologies—I was struck by the contrast between my experiences of digital border control tools and the experiences of those whom these tools are aimed at 'deterring' and stopping (Ahmed and Tondo, 2021). Why did the colour of my passport and skin determine whether a biometric passport control gate appeared as a convenient tool or as an insurmountable obstacle (Buolamwini and Gebru, 2018)? I felt a strong sense of unease not only at the privilege evident in my experiences of border control, but also at how new border control technologies were discussed in a policy context mainly in terms of facilitation, convenience, reliability, and 'progress' (European Commission, 2022; IOM, 2018a). Where exactly did the politics of unequal global mobility figure amid this optimistic tech talk?

Drawing on feminist-pragmatist theories of critical social analysis, I use the term 'unease' to describe my emotional response to these issues, to capture the negative yet indeterminate character of this feeling (Wille, 2020). Feelings such as 'anger' or 'disgust' would suggest a much clearer normative orientation to the problems at hand, yet I have not always been able to move from unease regarding the politics of unequal mobility to a clear plan of action or political stance on borders more broadly. According to Katrin Wille (2020: 2), unease can act as a useful catalyst for more sustained critical analysis of oppressive, unfair, or uncomfortable situations; the sentiment of unease is 'an unstable, hesitating evaluation' arising from a negative response to 'habitualized power asymmetries that attack the epistemic authority of some'. Ultimately, engaging with and cultivating a sense of unease towards exclusionary and hierarchical relationships can motivate individuals and groups to critique, call attention to, and seek to dismantle such social structures.

In his book on the securitization of migration and asylum in Europe, Jef Huysmans (2006: xi) recounts how his emotional response to a language of securitization motivated his research, even though it was not initially clear what political or ethical orientation this emotional response should engender: 'there was something awkward about analyzing migration issues through a security lens, irrespective of whether the intention was to support the idea that migration was a real threat or to argue that the fear of migration rested on a misperception.' So too, I felt—and continue to feel—that there is 'something awkward' about how border control technologies are deployed in the context of global inequalities. Nonetheless, I have often found it difficult to formulate a clear plan of action in response to this feeling of unease. Should we do away with borders entirely? Are all attempts to facilitate cross-border mobility for some, while increasing scrutiny for others, irredeemably unjust or racist?

I suspect some academics and activists will criticize the indeterminacy of my emotional response to questions relating to border control. Indeed, while carrying out this research and writing this book, I have already faced critical questions from other academics regarding what they view as a lack of criticism in my orientation toward the International Organization for Migration (IOM). In response to such criticism, I contend that a feeling of unease, understood as a negative but politically indeterminate emotion, should not be discounted as a motivation for action. As I outline in more detail below, expressing unease rather than outright hostility in my interactions with IOM officials has, in my view, paved the way for productive critical engagement with the organization by allowing me to influence their assessments of the limitations and challenges relating to a system such as the Migration Information and Data Analysis System (MIDAS). In this way, unease can productively guide researchers seeking to balancing criticality on one hand with research access and policy influence on the other hand (Bosworth et al., 2018a; Kalir et al., 2019).

Eric Van Rythoven (2021) has demonstrated how unease, once it begins to take hold in public discourse relating to a particular social issue, can bring about political change by forcing decision-makers to distance themselves from discourses that generate a broadly negative, if vague, emotional response among the general public. Van Rythoven (2021: 263) has argued that 'unease matters' because it can highlight 'starkly asymmetrical power relations' as well as continuities between current social problems and historical practices that have already been condemned as unjust. Unease may not always bring about an instant termination of questionable political practices, nor immediately lead to the recognition of a clear plan for future action, but it can motivate us to engage in social inquiry to uncover what precisely is causing this emotional response, and what might be politically practicable strategies for addressing those causes.

Although my prior assumptions about border control have been repeatedly challenged by my empirical findings, as I outline below, being transparent about the motivations for this research is intellectually honest and crucial for 'unmastering research' (van Wingerden, 2022). Pre-existing beliefs are also a key component within the pragmatist research paradigm within which I situate this research. In this view, inquiry begins when prior beliefs are challenged by a problematic situation. Such challenges can manifest as cognitive dissonance and give rise to an emotional response: 'Emotions and preferences operate throughout the inquiry process, starting most notably with a *feeling* that something is problematic in a situation' (Morgan, 2013: 1048, original emphasis).

Pragmatist inquiry, retroduction, and knowledge production

While social scientists occasionally refer to 'pragmatic sensibilities' in their methodological discussions (Seale et al., 2004: 5), pragmatism is rarely discussed as an overarching research paradigm. Johannes Wheeldon (2015: 399) has argued that the term 'pragmatic' is commonly used by criminologists as a 'criminological slur', particularly when criticizing scholarship that focuses on the practicalities of criminal justice and crime control rather than theoretical or normative considerations. These negative connotations are not new. More than a century ago, pragmatist Charles Sanders Peirce (1998: 335; Bacon, 2012: 43) so detested the colloquial usage of the term 'pragmatic' that he sought to distance himself from it by renaming his position 'pragmaticism', a name 'ugly enough to be safe from kidnappers'.

Notwithstanding the scepticism of a pragmatic orientation toward criminological research, a problem-oriented and practical attitude—what Gadd, Karstedt, and Messner (2012: 6) term a 'pragmatic but not prescriptive' approach—remains prevalent among criminological researchers seeking the best methodological tools for making sense of their research topics. Situating this research within a pragmatist research paradigm is not so much a thoroughly innovative methodological 'first' (Liboiron, 2021) as it is an attempt to 'explicitly address the assumptions' (Bosworth and Hoyle, 2011: 5) already underpinning much criminological scholarship.

Now, what can the explicit designation of pragmatism as a research paradigm contribute to methodological discussions in the field of border criminology, and how does this paradigm relate to dominant alternatives? A core tenet of pragmatism is the view of knowledge as a dynamic relationship between pre-existing beliefs and practical actions or experiences. In this view, knowledge is not the product of the researcher dispassionately examining empirical data in order to generate descriptions that more or less accurately 'mirror' or 'reflect' objective reality (Rorty, 2017). Rather, all knowledge claims are specific to a particular problematic context, and their 'truthfulness' depends on their practical consequences in terms of solving or alleviating those specific problems (Pihlström, 2021: 151–152). What appears as a problem to one community of researchers may appear meaningless or unimportant to another. The point of creating new knowledge is not to obtain a more 'accurate picture representation' of reality, but 'to deal with felt problems and difficulties' (Hickman, 2001: 27–28).

In contrast to dominant forms of inference in the social sciences, which can be described as deductive or inductive reasoning, this approach to research can be characterized as 'retroductive' (Giese and Schnapp, 2021). While deduction begins with a hypothesis that is tested against empirical data, and induction aims to create generalizations based on systematic observations, retroduction seeks to create new interpretations of social problems by moving back and forth between existing explanations and observations of individual cases (Giese and Schnapp, 2021: 78). Retroductive reasoning seeks, according to Christian Beighton (2019),

> to find new factors to a well-known problem. Often, this means redefining and reconceptualizing the problem itself by assembling or discovering, based on an interpretation of collected data, combinations of features for which there is no appropriate explanation or rule.

The distinctiveness of this view from a positivist understanding of scientific knowledge as accurately mirroring objective reality is clear, but its relation to constructivist views on the socially constructed nature of knowledge is more complex. Criminologists have long recognized that the complexity and dynamic nature of the social world undermines attempts to uncover timeless, law-like regularities in offending and crime control practices. In short, 'crime is socially constructed, politically influenced and historically variable' (Newburn, 2017: 120). Nonetheless, the pragmatist conception of the socially constructed nature of knowledge is distinct from the dominant constructivist view in at least two key aspects.

First, for constructivists, the contextual nature of knowledge claims is dependent on the social meanings and self-interpretations of actors, which can be abstracted from a particular practical context (Carrier, 2011). For pragmatists, in contrast, the meaning of knowledge claims depends on the consequences of a given interpretation in terms of solving a particular practical problem: 'pragmatists' choice of one version of reality over another is governed by how well that choice results in anticipated or desired outcomes' (Kaushik and Walsh, 2019: 3). Although such problem-solving is an everyday occurrence, academic research is nonetheless set apart from quotidian practices as 'a process of inquiry that is performed more carefully and more self-consciously than most other responses to problematic situations' (Morgan, 2013: 1047).

Second, constructivist perspectives privilege the social dimensions of knowledge and avoid a focus on material or 'external' reality: 'the *appearance of substance* is just that, a constructed identity, a performative accomplishment which the mundane social audience, including the actors themselves, come to believe and to perform in the mode of belief' (Butler, 2007: 192, original emphasis). In contrast to focusing solely on the 'construction of social problems' (Goode and Ben-Yehuda, 2009), pragmatist perspectives hold onto the notion of an empirically knowable external world as one criterion for evaluating truth claims. Whereas critical criminologists have stressed the 'inter-subjective' nature of knowledge about crimes and harms (Yar, 2012: 59), in the pragmatist view these intersubjective understandings must be evaluated with reference to the external world in order to establish warranted assertions. Neither material reality nor social construction are accorded a privileged position as ultimate arbiters of truth. According to Donald Davidson's (2001) formulation, knowledge is the product of a tripartite relationship between knowledge of ourselves, knowledge of the material world around us, and knowledge of other people and what they think. In this view, as Michael Bacon (2012: 87) has explained:

> The three varieties of knowledge are interrelated, and none can be had without the other two [. . .] we can only attribute thoughts to others if we know our own thoughts, because that attribution is a matter of matching their behavior with our own. And both require a third element, namely knowledge of our shared environment.

This view of knowledge embraces neither an uncritical positivist view on 'external reality', nor a constructivist focus on intersubjectivity that obscures the causal impact of the material world around us. Instead, it provides standards for evaluating competing truth claims without basing these standards on a supposedly authoritative 'view from nowhere' (Haraway, 1988). Situating my research within the pragmatist research paradigm has the practical benefit of allowing me to critically analyse both the intersubjective and material political stakes of digital crimmigration control technologies. Beyond this book, the pragmatist research paradigm can also provide epistemic and methodological foundations for two pressing practical disciplinary problems: democratizing and decolonizing border criminology.

'Unmastering research': Democratization, decolonization, and positionality

In the context of the increasingly global nature of several criminologically relevant social problems, Katja Franko (Franko Aas, 2012b: 16) has argued that 'developing more democratic epistemologies is not only a question of epistemological justice, but increasingly also an analytical imperative and an opportunity for theoretical innovation'. Pragmatist authors such as Molly Cochran (2002: 526) have similarly noted how a key problem for academic knowledge production in a global age—and in the context of continuing postcolonial hierarchies—is 'how to maintain the objectivity of inquiry while exercising ethical judgement and without effectively imposing one particular set of cultural values upon others'.

I have outlined above how pragmatism eschews claims to an authoritative and value-neutral 'view from nowhere'. This perspective is inherently democratic due to its view on the problem-oriented contextuality of knowledge claims. Feminist pragmatists such as Shannon Sullivan (2001: 5) have been particularly insightful in highlighting how pragmatism naturally promotes more 'pluralistic' forms of knowledge production. Cochran (2002: 542) has similarly argued that, if knowledge is understood as the attempt to solve particular social problems, it follows that these attempts are likely to be misguided unless the views of all social actors involved in these practices are properly understood and considered.

Whereas constructivist and 'postmodern' approaches struggle to establish new grounds for deliberating between competing cultural perspectives after deconstructing traditional universalist views (Beirne, 1983; Carrier, 2011), the pragmatist focus on resolving social problems sidesteps ontological debates about relativism. In short, although there are no universally privileged perspectives on knowledge as such, there are perspectives which are better than others at addressing particular social problems—once we have agreed on which problems are worth solving and to what end—and that more closely correspond to individual beliefs and experiences (Morgan, 2013: 1050). The goal of inquiry is not to uncover universal causal laws, but rather to identify and engage the community to whom a particular social problem is relevant.

The democratic credentials of pragmatism also provide foundations for decolonizing the field of border criminology (Aliverti et al., 2021). In contemporary border criminology scholarship, expanding the community of inquirers means identifying and incorporating knowledge claims made outside of the Global North, as well as those which do not necessarily meet traditional Eurocentric and scientistic criteria of epistemic soundness. Challenging the epistemological bases of Northern-produced knowledge claims is a key dimension of decolonization (Tuck and Yang, 2012). Not only is pragmatism fundamentally committed to a thoroughgoing critique of epistemic essentialism—as reflected in Richard Rorty's (2021) characterization of the approach as 'anti-authoritarian'—but it also foregrounds the use of eclectic methodological tools to address particular social issues. In practice, this means engaging directly with marginalized and colonized populations, such as Southern actors and indigenous peoples, when constructing claims about decolonial forms of knowledge production (Tucker, 2018). Feminist pragmatist Amrita Banerjee (2012: 83–84), in her discussion of decolonization, characterizes the goal of such research practices as 'interactive plurality', which highlights the 'politics of location' by focusing on the 'agency and action' of Southern populations. Foregrounding Southern agency is the focus of Chapter 6 of this book.

A key theme in discussions about decolonizing criminology has been the recognition of 'the importance of identity and positionality of criminologists for shaping methodologies and findings (in terms of their classed, gendered and racialized identities)' (Aliverti et al., 2021: 300). The notion of positionality in this context highlights the roles that the researcher's 'age, class, ethnicity, gender, language, marital status, nationality, parental status, profession, and religious beliefs play throughout the research process' (Bilgen et al., 2021: 523). In criminology, statements about positionality are seen as crucial acknowledgements of the socially situated and value-laden nature of criminological research.

Discussions about positionality are, of course, a welcome rectification to social science scholarship that overlooked the role of the researcher entirely. However, critical authors have recently argued that the commonality of positionality statements now risks lapsing into a box-ticking exercise, through which researchers implicitly reaffirm their authoritative status precisely by claiming to dispassionately observe the power relations that underpin their knowledge claims. As Van Wingerden (2022: 4) has explained:

> The crux is that the self-awareness inherent in positionality claims implies that it is possible to consciously survey power relations—almost as if from a distance—and situate yourself in them. [. . .] Self-critical and self-conscious positioning is less an uncovering of power relations than a construction and objectification of the self in relation to others.

In other words, the concept of positionality is at risk of becoming related more to what Seale and colleagues (2004: 7) have termed the 'political role of methodology' rather than the 'procedural one'. The former dimension describes how methodological discussions serve to establish the researcher's expertise and authority, whereas the latter relates to how methodological considerations shape research in practice.

Jasmine Gani and Rabea Khan (2024: 8) have levelled serious criticisms against reflexivity statements that are purely performative, and which end up—either unwittingly or intentionally—reifying privilege through a 'cathartic recentering of the (white) researcher'. Such critiques of redemptive positionality statements present serious challenges to a white, male, Global North-based researcher (such as myself) seeking to critically analyse digital crimmigration control technologies from a postcolonial perspective. Gani and Khan acknowledge that there is no straightforward, easy solution to the uneasy relationship between positionality statements and the reification of postcolonial power relations. They advocate 'reflection, a centering of humility, and resistance to the temptation of performance; followed by action in the form of material and intellectual reparations' (Gani and Khan, 2024: 11).

My account of how feelings of unease motivated this research was inspired by critical feminist authors' calls to be reflexive throughout the research process, while acknowledging that doing so 'is uncomfortable—or it should be' (Enloe, 2016: 258). Below, I highlight how the research process took unexpected turns, how my expectations regarding potential findings have been upended by my observations in the field, and how my position as an authoritative researcher has been thoroughly challenged through professional and personal interactions with my interlocutors at the IOM and the Nigeria Immigration Service (NIS). My stance of unease towards the IOM's practices allowed me to engage with the organization's officials critically but productively; alongside my fieldwork, I was asked to author an independent report of the IOM's roll-out of MIDAS in Nigeria. The report evaluated the system's limitations and challenges from legal, operational, and technical perspectives, and has informed the IOM's deployment of MIDAS in other countries later on. The research process also formed the basis for engagement with civil society actors' attempts to produce fairer, more limited, and rights-oriented digital border controls and humanitarian practices (Singler, 2024b; Tsui et al., 2023). In my academic work, I have actively sought out opportunities to collaborate with Nigerian academics in order to directly engage with and promote local expert knowledge (Oxford Law Faculty, 2023; Singler and Babalola, 2024).

Although the reflexive discussion in this chapter has unavoidably adopted the first-person singular 'I' to explain how my subjectivity has shaped the research process, my intention has not been to place myself at the centre of the research findings, but rather to explicitly position this research as normatively oriented towards the critique and dismantling of continued postcolonial racial and class hierarchies. This chapter was inspired by Gani and Khan's (2024) call for reflection and humility. Although 'material and intellectual reparations' are a matter of continued practice and hard work, rather than a one-off achievement, my hope is that my actions thus far demonstrate my commitment to the projects of decolonization and democratization both within the field of academic research and beyond.

This reflexive and practical approach to dealing with the complicated problem of positionality is again based on the broader ontological and epistemological assumptions of pragmatism. This perspective does not view the acknowledgement of positionality as a matter of 'trading a detached, distant, and hierarchical stance for an intimate, close, and equitable position' (Israel and Hay, 2012; Preissle and Han, 2012: 599). Rather, there is no such thing as a 'detached' perspective from which to observe the nature of 'cultural constructs [. . .] once and for all' (Sullivan, 2001: 36). Knowledge is always necessarily social and specific to a particular perceived social problem. Given the retroductive orientation of pragmatist inquiry, prior beliefs can be called into question in unpredictable ways by empirical circumstances, forcing the researcher to re-evaluate the theoretical, empirical, and methodological dimensions of their project during the research. In short, a pragmatist perspective avoids uncritical positionality statements not by seeking to excise uncertainty and unpredictability from the research process, but rather embracing them as key components of academic inquiry. My account of how my feeling of unease motivated and informed my research is not followed by a discussion of the steps taken to mitigate my role in the research. Rather, in this chapter I advocate 'unmastering research' in the sense of foregrounding 'the dynamic and often unpredictable interactions and relationships that constitute research, which remain shaped by ethical decisions made in the process' (van Wingerden, 2022: 5).

Below, I describe how my identity as an Oxford-educated white man impacted the research project in practice. The practicalities of the research often took unexpected turns, and at times I felt that my educational background, gender identity, and ethnicity put me in a unique position to find new ways of continuing the research successfully. My research has been thoroughly shaped by my 'positionality', yet I do not have access to an external perspective from which to dispassionately determine how the research project would have turned out had I not benefited from the forms of privilege that I possess. Nonetheless, I offer a detailed account of how the research project developed in practice, and reflections on how my identity impacted that process, in the hope that this will allow readers to assess whether the claims I make in subsequent chapters are warranted and useful for better understanding the kinds of social problems this book seeks to address.

Research in practice: Access, unpredictability, and luck

Having selected an appropriate case study for critically examining the analytical issues set out in Chapter 2, I set out to collect empirical data by engaging senior officials from the IOM's Immigration and Border Management (IBM) unit. Due to the politicized nature of border control and the 'club-like' nature of transnational policymaking and international organizations (Barnett and Coleman, 2005: 609; Keohane and Nye, 2002), a strategy of 'cold calling' was unlikely to result in research access. Instead, as criminologists such as Emma Wincup (2017: 62) have argued, identifying 'gatekeepers' who have 'the power to open up or block off access' is crucial in the early stages of research.

Already at that early stage, my personal privilege relating to my educational and institutional status contributed to facilitating my research. After discussing my proposed research with my academic colleagues, I was immediately put in touch with multiple researchers and practitioners who had direct links to the IOM and other UN agencies. These individuals provided me with contact information and introductions to officials with direct experience of working on MIDAS. It is impossible for me to know how easy or hard such networking would have been at other academic institutions. Nonetheless, it seemed to me that my affiliation with the University of Oxford attached to my research project added an air of authority and expertise that was not necessarily merited by my research experience at that time. In spite of the IOM's reputation of being 'not particularly transparent' (Klabbers, 2019: 389), it did not take me long to identify relevant gatekeepers who could make or break the empirical research project.

My first discussion with an IOM official was with one of the country office employees to whom I had been introduced. This early discussion was long and challenging, and mainly consisted of me trying to prove my expertise to the official in the hopes that they would agree to facilitate the research. William Harvey (2011) has noted how elite interviews often include an element of 'testing' the researcher's expertise. This official asked me a host of technical questions to probe my pre-existing knowledge of MIDAS as well as topics such as the constitution of the IOM. By passing these spontaneous 'tests', I established rapport with the official, whose tone slowly changed from curt to jovial during the call. Once I had passed this initial assessment of expertise, I found myself 'inside' the network of IOM officials working on MIDAS, as the official agreed to facilitate my research by putting me in touch directly with their colleagues in Geneva. As Sara Delamont (2004: 213) has argued, it seemed that 'the harder it is to gain access, the more likely the work will be rewarding once "inside" '.

It is important to stress how transformational this positive initial contact with the IOM was for the remainder of the research project. I later found that the group of MIDAS-related senior officials within the organization is small enough that most individuals know each other on a first-name basis. A negative interaction with any of these officials may well have resulted in insurmountable reputational damage that could have prevented the interview- and fieldwork-based components of the research. Barak Kalir (2019: 85) has noted that 'the role that luck might have played in any successful attempt to get access to challenging research sites is usually unconsciously ignored or deliberately omitted from methodological accounts', despite the significance of luck in enabling successful research projects. I was most certainly lucky in being able to access a network of colleagues with links to the IOM, and in emerging from my initial contact with the organization unscathed and with the support of my first interlocutor. In some ways these outcomes reflected institutional privilege, yet it is also the case that 'luck takes nothing away from our competency as professional researchers and the need for a robust methodology and much footwork' (Kalir, 2019: 86). Building rapport with the IOM officials to whom I spoke often depended on the successful demonstration of expertise based on extensive background research. Nonetheless, the research was also enabled in large part by luck, and by the grace of my IOM contacts who agreed to facilitate my research.

Having gained research access to the senior levels of the IOM, in particular the IBM unit in Geneva, I initially planned to travel to their offices and carry out the elite interviews in person. At this stage, my research was severely disrupted by travel restrictions relating to the global Covid-19 pandemic.[1] Faced with uncertainty regarding whether and when travel to Geneva would become possible again, I considered carrying out the interviews online. Based on my previous experiences of elite interviews, I intuitively felt that rapport was often established while walking from the lobby to the office, or grabbing a coffee together before an interview. I was sceptical as to whether interviewees would feel comfortable disclosing sensitive information online, and whether I would be able to establish a relationship of trust mediated by computer screens and an often spotty internet connection. Methodological literature on the value of online and telephone interviews, however, eased my concerns by suggesting that these methods 'have the potential to mirror face-to-face interactions for those that are geographically dispersed' (Novick, 2008; Sullivan, 2012: 54). Jessica Sullivan's (2012) work was helpful in highlighting how online interviewing could present an opportunity as well, by allowing researchers to expand the pool of interviewees to geographically otherwise inaccessible areas.

In response to the Covid-19 pandemic I, like many others, was forced to reformulate my empirical research plans (Richardson et al., 2021). I chose to begin by conducting online rather than in-person interviews, and expanded my pool of interviewees from the IOM offices in Geneva to all of the organization's country offices that had deployed the MIDAS system. I had also probed the possibility of carrying out fieldwork at the IOM's African

[1] It goes without saying that disruptions to my research are unimportant in the context of a deadly pandemic that has cost millions of lives and caused hardship to so many across the globe. Nonetheless, the pandemic did cause significant methodological disruptions that merit discussion in this chapter. I offer this account in order to explain how the research process developed while recognizing the privilege inherent in experiencing Covid-19 mainly in terms of disruptions to my research, rather than as severe physical or emotional distress, not to mention the pains of losing a loved one.

Capacity Building Center (ACBC) in Moshi, Tanzania. However, I was forced to place these plans on hold and eventually abandon them entirely as travel restrictions to Tanzania remained in place for an extended period. As I inquired into conducting fieldwork at an IOM field office, my contacts in the organization suggested Nigeria as an alternative location, largely due to the fact they were searching for a fixed-term consultant to author a report on MIDAS. This *quid pro quo* arrangement was necessary for the organization to support my fieldwork to the extent that it did.

Here, again, luck shaped my research project, as it turned out that these Covid-related disruptions ultimately benefited the project in several ways. Expanding my interview pool to include officials from country offices was immensely helpful in gathering information on how MIDAS was rolled out in practice, to what extent the system transformed practices on the ground, and how IOM officials experienced their interactions with state agencies in a variety of country contexts. Changing fieldwork locations from Tanzania to Nigeria was also fortuitous in two ways. First, although the ACBC is mentioned repeatedly in official IOM documentation as a key site for training African state border control agencies in the use of MIDAS, I later learned that in fact most trainings were carried out *in situ* in the Member States deploying MIDAS. An IOM official in Abuja later joked: 'you should thank the academic gods you're in Nigeria' (Field diary, 6 September 2021). Nigeria has the most extensive roll-out of MIDAS, providing a rich corpus of technical documentation and first-hand experiences of how the system was deployed on the ground.

A second fortuitous outcome of travelling to Nigeria instead of Tanzania was the institutional support from the IOM and the United Nations that I received as a hired consultant. Above, I explained how my stance of unease allowed me to engage with IOM officials critically yet productively. Thankfully, this relationship—combined with the openness of the organization's officials to constructive criticism—resulted in an arrangement in which I was granted field access in exchange for authoring an independent report on the legal, operational, and technical dimensions of MIDAS in Nigeria. Under the terms of our agreement, the IOM would not censor the findings and recommendations of my report, which has informed their deployment of the MIDAS system in other African countries later on.

Mateja Peter and Francesco Strazzari (2017: 1536) have highlighted how the increasing 'securitization of research' has created a context in which, 'to avoid future liability under their duty of care, universities and research institutes want to make sure that staff members sent abroad are informed and prepared'. At the time of my research, Nigeria could certainly have been categorized as a 'zone of danger' (Peter and Strazzari, 2017: 1545) owing to the fraught security situation in the Boko Haram-controlled Northeast of the country as well as an increase in kidnappings in Abuja in 2021 (Paquette, 2021). However, as an IOM consultant, I was subject to UN security procedures in the country, and was provided local transport in a white UN SUV. My in-country IOM contacts also arranged safe accommodation in what was called 'The Compound', which I would not have been able to access without their assistance.

Once I arrived in Abuja, my field observations largely proceeded in a routine fashion. From around 8:30am to 6pm Monday–Friday, I sat in the office, analysed MIDAS-related documentation, spoke with IOM officials, and observed meetings between the IOM and Nigerian state agencies. Occasionally, I would accompany my IOM contacts to meetings with Nigerian officials at other locations, such as the headquarters of the NIS outside of Abuja and various workshops and training sessions at other venues around the city. In the evenings and weekends, I returned to the compound to work on my research.

Thus far, I have described how my research developed empirically, yet the project also took many unexpected theoretical and emotional turns, which it is also important to highlight to avoid the 'methodological lie' of presenting the research as entirely predictable (Bosworth and Hoyle, 2011). A sense of emotional vulnerability arose from my outsider status when conducting fieldwork, as well as from the potential postcolonial dynamics underpinning a Northern, white researcher examining political practices in the Global South. My identity was not to be forgotten, as I was affectionately called 'white boy Sam' by the local UN drivers I befriended during my stay. Before travelling to Nigeria, I was aware of how concerns relating to the reproduction of the 'colonial gaze' have 'paralyzed some scholars into avoiding fieldwork' entirely (Sultana, 2007: 375). However, as Farhana Sultana (2007: 376) has argued, 'acknowledging one's own positionality or subjectivity should not mean abandoning work'. I opted to adhere to best practices in critical research methodology by adopting a stance of critical reflexivity regarding my personal and institutional positionality as well as my intellectual and political dispositions (Salter, 2013: 20–22). In practice, such reflection quickly resulted in the observation that a majority of senior IOM and other UN officials in the compound were also white Europeans; the postcolonial underpinnings of white 'international experts' teaching

Southern countries how to do border control indeed became a crucial theme in my research, which I explore more fully in Chapter 7. More generally, this chapter is a result of reflecting upon the impact of my identity on the research, and how such reflection shaped the research process in important ways.

I also felt emotionally vulnerable in the sense that I felt intellectually out of place interacting mainly with border control professionals both in and out the office while in Abuja. Many of these individuals came from law enforcement and military backgrounds, and generally viewed migration and border control through the lens of security and control. My views on border control were often dismissed as 'academic' in a pejorative sense, or as idealistic. Such discussions were emotionally challenging, but also immensely important for the development of the theoretical framework developed in this book. The repeated challenges to my views on migration and border control technologies inspired me to re-evaluate my earlier theoretical approach—which had been largely based on 'assemblage' theories and posthumanist perspectives—and to explore alternatives that focused on the differences that particular tools and worldviews made to social practices, and on how we might offer justifications for competing worldviews without lapsing into cultural relativism or basing our claims on their supposed absolute 'truthfulness'. The result of that critical reflection is the theoretical framework outlined in Chapter 3, and situating this book within the pragmatist research paradigm as described above. In this sense, my social encounters in the field by no means demonstrated my mastery of my research topic. Rather, they can be positively described as 'catastrophic encounters' (Gallagher, 2016) in that they were able to 'unsettle the researcher's deeply held beliefs about the world and the self, and thereby have effects far beyond the researcher's control' (van Wingerden, 2022: 5).

Conclusion

This chapter has situated this book within the research paradigm of pragmatism. In line with the attempt to 'unmaster research', I have provided an account of the research process as it developed from prior motivations through to empirical fieldwork and subsequent interpretations, often in unpredictable ways. This account shows how, rather than successfully mastering my research topic, my experience was often characterized by an intellectual, emotional, and physical vulnerability arising from my lack of control of the research process. As Jess Linz and Anna Secor (2021: 110) have argued, 'vulnerability is quite opposite to mastery'. Indeed, much of the research was only possible thanks to academic colleagues as well as my IOM contacts—and thanks to a significant amount of luck, as well—rather than being the sole result of my own independent efforts.

This does not mean I simply tagged along for the ride, or that anyone else would have completed the research in the same way and with the same outcomes. I also faced obstacles that took considerable conscious effort to overcome, and the research itself was shaped by my personal prior beliefs, interests, and assumptions, as well as by my personality. Inspired by the critical work of Gani and Khan (2024) and others regarding the limitations of positionality statements, I have offered these reflections to ensure that I have been as transparent as possible about the subjective and unpredictable factors that shaped the research process, and which inescapably underpin the theoretical and empirical arguments put forth in subsequent chapters. My hope is that this transparency will persuade others to agree that my interpretations of empirical data in this book are warranted based on the empirical evidence I have gathered.

These knowledge claims may still not qualify as timeless truths, but they correspond to my subjective views, to the material environment, and to the intersubjective dimension between me and the reader—at least for the time being. As pragmatist Richard Rorty (2021: 48) has put it, timeless, absolute truth

> is too sublime, so to speak, to be either recognized or aimed at. Justification is merely beautiful, but it is recognizable, and therefore capable of being systematically worked for. Sometimes, with luck justification is even achieved. But that achievement is usually only temporary, since sooner or later, with luck, some new objections to the temporarily justified belief will be developed.

This view is in line with the pragmatist conception of the limits of knowledge production in general, and it is compatible with a normative orientation that views academic knowledge as an attempt to address and reconceptualize pressing social problems such as social exclusion at the border. Insofar as academic criminological research constitutes a type of expert knowledge regarding criminal justice and border control practices, this expertise should not aim at the creation of authoritative truth claims. Instead, critical research should uncover what social and political assumptions underpin contemporary practices of digital crimmigration control, what alternative worldviews have been marginalized in the process of developing new technologies, and how we might go about critiquing and reshaping these technologized practices. As Larry Hickman (2001: 6) has argued, drawing on the work of John Dewey, 'the role of the expert in democratic societies is not to make policy or to tell people what to think, but to alert people to possible ways in which their thinking about matters of importance may be improved'. This pragmatist view of expertise centres reflexivity and intellectual humility when producing the kind of critical arguments that I present in Part II of this book. This perspective also provides the foundations for critiquing the IOM's claims to expertise in the field of migration management, a task to which I turn in subsequent chapters.

PART II

MIDAS

5 MIDAS and the Performative Dimensions of Global Migration Management

I never practice, I only perform.

—Chance the Rapper (2016)

Introduction

In the first part of this book, I outlined some key reasons why migration management, criminal justice, and digital technologies should be critically analysed together. Border criminologists have highlighted the increasing centrality of immigration law and migration control to contemporary practices of punishment, control, and social exclusion (Bosworth et al., 2018b; Franko Aas and Bosworth, 2013). In an age of globalization, states have deployed the criminal justice system to control migration and to discipline migrants, while also utilizing the legal frameworks and practices of immigration control in a penal manner (Bosworth, 2008; Hernández, 2018; Stumpf, 2006). This merger of criminal justice and migration control is now regularly referred to as 'crimmigration control' (Bowling and Westenra, 2018), and citizenship has become 'a potent tool by which those at the margins of the political community are policed by the state' (Zedner, 2010: 382). However, the global scale of contemporary forms of punishment and control is distinct from earlier statist forms of penal practice, challenging the field of criminology to re-evaluate its earlier commitments to state-centric theorizing by asking: 'how does international criminal justice challenge conventional ideas of sovereignty, the penal state and of penal power in a globalizing context?' (Lohne, 2020: 146).

In addition to overcoming state-centrism, the previous chapters indicated a need to examine similarities and differences between the Global

Outsourcing Crimmigration Control. Samuel Singler, Oxford University Press. © Samuel Singler 2025.
DOI: 10.1093/9780198927525.003.0005

North and South: existing scholarship has shown that Southern actors actively respond to and reshape Northern logics of border control when translating them to local contexts (Mehta, 2016; Vigneswaran, 2013). This Southern agency is enacted against the backdrop of postcolonial global hierarchies and dominant Northern norms of sovereign authority (Stambøl, 2021b). A key dimension of contemporary practices of border control, through which norms of territorial sovereignty are being reshaped, is the deployment of novel border control technologies (Frowd, 2020). As Katja Franko (2020: 25) has argued: 'the exercise of power, including in the penal domain, is essentially technological. Contemporary border control systems aim to create bodies which are fused with technology.'

In this chapter, I begin the task of applying the framework presented in Chapter 3 to the empirical case of the International Organization for Migration (IOM) and its Migration Information and Data Analysis System (MIDAS), on which I focus throughout the remainder of this book. Border criminologists have conducted illuminating research into the role of non-state actors such as private corporations and non-governmental organizations in shaping crimmigration control practices (Bhatia and Canning, 2020; Hiemstra and Conlon, 2017; Infantino, 2016, 2019; Martin, 2017). Nonetheless, the role of the IOM in shaping migration control practices on a global level has thus far received only limited academic attention, usually by scholars of migration studies and international political sociology (Bartels, 2018; Dini, 2018; Fine, 2018; Frowd, 2020; Geiger and Pécoud, 2014; Pécoud, 2018). If indeed migration control is a key dimension of contemporary penal power which operates at the scale of 'the global', then a critical examination of transnational actors such as IOM is relevant to the contemporary project of border criminology. MIDAS, in turn, has been mentioned in passing in recent scholarship as 'a key part of the IOM's positioning as a neutral, technical provider of border management solutions for states who may not be able to afford them' (Cold-Ravnkilde, 2021; Frowd, 2018: 1667). However, the system has not yet received much sustained academic attention (Singler, 2024a).

This chapter demonstrates the utility of analysing the performative effects of the development and deployment of MIDAS. The discussion below sets the stage for further empirical examination of the deployment of MIDAS on the ground in Nigeria, as well as a pragmatist analysis of the political effects of the technology—tasks to which I turn in Chapters 6–8. A performative analysis of this system foregrounds some of the key political and theoretical stakes in border criminology research discussed in previous chapters: it resists Northern-centric and state-centric readings of global migration control practices, expanding the 'spatial imagination' of criminology (Franko Aas, 2012a: 236); it highlights complex and emergent forms of both human and non-human agency, while retaining an intimate focus on questions of power and politics; and, particularly when combined with a pragmatist perspective in following chapters, it allows for a more thoroughgoing normative critique of contemporary migration control and transnational criminal justice practices on a global level.

Below, I analyse the multidimensional performative effects of MIDAS in terms of the beneficiary states, the IOM, and the technical devices themselves. For beneficiary states, the deployment of the system constitutes a performance of sovereign territorial power, affirming membership in the international society of (biometrically capable) states. For the IOM, developing and deploying MIDAS and carrying out training sessions operate as performances of pedagogical competence, technical expertise, and political neutrality. Finally, the technical components of the system itself performatively act upon their targets, constituting 'the migrant' as a governable, potentially risky subject and 'migration' as a problem amenable to depoliticized techno-solutionist interventions. Before turning to the performative analysis, this chapter begins with an introduction of the IOM and MIDAS, situating them within the broader performative field of global migration management.

IOM, MIDAS, and global migration management

The roots of the IOM reach back to the creation of the Provisional Intergovernmental Committee for the Movements of Migrants from Europe in 1951, renamed the Intergovernmental Committee for European Migration a few months later (Pécoud, 2018: 1624). These names reflect the original goal of the organization: the post-war resettlement of displaced populations within Europe with a 'focus on logistics and transportation', that is, the operational aspects of migration control rather than protection or human rights considerations (Geiger and Pécoud, 2014: 868). The latter issues fell under the respective purviews of the International Labour Organization (ILO), concerned with the management of migrant workers, and the United Nations High Commissioner for Refugees (UNHCR), focused on the protection of refugees and asylum seekers.

The focus of the IOM on the operational dimensions of migration control remains crucial to its claims of political impartiality today, yet migration scholars have argued that from its inception the IOM has been heavily politicized (Georgi, 2010). The creation of the IOM as a separate, non-UN organization was linked to the political interests of wealthy Northern states in 'the actual transportation of people, rather than their human rights protection', as well as concerns on the part of the United States regarding potential communist influences within the UN (Pécoud, 2018: 1624). In that context, the IOM was created as 'the UNHCR's operational, United States-controlled counterpart' (Parsanoglou, 2015: 64). The institutional division of labour between the IOM, ILO, and UNHCR—along with the accompanying differences in normative and operational focus—still exists today.

Although the IOM became a 'UN-related organization' in 2016, its mandate calls into question the extent to which its new status will result in any significant shifts to its operational or normative agendas (Korneev, 2018). A notable omission from its constitution is any reference to the vulnerability or human rights of migrants. In spite of its newfound affiliation with the UN, the IOM is 'not bound by the human rights framework that forms the basis of the UN's work' (Pécoud, 2018: 1625). Overall, the constitution allows for the positioning of the IOM as a provider 'of migration-related services that governments find themselves unable or unwilling to carry out for legal and political purposes' (Ashutosh and Mountz, 2011: 22). This positioning has allowed the organization, despite its occasional championing of humanitarian ideals, to operate in legal and geographical grey areas when carrying out operations such as migrant detention and deportation in and from Indonesia on behalf of the Australian government as well as Canadian-funded labour brokerage schemes in the Philippines (Barber and Bryan, 2018; Ashutosh and Mountz, 2011).

It remains to be seen how resistant the IOM will be in the future to criticisms of its lack of a formalized commitment to humanitarian ideals, particularly as the organization becomes increasingly wedded to its recent self-fashioning as the 'UN Migration Agency' (IOM, 2019: xv). However, some critical authors have recently suggested that, rather than exerting pressure on the IOM to promote human rights in its work, closer cooperation with the UN might in fact undermine such a prospect. According to Anne Koch (2014: 919), cooperation between the UNHCR and the IOM can be characterized as 'normative task-sharing', which 'allows for a situation in which a humanitarian agency retains the moral authority to judge certain return procedures acceptable or non-acceptable, while cooperating with an operations agency that carries out returns of dubious voluntariness with the moral support of this first actor'. In similar vein, Asher Lazarus Hirsch and Cameron Doig (2018: 685) have argued that 'the IOM may actually capitalize on the UN's perceived legitimacy to deflect criticisms of its alleged rights violations'.

These criticisms notwithstanding, it is important to note that the IOM has engaged in humanitarian activities, for instance in the aftermath of the 2010 earthquake in Haiti. While critical of the IOM's mandate, Jan Klabbers (2019: 394) has nonetheless suggested that 'it would be grossly unfair to claim that the IOM does not have a humanitarian mission'. Philippe Frowd (2018) has also argued that assessing the IOM's commitment to humanitarian ideals is more complicated than simply condemning those of its activities which are clearly not in line with the human rights framework of the UN. According to Frowd, rather than seeking to conclusively show that the IOM either is or is not committed to humanitarian ideals, research should focus on how exactly humanitarian narratives shape and operate within the broader field of 'borderwork' carried out by the IOM. Below, I analyse how IOM practitioners themselves performatively enacted the IOM's political neutrality within the contentious field of global migration management. In Chapter 7, I demonstrate how discourses related to the humanitarian mission of the IOM, as well as its supposed human rights expertise, were central to the deployment of MIDAS in Nigeria.

In recent years, a key component of the IOM's work in the Global South has been the provision of MIDAS free of charge to the organization's Member States. MIDAS is a biometric border management information system that gathers and stores biographical and biometric data, travel document information, entry/exit data, visa data, and vehicle/flight/vessel data (IOM, 2018b). It gathers passenger data through a fingerprint scanner, a document scanner, and a webcam for facial recognition, and then stores these in a centralized depository of all traveller data. The IOM (2018b: 2) has characterized MIDAS as a 'high-quality, user-friendly and fully customizable border management information system (BMIS) for States in need of a cost-effective and comprehensive solution', and argued that the system 'enables States to more effectively monitor those entering and exiting their territory while providing a sound statistical basis for migration policy-related planning'. At the discretion of beneficiary states, MIDAS can be configured to check passenger data against national and international alert lists, although the extent of such interoperability varies significantly between states. The IOM has argued that digital border management information systems are crucial to facilitating 'orderly, safe, regular and responsible migration and mobility of people' (IOM, 2018a: 2). According to the organization, biometric technology specifically 'is vital for protecting identity and preventing identity or entitlement fraud', facilitating 'regular and safe cross-border mobility and migration', and enhancing 'security in migration and border management processes' (IOM, 2018a: 3).

Currently operational in 29 countries in the Global South, mainly in Africa, MIDAS has been the source of some concern among journalists and activists, who have argued that it is the latest component of 'the EU's strategy in the war on migration' aimed at reducing obstacles to deportation from the EU to Africa (Privacy International, 2019; Zandonini, 2019). These concerns highlight how MIDAS links directly to the research themes identified in previous chapters. The collection and analysis of biometric data has become a central facet of deterritorialized sovereign power in the Global North (Muller, 2010), and migration studies scholars have argued that expanding these practices to the Global South has been driven by a desire to replicate and legitimize Western conceptions of sovereignty at a global level (Dini, 2018). As a novel technical system that has only recently been introduced in the Global South, MIDAS also provides a useful case for analysing how the introduction of novel technical tools can shape border control practices both in ways intended by their designers—highlighting the politics of technological design—and by exerting performative effects of their own, unintended by their designers (Wood, 2021).

The framework of performativity outlined in Chapter 3 suggests that MIDAS should not be conceptualized merely as a neutral technical tool that human actors have used instrumentally to obtain pre-existing political goals. Rather, an analysis of the performative effects of MIDAS demonstrates that border security technologies have 'productive dimensions', in the sense that 'productive technologies of power matter politically insofar as they contribute to the constitution of new domains of political intervention and new modalities of divisibility' (Jacobsen, 2015: 44). This insight does not excise human agency from the analysis, but rather seeks to incorporate MIDAS as one component within the broader socio-technical configuration of global crimmigration control. In the following sections, I analyse three distinct dimensions of the performative effects of MIDAS: performances of (biometric) sovereign statehood by beneficiary states; performances of neutrality and expertise by the IOM; and the performative constitution of 'migration' as a governable, depoliticized 'problem' by the technical components of MIDAS itself.

Southern agency and biometric statehood

Authors across a number of social science disciplines have analysed the impact of globalization on state power and sovereignty (Agnew, 2017; Ku and Yoo, 2013). Following earlier arguments about the 'waning' and 'hollowing out' of the state (Brown, 2017b; Rhodes, 1994), more recent scholarship has suggested that the 'disassembling' of the state has not necessarily undermined sovereign power (Sassen, 2007). On one hand, state power often underwrites processes of privatization and transnationalization, allowing states to govern '*through* the distance' by 'decentralizing responsibility and putting policy recipients at a distance' (Infantino, 2016: 4, 79, original emphasis). On the other hand, even in an age of transnational mobility for some and the diffusion and disassembling of state authority, territorial borders continue to matter as zones of high security scrutiny and limited judicial safeguards against state power (Zedner, 2019). More broadly, in spite of the deterritorialization of state power, the norm of territorial sovereignty continues to structure contemporary practices of crimmigration control and transnational criminal justice, which are based on the presumptive legitimacy of an 'international community' of sovereign territorial states (Leader, 2020).

Questions of sovereign power and territoriality are complex in the context of African states, which historically have occupied a marginal position in Western-centric international political theory (Abrahamsen, 2017) and whose 'statehood' has repeatedly been called into question when evaluated against the norm of territorial sovereignty (Grovogui, 2002; Jackson and Rosberg, 1986). Although a Northern-centric attitude is immediately evident in interpreting African statehood as a 'failure' to live up to Northern realities, so too can presenting sovereign territoriality in Africa as a wholly colonial imposition deny agency of local political actors. According to Camille Lefebvre (2011: 202), such critiques, 'by marking African territorial organization with the stamp of colonial artificiality [. . .] denied Africa of a history which could, with time, have served a national or political discourse'. To avoid these pitfalls, a performative analysis of MIDAS can illuminate how African states have engaged in politically significant performances of sovereign territoriality. As Darshan Vigneswaran (2013) has argued in the context of South Africa, local political actors have significant influence over crimmigration control efforts by Northern and transnational actors, who are rarely able to impose their practices in the absence of willing local partners.

The agency of African states was immediately apparent in IOM officials' views on the relationship between the IOM and beneficiary states. As an intergovernmental organization, the IOM viewed its operational mandate as entirely determined by its Member States:

> There's one point we cannot forget, and this is important for us: there's a line you cannot cross, it's state sovereignty. We cannot tell, let's say, [country], 'You have to do this, this and this.' They do whatever they want, they are a sovereign country. (José, interview, 2 March 2021)

Many African states directly requested MIDAS. The system was not necessarily proposed or imposed by the IOM or its Northern donors: 'The government is advocating for MIDAS [. . .] IOM developed a project after a discussion with the government. IOM develops projects, and the government identifies the border posts where they want MIDAS to be installed' (Tom, interview, 24 February 2021). In several countries, the deployment of MIDAS was shaped by local political struggles and economic interests, with election cycles, interinstitutional competition, and sometimes corruption influencing whether the local government is willing to allow the IOM to operate within the country. In sharp contrast to journalistic accounts which presented MIDAS as a tool for facilitating deportations from Europe to Africa (Privacy International, 2019; Zandonini, 2019), all MIDAS data was fully owned by beneficiary states (IOM, 2018b). States zealously guarded against the IOM's efforts to promote greater international interoperability between systems, and against the efforts of regional political organizations such as the Economic Community of West African States (ECOWAS) to promote regional data-sharing activities:

> In regional meetings both in the West and in the East, well, the issue of data comes up quite regularly, always in the same terms, but without any progress [. . .] [Recipient states] didn't have enough reassurance on how these data were dealt with at the regional level. This is not something that they explicitly say, but this is what you may feel from the reticence to actually push forward these activities. And this is not just external stakeholders, like financial and technical partners like IOM or a donor, but it's also for example towards ECOWAS. (Maria, interview, 10 March 2021)

It was not only that African states already possessed enough capability to resist external interventions and exert their own influence; deploying MIDAS and limiting external intervention and integration performatively enacted the territorial sovereignty of these states. In this sense, 'there is no sovereign state or state identity behind expressions of state sovereignty' (Weber, 1998: 90). That the deployment of MIDAS constituted a performance of territorial statehood was particularly apparent in cases where the gap between this performance and the recognizable material effects on the ground was particularly wide. Even in contexts where the selection of border posts to be equipped with MIDAS seemed not to be based on capacity-building considerations, and 'systems are really underused' (Maria, interview, 10 March 2021), states still brandished MIDAS to enact their membership in the international community of territorial states by showing that 'they can control their borders too' (Jayden, interview, 6 April 2021).

While it is important to highlight the agency of African states in deploying MIDAS performatively, this policy choice should also be contextualized within the broader structuring effects of existing global discourses, practices, and materialities relating to sovereign power. In other words, performances of territorial statehood in Africa partly gained political significance through 'integration (at a regulatory level) and emulation (at a normative level)' of existing global norms (Frowd, 2020: 4). In the age of digital border controls, the norm of sovereign territoriality that African states performatively enacted was one of *biometric statehood*. In the context of globalization, states conceptualized cross-border movements as both 'integral to trans-boundary communities [and] international commerce and trade' and 'something dangerous, threatening and potentially risky' (Muller, 2010: 15). Rather than stopping migration, states sought new technological solutions to 'order' or 'manage' cross-border movements through the 'social sorting' of potentially risky identities, in a quest to simultaneously facilitate mobility and increase security (Jones, 2009; Lyon, 2003). Biometric identification technologies have been particularly 'vital in identifying the undesirable populations in the new global order', due to the perception of biometrics as 'almost impossible to forge because our bodies, or rather than the information extracted from our bodies, are unique tokens of identification' (Franko Aas, 2006: 145–146). Although states asked the IOM to install MIDAS partly due to the perception that the system 'is going to strengthen the security part [of borders] very much' (Amare, interview, 31 March 2021), it was more precisely the logic of 'social sorting' associated with biometric systems that was appealing to them: 'There is always the need for the government to make sure that, you know, to let the good guys in and keep the bad guys out, something like that. So, this is what the use of biometrics is all about' (José, interview, 2 March 2021).

African state agencies' performative deployment of MIDAS aimed to affirm membership in the international community of biometrically capable states, not only through demonstrating security capacity but more generally by demonstrating their capacity in terms of 'embracing' their citizens and making their territory and population 'legible' (Frowd, 2020; Torpey, 2000; Scott, 1998). The goal of increasing legibility was apparent in that 'the objective is not only to enhance [. . .] border security' (Luca, interview, 3 March 2021) but to manage and order cross-border movements for the purposes of trade, taxation, and protection:

> What we've managed to do with MIDAS has been to capture what these little trends look like, how they change, how we can facilitate trade, how trade helps development [. . .] We've managed to regulate migration movements, registrations of people in border communities; all of this data eventually feeds into welfare, feeds into displacement and humanitarian responses. (Diego, interview, 16 February 2021)

MIDAS was also seen as a potential first step towards a more general project of making the population legible to the state through the introduction of a national biometric database of citizens: 'if you want [. . .] a massive national registration, you can already use what's there, and you may go backwards and go from MIDAS to from National ID registration' (Mohammed, interview, 22 February 2021). In Chapter 8, I discuss in more detail this complicated relationship between MIDAS and other national biometric registration systems in the Nigerian context.

The extent to which these performances of biometric statehood were structured by existing international norms and standards was evident in the routine characterization of biometric border controls as 'a step forward' and 'modern' (José, interview, 2 March 2021). Being 'left behind'—that is, not having a biometric border management information system—was a cause of embarrassment and 'jealousy', and 'there is this sort of emulation aspect' in requesting MIDAS once neighbouring states have adopted the system (Louise, interview, 9 March 2021). Indeed, many African states requested MIDAS even when IOM officials were not convinced that a biometric border management information system would be a suitable solution to country-specific issues: 'I think in many states where we have MIDAS projects, I'm not sure if it really lacks biometric data collection at the borders to increase security in their country' (Zahra, interview, 19 March 2021). Despite such scepticism on the part of the IOM, states themselves were 'proud' to demonstrate their biometric statehood through the deployment of MIDAS: 'I think for them, it's a sovereignty tool [. . .] They're quite proud to have their own system' (Mohammed, interview, 22 February 2021).

The lens of performativity allows us to conceptualize assertions of biometric statehood by African states as more than 'fake' or 'superficial'. Although there was often an empirical gap between public discourses of biometric capability and operational realities on the ground, the deployment of MIDAS had very real effects in constituting the biometric statehood of the beneficiary states. Chance the Rapper's (2016) lyric included in the epigraph of this chapter can be used to capture the importance of these performances independently of the practical impacts of new border technologies: 'I never practice, I only perform.' As Ferenc David Markó (2016: 126) has argued in the context of South Sudan, states in Africa have deployed biometric identity management systems 'to convey the image of a modern, "non-failed" state to the international community' even when the practical promises of these systems 'remain unfulfilled'. African states were not simply 'passive recipients' of MIDAS (Bartels, 2018: 64) but rather active agents who adopted, modified, and naturalized the norm of biometric statehood through their performative deployment of this system. A recognition of this agency is crucial to the avoidance of Western-centric theorizing in border criminology and transnational criminal justice (Franko Aas, 2012b). Nonetheless, Southern states' agency did not exist in a vacuum. It was conditioned by the contemporary global norm of biometric statehood. It is to an analysis of the role of the IOM in producing, reaffirming, and spreading this norm that I now turn.

Pedagogical performances: Neutrality, expertise, and solutionism in the IOM

Scholars of transnational criminal justice have highlighted the centrality of transnational actors and intergovernmental organizations in producing the 'rules, norms and standards that condition global practices of governance, care, and control' (Lohne and Sandvik, 2017: 14). The IOM has produced and disseminated norms relating to 'the orderly and humane management of migration' by 'providing services and advice to governments and migrants' (IOM, 2021a). Yet this language of 'services and advice' has obscured the significant political impact that the organization's activities have had on migration control. As others have argued, the IOM has contributed to the normalization of exclusionary migration control practices (Fine, 2018), reified state power to the detriment of undocumented migrants (Dini, 2018), legitimized a 'post-imperial' global order (Andrijasevic and Walters, 2010), and carried out 'migration-related services that governments find themselves unable or unwilling to carry out for legal and political purposes' (Ashutosh and Mountz, 2011: 22).

How has the IOM been able to continue presenting itself as a neutral service-provider despite these outcomes? Analysing its public discourses, operational practices, and technical tools from a performative perspective suggested that the organization's political reputation of neutrality was the product of 'a lot of hard work' (Weber, 1998: 79). More specifically, the IOM enacted its organizational identity as a politically neutral actor through *pedagogical performances* of migration management. In doing so, the organization has expanded its political influence in shaping global migration control practices, while simultaneously undermining external calls for political responsibility and accountability. IOM officials explicitly viewed their work in pedagogical terms, describing their role as 'teaching states about security' and giving 'briefings and lectures . . to make people understand how you cannot possibly live in a modern world today without digitized information, and how it benefits you' (Diego, interview, 16 February 2021).

However, this pedagogical orientation did not automatically confer upon the teacher the status of neutrality. As Philippe Frowd (2020: 72) has argued, the IOM's educational practices were 'dependent on the prior existence of an unequal distribution of capital between teacher and learner, which the pedagogical act maintains or even exacerbates. At its root, the politics of border control pedagogy is paternalistic.' Indeed, the organization's employees were acutely aware of the 'post-imperial' implications of its position as a mainly Northern-funded actor operating in the Global South: 'We're not dealing with colonial children, but we're dealing with the children of colonial children, and the impact of that. There is a suspicion [of our] computer systems' (Diego, interview, 16 February 2021). Moreover, officials recognized that the global standard of biometric statehood has been heavily influenced by the political concerns of powerful donors such as the United States:

> I think this goes back to all the security resolutions, which came after 9/11. And I mean, I don't necessarily agree with that. I don't think

> biometrics are the way to go for migration. [. . .] I would also say that the US played quite a big role in that [. . .] the US is the biggest single donor. [. . .] I think that this has played a major role in developing this norm of having biometric data systems for border controls. (Zahra, interview, 19 March 2021)

This unease towards the post-imperial implications of the IOM's work was further reflected in officials' acknowledgement that the development of new border technologies effectively instituted what Matthew Longo (2018: 205) has termed a 'global firewall' whereby 'states that have data on their citizens are able to align forces and trust each other, whereas those that are data "dark" are vilified and excluded'. As IOM official José described this issue:

> When you launch all these new technologies, you have, European Union can do it. You have US, Canada, and you know, New Zealand, Australia, China, and Singapore that can do it. But what about the rest? What about the African continent? Nobody will be able to do it. We're talking about 44, 45 countries. So, if they don't do it, you don't trust [them]. (Interview, 2 March 2021)

Additional performative work was required to present the IOM as politically neutral and avoid the label of a 'post-imperial' institution. To this end, the organization's employees positioned the IOM as not only a border control educator but more specifically as a technical expert organization. Kjersti Lohne (2020: 157) has argued that transnational criminal justice actors such as the International Criminal Court have legitimized and depoliticized their interventions through 'non-democratic claims to efficiency, economics, rationality—and humanitarianism'. Indeed, IOM officials routinely described the organization as promoting efficiency and rationality in border management, and characterized the IOM as 'proud of being a non-norm setting organization' (Zahra, interview, 19 March 2021). Rather than actively shaping the politics of migration control through its interventions, according to officials the IOM instead simply listened when 'every country tells us exactly what they want [. . .] after that, we don't manage the system, we don't want the system, we don't own the system. We train people to work on the system' (José, interview, 2 March 2021).

A key motif in the IOM's performances of neutrality was its relationship to the United Nations. Kate Leader (2020: 248) has noted how transnational criminal justice actors that do not possess formal UN status increase their international legitimacy by emphasizing their links to the UN. The IOM was no exception, occupying the ambiguous position of a 'UN-related organization'. This means that it was 'not bound by the human rights framework that forms the basis of the UN's work' (Pécoud, 2018: 1625). Yet the IOM (2019) attached the title 'UN Migration' to its name in official documents, while IOM officials oscillated between describing the organization as 'a UN agency' (Amare, interview, 31 March 2021) and highlighting 'the history of IOM not being a UN agency' (Zahra, interview, 19 March 2021). Officials recognized the positive reputational effects of being affiliated with the UN: 'the [country] government entrusted IOM, because the government of [country] has trusted the UN and is getting a lot of support from the UN. That being the case, they thought it wise that they can trust to work with a UN agency' (Amare, interview, 31 March 2021).

The IOM's claims to neutrality hinged on its professed technical expertise. Although systems such as MIDAS played a crucial role in entrenching and naturalizing the norm of territorial sovereignty (Ashutosh and Mountz, 2011), IOM officials represented these systems as components of a neutral technical project of providing 'training and capacity building for the government' (Tom, interview, 24 February 2021). These demonstrations of technical expertise were not merely 'superficial', but constituted the IOM as a neutral, technical expert of 'migration management', with whom beneficiary states were more willing to work compared to donor countries:

> MIDAS is rolled out in [country], and it's funded by the Americans [but] the government does not want the Americans there [. . .] the US was not really present, they never negotiated, or they never met with the [local authorities] directly. It was really through IOM. So I think sometimes it also changes how present the donor is, in the view of the receiving government. (Zahra, interview, 19 March 2021)

The performative nature of the IOM's provision of technical equipment and assistance to countries was reflected in the 'solutionist' attitude of the organization towards these technical capacity-building projects. Evgeny Morozov (2013: 6) has used the term 'solutionism' to refer to a preoccupation with narrow, technical fixes 'to problems that, on careful examination, do not have to be defined in the singular and all-encompassing ways that "solutionists" have defined them; what's contentious, then, is not their proposed solution but their very definition of the problem itself'. IOM officials recognized the importance of framing migration control as a technical issue to which MIDAS is the solution:

> Sometimes it's a bit seen as this technical solution to security problems. And I think when we roll out MIDAS projects, for instance, we argue that it has stabilizing effects [. . .] Just the framing of it, I think it can come across as quite a solutionist approach to fragile states. (Katrina, interview, 17 February 2021)

In essence, the IOM acted as a solutionist policy 'entrepreneur' that was 'capable of seizing opportunities and responding innovatively to them' (Geiger and Pécoud, 2014: 870). Importantly, this solutionist entrepreneurialism served to constitute the organization as the authoritative, neutral expert to be trusted with providing technical solutions to the 'problem' of migration. MIDAS was offered as a 'foundational building system for Member States' to begin gathering and analysing migration data, and 'all of this data eventually allows us to actually put on more projects' by suggesting potential avenues for further technical solutions (Diego, interview, 16 February 2021).

Despite the pejorative connotations of the term 'solutionism', viewing these activities by the IOM as performative is not meant to suggest that IOM officials are acting out a 'role' that is in some way 'fake'. The IOM is a self-avowedly multidimensional organization, whose work often reflects a 'genuine but overly formalist humanitarianism' (Frowd, 2018: 1658). Officials and departments within the IOM disagreed over the political and normative implications of MIDAS projects: 'We have huge discussions with colleagues from the humanitarian side [. . .] because they don't agree at all with some of the projects that IBM is undertaking' (Zahra, interview, 19 March 2021).

Attempting to avoid 'post-imperial' influence on beneficiary states while simultaneously promoting global human rights standards forced the IOM into a difficult balancing act. The appearance of technical neutrality allowed the organization to escape this bind. For instance, in her report on digital border technologies, UN Special Rapporteur E. Tendayi Achiume (OHCHR, 2020: 20) called on the IOM to mandate equality and non-discrimination protections when offering systems such as MIDAS to Member States, 'and prohibit adoption of technologies that cannot be shown to meet equality and non-discrimination requirements'. One IOM official highlighted how the report had ignited internal debates within the organization, in which the normative desirability of imposing international human rights standards upon Member States was pitted against the need to avoid post-imperial violations of the sovereignty of African states:

> Something that comes up quite often in these discussions [is] 'How far can we go? How much can we recommend, also, in terms of data protection?' Because many times it's also seen as this, 'Oh, just because the Europeans have this really nice and comprehensive framework now, this is not something that we can impose on other Member States'. (Katrina, interview, 17 February 2021)

Ultimately, this tension was resolved through the IOM's pedagogical performances which constituted the organization as a neutral expert that offers MIDAS as a 'solution' to the supposedly technical issue of migration control. Although we have seen that the constitution of the IOM as a neutral, technical expert required a significant effort from the organization's employees, it was also apparent that the technological nature of its interventions—particularly the provision biometric governance through MIDAS—itself conferred legitimacy to the IOM's claims to neutrality. This technical focus suggests that a final performative dimension of MIDAS related to the non-human technical systems themselves.

Subjectification, governability, and depoliticization: The constitutive effects of MIDAS

Applying the framework of performativity to border security devices themselves highlights the independent political effects of technical systems. Doing so need not imply intentionality of non-human objects, but rather brings into view how technical systems 'make a difference' within broader socio-technical configurations (Amicelle et al., 2015: 297). Neither should a focus on non-human agency obscure the ethical and political accountability of humans who deploy technologies, as I argued in Chapter 3. Rather, a performative reading of MIDAS can contribute to the broader project of theorizing 'processes of subject formation' within the context of crimmigration control (Squire, 2017: 262).

To view technical systems as having performative, constitutive effects is to argue that technology is neither objective and neutral nor merely instrumental to human political interests. Technologies are 'influenced by the ambitions of their generators, the cultural mentalities and personal interest of their operators and the demands of their consumers' (Zedner, 2009: 267), but they also have 'constitutive agency' (Jacobsen, 2015: 48) in that they produce, structure, and modify the political contexts in which they operate. We have seen above how African states and the IOM deployed MIDAS performatively to constitute themselves as particular kinds of actors. Yet, criminologists have noted that in addition to their instrumental and performative use by human actors, technologies modify human practices and produce the subjects and fields of action upon which they operate. For instance, in his analysis of risk-assessment technologies, Robert Werth (2019: 341) has noted how they 'exert performative effects through automatic, institutional, and bureaucratic mechanisms independent of, and sometimes in opposition to, beliefs' of human users.

Scholars of policing and borders have highlighted how security technologies exert performative effects on practices of control through mechanisms such as the creation of feedback loops which feed into technological solutionism (Martins and Jumbert, 2022), connotations of neutrality and teleological 'progress' (Dauchy, 2023; Frowd, 2020), and a reputation of infallibility when compared to humans (Ajana, 2013). These mechanisms were readily apparent in IOM officials' views on the nature of MIDAS. First, the notion of a feedback loop (O'Neil, 2016) highlights how the deployment of the system contributed to the identification of new information gaps that called for the expansion of MIDAS and interlinking it with other systems in the future:

> Our first step was first to get all border posts first computerized, second to get them provincially connected, then to get them centrally connected, and then work with the East African Community and the intergovernmental authority by placing central databases at those HQs, and allow for the representatives of Member States that are based at the EAC to monitor their own migration flows from a central data point. (Diego, interview, 16 February 2021)

In this context, MIDAS was routinely referred to as a 'foundational building system' that subsequently 'facilitates newer systems' (Diego, interview, 16 February 2021).

Second, these expansionist views related to how novel digital technologies were imbued with connotations of technical neutrality and teleological progress. The adoption and expansion of the system was viewed as a natural 'step forward', which was the result of not political decisions but rather an accurate understanding of 'what are the advantages, disadvantages, and real possibilities' of the system (Maria, interview, 10 March 2021). Conversely, choosing not to deploy the system was attributed to a 'lack of [awareness] of the potential of MIDAS' (Georgio, interview, 3 March 2021).

Third, the supposed infallibility of biometrics played a significant role in the legitimization of MIDAS. Scientific research into the reliability of biometrics has suggested that

> [e]fficiency gains are often overstated and fail to take into account an automated border control mechanisms' true ability to process travelers relying instead on the theoretical matching accuracy of a facial recognition algorithm while ignoring real-world accuracy challenges and related but extraneous factors. (Israel, 2020: xv; see also Buolamwini and Gebru, 2018; OHCHR, 2020)

Nonetheless, IOM officials argued that, compared to non-digital methods, biometric border controls were infallible: 'the level of accuracy, it's amazing. And the level of certainty and integrity of the passport or visa, and the data inside the passport, is almost one hundred percent' (José, interview, 2 March 2021). Perceptions of the infallibility of biometric technologies were crucial to the widespread adoption of MIDAS: 'the sense of really one hundred percent or seemingly one hundred percent identifying a person by your bodily features, I think this is something that's, yeah, on a security lens, very attractive' (Zahra, interview, 19 March 2021).

Through the mechanisms of feedback loops, connotations of neutrality and progress, and the supposed infallibility of biometrics, MIDAS exerted its performative effects. What, then, were these performative effects? Werth (2019) has shown how risk-assessment technologies constitute the 'penal subjects' upon which they operate as necessarily 'risky' individuals, and so too biometric border controls constituted a particular kind of political subject. According to IOM official Tom, MIDAS allowed states to 'understand what is a migrant' (Tom, interview, 24 February 2021). The notion that the system performatively produced migrant subjects was reflected in the description of border-crossers who remain unidentified by biometric systems as 'people that do not exist' (Michael, interview, 8 March 2021). Describing individuals as 'identity-less [...] presupposes that they do not have the kind of identity required by state bureaucracy: a stable, objective, unambiguous and thing-like identity' expressed in biometric identifiers (Franko Aas, 2006: 147). By enacting a logic of risk and control related to the 'accurate' identification of individuals at the border, the technical devices constituted the 'migrant' as suspicious and potentially risky. The system was argued 'to prevent, you know, criminal activities, counterterrorism, and this kind of transnational crime, and of course, improving the control and the security of the country' (Luca, interview, 3 March 2021).

However, focusing on how MIDAS constituted marginalized subjects as suspicious gives only a partial view of the system's performative effects. In addition to marking out some migrants as suspicious, novel border control technologies constituted the 'trusted' traveller by making all border-crossers equally 'visible'. It is important to recognize that this visibility can have both inclusionary and exclusionary effects (Martin and Taylor, 2021: 51). More broadly, MIDAS constituted 'migration' itself as a governable 'problem' amenable to techno-solutionist interventions. Rather than simply 'securitizing' migration in terms of threats and risk, the technology contributed to 'a global system of standardized identification and [. . .] the *global intelligibility* of populations' (Franko, 2020: 28, original emphasis). By framing migration in terms of infallible, neutral technologies, the IOM's new technology brought 'migration into being as an object of global governance and perform[ed] it as a *global reality* to manage in technical and pragmatic ways' (Robinson, 2018: 421, original emphasis). According to the organization's officials, by adopting MIDAS, African 'states saw and realized that a computerized border has much more to do than just security' (Diego, interview, 16 February 2021). Not all migration is risky or deviant, but all unordered migration is risky and deviant. In effect, the system constituted migration as a field of governance, which was problematic unless it was statist in the sense of being made visible, ordered, and regulated by state power. Cross-border movements themselves were not necessarily problematic and could indeed be a 'win-win-win [. . .] if migration is orderly'; the problem was 'movements that are not registered in MIDAS' (Tom, interview, 24 February 2021).

Conclusion

Uncovering the politics of global crimmigration control practices is central to the projects of border criminology and transnational criminal justice. A performative analysis of transnational actors operating in this field—as well as the border control devices they have developed and deployed—can be useful to this academic endeavour, and provides the foundations for a more thoroughgoing normative critique of technologized crimmigration control. Performativity can highlight the political stakes inherent in questions about ontology, agency, and subjectivity (Squire, 2017). Claims about accuracy, identification, and technicality implicitly rest upon ontological and political assumptions about the possibility and desirability of technological and biometric governance in the context of migration control. Rather than making claims about the accuracy of biometric technologies or the actuality of dangers posed by migrants—which conform with the ontological assumptions made by technical experts themselves about the 'calculability' (Amoore, 2014) of migration-related problems—performativity provides a basis for contesting crimmigration practices on the level of the social and political assumptions that underpin the deployment of technologies such as MIDAS.

In enacting migration as an object specifically of 'global governance', MIDAS paved the way for migration control interventions by transnational actors such as the IOM. In doing so, the system simultaneously depoliticized these interventions due to its technical nature. As Katja Franko (2020: 29) has argued, global crimmigration control practices are 'of central importance to the preservation of the current social order and to the global allocation of resources. They are vital techniques for maintaining the existing divisions between the Global North and South.' Yet, the relationship between crimmigration control and global hierarchy—which at times threatened to become evident in IOM officials' unease toward the 'post-imperial' nature of the organization's work—was obscured beneath the supposed neutrality of techno-solutionist interventions.

Through a discussion of elite interviews with IOM officials, this chapter has demonstrated the utility of analysing the performative dimensions of MIDAS. However, the discussion above also indicated the need for further empirical and theoretical analysis in later chapters. Thus far, the analysis has been based primarily on accounts by IOM officials. These accounts were limited in the sense that Southern actors' understandings of IOM practices and of the political effects of deploying MIDAS may differ in important ways from IOM officials' perceptions. Considering the pragmatist recognition of the context-specificity and situatedness of knowledge claims (Hickman, 2007), a more complete analysis of how Southern agency has shaped the IOM's deployment of MIDAS in Nigeria requires direct engagement with Nigerian actors themselves, as well as observations of interactions between IOM officials and their Nigerian counterparts in Abuja. Chapter 6 analyses Nigerian state actors' performances of biometric statehood in a broader historical and social context, and examines the MIDAS-related practices of Nigerian officials on the ground. Chapter 7 discusses these field observations from the perspective of the IOM, focusing particularly on the pedagogical practices of IOM officials directly engaging with their Nigerian partners. Chapters 6 and 7 not only discuss further empirical evidence, but also conceptually advance the discussion of performativity outlined in this chapter by drawing on the insights of a pragmatist perspective on technology.

The analysis above regarding the performative effects of the technical components of MIDAS also indicated the need for deeper examination of human–technology relations in the development and deployment of MIDAS. A pragmatist perspective will be helpful in teasing out the distinctions between the performative effects of technology and the political deliberation that sets their human designers and operators apart from the technical tools themselves. As discussed in Chapter 3, such a distinction requires a more sustained analysis of how MIDAS itself impacted 'decisions taken *within* a structure' while uncovering the moments of dislocation in which humans made decisions '*about* a structure' (Howarth, 2013: 185, original emphasis). Such an analysis is the focus of Chapter 8.

6

'Who is in charge here': Territory, Extraversion, and Local Agency in the IOM's Capacity-building Practices in Nigeria

> *Nigeria is not a nation; it is a mere geographical expression. There are no 'Nigerians' in the same sense as there are 'English' or 'Welsh' or 'French'. The word Nigeria is merely a distinctive appellation to distinguish those who live within the boundaries of Nigeria from those who do not.*
>
> —Chief Obafemi Awolowo (1947: 47–48)

> *In the chaos of relations among individuals, groups, class fractions and classes, the State tends to impose a rationality, its own, which has space as its privileged instrument.*
>
> —Henri Lefebvre (2009: 226)

Constructing the boundaries of the state

Territory is a key component of modern statehood. Contemporary states are distinct from previous forms of political authority in that they lay claim to sovereignty over an exclusive geographical area demarcated by linear boundaries. Max Weber's (2009: 78) classic definition of the state specified that the state's 'monopoly on the legitimate use of physical force' was wielded 'within a given territory'. In contrast, political authority in earlier polities and empires emanated outward from urban centres and often overlapped among several rulers and religious authorities. Law, previously, 'was applied to peoples rather than to states or territories' (Branch, 2014: 25), whereas the rationality of modern states has 'space as its privileged instrument'

Outsourcing Crimmigration Control. Samuel Singler, Oxford University Press. © Samuel Singler 2025.
DOI: 10.1093/9780198927525.003.0006

(Lefebvre, 2009: 226). Today, dominant conceptualizations of political and legal authority in general, and criminal law specifically, are geographically bounded. In this context, Emma Kaufman (2022: 362) has argued that 'crime is an idea tied to a location'.

Many authors have shown how the modern conception of territorially exclusive sovereignty has historically been undermined in practice by cross-border movements, sub- and supranational political arrangements, and external control and influence (Agnew, 2015; Beaulac, 2000; Osiander, 2001). Nonetheless, claims to territorial authority remain key markers of sovereign statehood in public discourse and political practice. The ubiquity of equating the geographical boundaries of the state with the limits of society has long impacted academic research as well, resulting in the 'territorial trap' or 'methodological nationalism', in other words the privileging of the nation-state as 'the natural unit of criminological inquiry' (Franko Aas, 2007: 286).

This chapter contributes to existing border criminology scholarship that problematizes territorial statehood (Franko Aas, 2012b; Stambøl and Solhjell, 2021; Valverde, 2011) not by focusing on the empirical falsity of claims to exclusive territorial control (Olonisakin et al., 2018), but rather by critically examining how Nigerian federal authorities actively construct the territoriality of the Nigerian state through their collaboration with the International Organization for Migration (IOM) and their deployment of the organization's Migration Information and Data Analysis System (MIDAS). In the previous chapter, I argued that several states have utilized MIDAS to perform their biometric statehood to an international audience. In this chapter I analyse such performances by Nigerian federal authorities, placing these practices within a broader historical context of territorial sovereignty in postcolonial Africa. In doing so, I highlight the political stakes of the deployment of a biometric border control system by these authorities, both domestically and internationally, by conceptualizing them as an example of 'extraversion' (Bayart, 1993). Authors focused on postcolonial politics in Africa have used this term to describe practices whereby local elites utilize 'their dependent relationship with the external world to appropriate resources and authority in order to establish or reinforce their power over domestic competitors' (Peiffer and Englebert, 2012: 361; Bayart and Ellis, 2000). Below, I demonstrate how Nigerian federal authorities leverage their relationship with the IOM, actively outsourcing the development of crimmigration control practices to the organization, as a deliberate strategy to strengthen their claims to political authority and legitimacy both domestically and internationally.

New technologies—and their deployment in colonial and postcolonial contexts—have long been an important force shaping dominant understandings and practices of territorial sovereignty, as demonstrated by the history of mapmaking techniques and technical tools such as the astrolabe (Branch, 2010; Goettlich, 2019). Linear conceptions of territory 'appeared first in the representational space of maps and only subsequently in political practices on the ground' (Branch, 2014: 3). As Matthew Longo (2018: 36) has argued, 'it is through technological advances in boundary-making that the state and border co-evolved'. Against this background, in this chapter I also ask what is novel about the deployment of MIDAS as a technical practice through which Nigerian federal authorities perform their statehood.

While the notion of performativity provides a useful framework for analysing how federal authorities actively constructed the territorial sovereignty of the Nigerian state, a pragmatist conception of technology guards against an over-emphasis on discursive performances by bringing into view how these practices were shaped by the broader material and technological context of contemporary digitized border control systems. This technological context partly determined the nature of Nigerian performances of territorial sovereignty, by shaping international norms regarding state authority. To qualify as full-fledged states in the eyes of the international community, Nigerian authorities sought to specifically demonstrate their biometric statehood. This kind of state power was characterized by the deployment of a biometric border control system that lives up to international technical standards and 'best practices' (Muller, 2010; Singler, 2021).

A pragmatist conception of technology as 'the invention, development, and cognitive deployment of tools and other artifacts, brought to bear on raw materials and intermediate stock parts, with a view to the resolution of perceived problems' (Hickman, 2001: 12) focuses the analysis on the interplay between technical tools and the perceived problems which human actors attempt to resolve within a broader global context of technological norms. Below, I argue that Nigerian federal authorities' deployment of MIDAS was shaped by postcolonial global hierarchies to the extent that international standards, 'best practices', and the technical components of the system were largely developed in the Global North and embodied Northern logics of territoriality and border control. However, I also demonstrate that perceptions of what social problems a biometric border control was meant to solve differed significantly between Nigerian federal authorities, the IOM, and the organization's Northern donor states.

The analysis below foregrounds the importance of Southern agency in shaping contemporary global practices of crimmigration control. While in subsequent chapters I focus on the political roles of the IOM and of the technical components of MIDAS itself, this chapter demonstrates that neither Northern states, nor international organizations, nor technical devices determined practices in the Global South. Conceptualizing crimmigration control as a global phenomenon requires an account of how Southern actors actively take part in, reinforce, reappropriate, reshape, and resist Northern-produced norms of border control (Šalamon et al., 2020). In the context of MIDAS specifically, an analysis of the agency of Nigerian federal authorities complicated views of the IOM as a 'post-imperial' organization able to impose policies upon its Southern recipient states (Andrijasevic and Walters, 2010; see also Vigneswaran, 2013). The analysis in this chapter contributes to the decolonization and Southernization of border criminology (Carrington et al., 2018; de Magalhães Gomes, 2021), by both situating Nigerian federal authorities' performances of biometric statehood within postcolonial global inequalities and highlighting how these authorities asserted their agency to reshape global norms and translate them into local practices. Central to such practices was the deployment of MIDAS to solve what federal authorities perceived as problems of domestic and international political authority and legitimacy. The system contributed to solving these problems by allowing state agencies to enact the dominant contemporary norm of territoriality: biometric statehood.

This chapter begins by situating contemporary performances of statehood in Nigeria within a broader historical and social context of postcolonial sovereignty in Africa. The relationship between territorial statehood and political authority is complex in the African context; Westphalian notions of territorial control were often colonial impositions, yet ones which later underpinned nationalist independence movements and statehood after decolonization (Lefebvre, 2011; Sharma, 2022). States in the Global South have figured in the literature on migration externalization as actors to whom Northern states outsource border controls (Frelick et al., 2016; Lavenex, 2016), but below I examine how Nigerian federal authorities themselves outsourced the development of crimmigration control practices to the IOM. These authorities productively utilized their relationship with the IOM, and strategically deferred to the organization in the context of migration management, in a process that can be characterized as extraversion. This analysis raises the question of how we should characterize the relationship between Nigerian federal authorities, the IOM, and the organization's Northern donors. In the final section, I evaluate whether Nigerian performances of biometric statehood were the result of a relationship of post-imperial dependence. I argue that while the broader context of global norms regarding biometric statehood was influenced by Northern policy interests and technical developments, nonetheless Nigerian authorities were able to significantly shape how, and to what extent, crimmigration control practices were translated into local contexts.

Postcolonial statehood and the international system

If the historical relationship between sovereign statehood and territorial boundaries has been dynamic and complex everywhere, it is particularly so on the African continent. In the European context, the development of national identities coterminous with state borders was far from natural, instead often representing the product of centuries of both public investment and coercive cultural homogenization through lawmaking and fighting wars (Tilly, 1992). In the wake of decolonization across the African continent, postcolonial states rarely had such a history of concerted nation-building. Oppressive colonial governance had focused more on resource extraction and the violent subjugation of local populations than on societal development, notwithstanding civilizational and paternalistic rhetoric in colonial public discourse (Anghie, 2004; Swatuk, 2001). As Ruben Eberlein (2006: 576) has explained:

> As in Europe, the historical roots of African state-making closely resemble organized crime, but with one decisive difference: the warlords of the Chartered Companies didn't invest their predatorily accumulated capital in the geographical entities they were aspiring to control, but transferred it to Europe or into racially confined enclave economies like plantation farming.

According to Christopher Clapham (1996: 19), after decolonization 'the territorial legitimacy of many of the newly independent states rested more on the establishment of their frontiers by prior international agreement between the former colonial powers than on any sense of nationhood or common identity among the peoples of the territory themselves'. Political elites in states such as Nigeria were well aware of this issue; in the run-up to Nigerian independence, nationalist leader Chief Obafemi Awolowo (1947: 47–48) argued that 'Nigeria is not a nation; it is a mere geographical expression'. In academic analyses of territorial statehood in Africa, it has become commonplace to highlight that 'the boundaries separating African states were created by colonialism, that these boundaries were arbitrarily drawn, and that they separated peoples, linguistic entities, and cultural and political communities that formed natural and homogeneous wholes before colonization' (Mbembe, 2000: 261).

However, focusing on the arbitrariness of borders in Africa risks Eurocentrically contrasting the African experience with an idealized view of nation-states in the Global North. Wars, secessionist movements, and indigenous peoples' right to self-determination all demonstrate that the fit between nation and territorial state has everywhere been constructed, more or less coercively (Barnsley and Bleiker, 2008; Leonard, 2005; Nichols, 2014; Oksanen, 2021). Moreover, in the African postcolonial context, these supposedly groundless and contentious boundaries have remained remarkably stable following decolonization. Wars of secession and other territorial conflicts have rarely resulted in changes to borders, and 'not a single boundary change has occurred in Africa since 1989 without the consent of concerned states. With the exception of Eritrea's negotiated exit from Ethiopia in 1993 and South Sudan's independence in 2011, Africa's borders remain fixed' (Seymour, 2013: 18). It is not clear that Nigeria should be characterized as a 'mere' geographical expression, as its boundaries have remained nearly unchanged for the entirety of the country's independence.[1]

Correcting these analytical shortcomings requires a conceptual shift away from Eurocentric ideals of nation-statehood towards an examination of how territorial statehood as a norm has been actively constructed. Instead of focusing on a supposed gap between *de jure* and *de facto* statehood (Jackson, 1986), the fixity of borders in Africa raises the question of how, why, with what political effects, and in what technological context

[1] The exception to this rule is the Bakassi Peninsula in the South-East of Nigeria, at the Nigeria–Cameroon border. Political control of this disputed territory was transferred from Nigeria to Cameroon in 2008 following lengthy deliberations by the International Court of Justice from 1994 to 2002 (see Babatola, 2012). However, the case of the Bakassi Peninsula does not undermine the broader claim here regarding the remarkable fixity of Nigerian borders; this territory was disputed by two states rather than the ethnic and cultural groups whose interests were given short shrift by the colonially imposed borders of Nigeria.

territoriality has been performed by state agencies. These analytical moves foreground the fact that statehood cannot be conceptualized with reference only to the internal aspects of geographically bounded societies. Rather, it is a category constructed with reference to, and in interaction with, the international society of sovereign states (Bull, 1977).

The weak governance structures of postcolonial states have often been analysed with reference to Eurocentric ideals of Westphalian statehood. In this view, state authority in Africa has been found lacking when compared to the idealized territorial state. Robert Jackson (1986) influentially conceptualized statehood in Africa as a manifestation of 'negative sovereignty', in other words sovereignty in title only, lacking the positive capacity for self-government. Jackson and Rosberg (1986: 2) argued that most 'African states exist primarily by means of international legitimacy. Their sovereignty derives far more from right than from fact.' This understanding of postcolonial statehood subsequently became the dominant framework in analyses of the politics and international relations of the continent. Rita Abrahamsen (2017: 134) has noted that '[t]he African state, it seems, can be almost endlessly pathologized as some deviant form of an ideal Weberian, Western state; suffice to mention the neopatrimonial state, the weak state, the failed state, the criminalized state, the quasi-sovereign state, and so on'.

Analyses of weak governance structures have been important to understanding the sources of conflict, health outcomes, and political processes of democratization in recent decades (Autesserre, 2010; Fearon, 2017; Fearon and Laitin, 2003; Harman, 2012). However, Siba Grovogui (2001: 44) has demonstrated how such analyses, whatever their authors' original 'humanitarian dispositions', can easily lead to 'the proposition that the solution to the post-colonial condition of Africa is to further disempower its states by imposing an overt or disguised form of international trusteeship'. In addition to such obviously deplorable policy implications, such analyses also commit the analytical error of conceptualizing statehood in purely internal terms. In this view, governing capacity is an internal characteristic that societies either possess or lack, and which seems to emerge organically as the result of social cohesion within state boundaries. Once successfully achieved, this governing capacity can be described positively as state sovereignty (Jackson, 2007).

However, the norm of sovereign statehood did not emerge organically when already bounded societies somehow achieved a sufficient level of internal cohesion. Rather, modern notions of sovereignty developed as an international norm through interactions between rulers within Europe, and later between European states and societies in the Global South (Anghie, 2004). State boundaries did not reflect the natural limits of societies: 'for a border to have any meaning it must be accepted and validated by other nation-states as well' (Mechlinski, 2010: 96). The criteria for statehood were decisively determined by the states that are already accepted members of the international society, and these criteria have historically justified colonial and postcolonial global inequalities by marking a 'standard of civilization' that initially excluded non-European societies. Given this historical background, 'since European sovereignty is presumed, the European issue is how conflicts between sovereign states may be resolved in the absence of an overarching sovereign; the problem for the non-European world, by contrast, is how to acquire sovereignty' (Anghie, 1999: 68).

Although views on 'weak' or otherwise deviant statehood in Africa have contributed to highlighting the political significance of international norms in shaping postcolonial conceptions of state sovereignty, by focusing on the internal determinants of state capacity they have perpetuated the myth that 'post-colonial sovereignty constitutes a historical deviation from Western norms, both as a juridical fiction and an empirical reality' (Grovogui, 2001: 30). This view has not only overlooked how 'sovereignty represents an historical mode of global governance intended to effect a moral order of identity and subjectivity' (Grovogui, 2001: 30), but has also contributed to the exclusion of Africa from the creation of knowledge about the international system. Viewed mainly through the lens of deviance from an idealized Eurocentric norm, states in Africa have not often figured in scholarship on international politics and criminology as potential sites for theoretical innovation (Abrahamsen, 2017; Comaroff and Comaroff, 2006; Franko Aas, 2012b). Existing literature on topics such as transitional justice in post-conflict settings, and postcolonial theory more generally, however, has highlighted the potential utility of incorporating insights from political experiences in Africa when theorizing contemporary statehood as well (Césaire, 2000; Fanon, 2001; Gahima, 2012; Loyle, 2018; Mbembe, 2001)

What has been the role of international norms regarding sovereignty in shaping postcolonial statehood in Africa, and what can the development of African states in turn tell us about these norms? The key components of sovereign statehood in the wake of decolonization were outlined in the United Nations General Assembly Declaration on the Granting of Independence to Colonial Countries and Peoples (McWhinney, 2008). Known as Resolution 1514, this declaration stated: 'Any attempt aimed at partial or total disruption of the national unity and territorial integrity of a country is incompatible with the purposes and principles of the Charter of the United Nations' (Seymour, 2013: 20). In this way, the territoriality of nation-states was codified into international law. As states have guarded their authority and legitimacy, 'the international community has generally been loath to permit the breakup of existing states or to admit new states to the club. The weight of international norms strongly favors the status quo, making both the birth of new states and the death of old ones, however decrepit, extremely rare' (Ahram, 2017: 348).

Of course, the extent to which the non-interference principle has in fact been upheld in the African context has been hotly contested throughout the second half of the twentieth century and the beginning of the twenty-first. Given the globally unequal distribution of economic, political, and cultural power, Northern states have been able to indirectly influence the internal policies of states in Africa through bilateral agreements, international aid, and the interventions of international organizations (Abrahamsen, 2000). Kwame Nkrumah (1965), the first president of independent Ghana, characterized such indirect influence as 'neo-colonialism' as early as the 1960s. More recently, authors such as David Williams and Tom Young (2012) have argued that—given the extent to which domestic policies are shaped by the agendas of international organizations such as the World Bank and the International Monetary Fund—the sovereignty of states in Africa has been severely undermined. Williams (2010: 25) describes this predicament succinctly: 'It is clear that sovereignty is no longer a guiding or constitutive norm in contemporary international politics, at least for a significant number of states.'

Yet, states in Africa have continued to assert their territorial sovereignty vigorously. They have done so both discursively, through political declarations about sovereign authority over any international or non-governmental organizations that operate within their borders, and practically, by exerting control over these organizations' activities and even expelling them, as was the case in Sudan in 2009 (Charbonneau, 2009). In many African states, migration control has been a particularly important practical domain for demonstrating territorial authority, precisely because of the weak governance capacity of states. For rural populations in states like Tanzania, migration control checkpoints at the border are the main sites of state visibility (Landau, 2005; Vigneswaran, 2013). In this context, William Brown (2013: 262) has argued that although the substantive policy autonomy of many African states has been curtailed by international interventions, nonetheless territorial sovereignty remains 'the central constitutive institution around which relations between African states and Western donors operate'. Indeed, African states have often productively leveraged their territorial sovereignty to navigate their relationships with Northern states, international organizations, and transnational corporations: 'Sovereignty as a right to rule is therefore critical to the ability of recipient states to exercise agency within the inequalities of the aid relationship' (Brown, 2013: 275).

Border control technologies and sovereign territoriality

Examining Southern agency is central to understanding crimmigration control as a global phenomenon, partly determined by postcolonial global hierarchies yet simultaneously shaped 'from below' by Southern actors themselves (Stambøl, 2021b; Stock et al., 2019). In this section, I place contemporary practices of border control in Nigeria within the historical context of postcolonial statehood in Africa. I then relate the findings from my qualitative interviews and non-participant observations in Abuja, Nigeria, where I spoke to officials from the Nigerian Immigration Service (NIS) and the Ministry of Justice (MoJ) and observed meetings, training sessions, and the everyday practices of NIS officials in cooperation with officials from the IOM. In so doing, I demonstrate how the development of crimmigration control practices in Nigeria—specifically, the roll-out of security-focused digital border control technologies and the merging of the legal and practical frameworks of migration control and criminal justice—was driven both by international pressures at a regional level and by policy input from the IOM. However, discussions with Nigerian federal officials showed that these authorities were not passive recipients or helpless victims of influence or control by external actors. Rather, outsourcing the development of border control frameworks to the IOM constituted a strategy of extraversion by NIS and MoJ officials. These officials leveraged their partnership with the IOM to enact international 'best practices' and technical standards in order to affirm the territorial sovereignty of the Nigerian federal state internationally as well as in relation to competing sources of domestic political authority. This partnership provided federal agencies with important reputational benefits that translated into domestic political power, even though partnering with a UN-affiliated organization offered fewer opportunities to accrue private economic awards through corruption compared to public–private partnerships.

The pragmatist conception of technology outlined in Chapter 3 suggested that the deployment of technical tools is shaped on the one hand by a broader technological context of established and 'habitualized tools, artifacts, and skills', and on the other hand a particular perception of the social problems that the adoption of new tools is meant to resolve (Hickman, 2001: 12). The notion of performativity, in turn, highlighted that the adoption of new technical tools can have political effects independently of their practical impact, by constituting the actors that deploy them. When applied to states, this view implies that 'there is no sovereign state or state identity behind expressions of state sovereignty' (Weber, 1998: 90). State agencies, through their deployment of discourses and practices relating to territorial sovereignty, continually perform their statehood in order to legitimize their political authority. In this section, I examine how federal officials attempted to solve the perceived problem of territorial political authority through the deployment of the system, and analyse the performative effects of these technological practices.

Territory and federal political authority in Nigeria

The territorial borders of Nigeria date back to 1914, when the British colonial government united the Southern and Northern Nigeria Protectorates to form a 'unified colonial state' (Falola and Heaton, 2014: 6). These borders were inherited by the newly independent Nigerian state in 1960, despite their spurious relation to any existing cultural or ethnic boundaries, as described by nationalist leader Obafemi Awolowo earlier in this chapter. Contemporary Nigerians still identify strongly with their local extended family and their ethnic group, of which there are hundreds within the territorial boundaries of the Nigerian state (Campbell and Page, 2018: 8). Domestic politics is profoundly shaped by religious and ethnic divisions. The population is roughly balanced between Muslims and Christians, mirroring the physical juxtaposition of the National Mosque and National Ecumenical Center in Abuja. Three major ethnic groups significantly shape national-level politics: the Hausa, Yoruba, and Igbo, who mainly reside in the North, West, and East of contemporary Nigeria respectively (Eze, 2016). The complexity of these religious and ethnic allegiances, combined with the relative weakness of nationalist sentiment, has resulted in characterizations of the country as 'one of the most deeply divided states on the African continent' (Onuoha, 2011: 407).

Similarly to its territorial borders, Nigeria's criminal justice system is also of colonial origin (Saleh-Hanna, 2008). The British colonial governors introduced criminal courts, imprisonment, and police institutions 'with the primary purpose of protecting British commercial interests in the country' (Otu, 1999: 294). British colonial criminal justice systems did not supersede local arrangements entirely; newly established police forces and English-style courts were mainly used to uphold British commercial interests, while local disputes and crimes were handled by 'traditional judicial institutions' and 'community-based' policing practices, under the banner of 'indirect rule' (Agbiboa, 2013: 259). Although the policy of indirect rule did not entirely dispense with local practices, it still undermined the political authority of local communities. Moreover, this approach should not be mistaken for a humanistic or progressive one: 'the police force in Nigeria was formed by British officials in an effort to protect themselves from the natives they were exploiting and oppressing, both economically and politically' (Otu, 1999: 304).

Political authority in independent Nigeria has been hotly contested, and the history of the state has been marked by periodic military coups and dictatorial takeovers followed by a democratic transition and partial liberalization from 1999 onward (Peiffer and Englebert, 2012: 360). Despite the past few decades of political democratization, Nigeria is characterized as only 'partly free' by Freedom House (2022) and was ranked 154th of 180 countries in the 2021 Corruption Perceptions Index (Transparency International, 2021).

Political contestation and corruption within the country have often been characterized by specifically territorial elements. Since independence, the states that make up the Federal Republic of Nigeria have 'witnessed an unprecedented reduction in their power and a high degree of centralization' (Onuoha, 2011). NIS officials in Abuja were keenly aware that the agency was a federal one, contrasting their role with those of local bureaucracies. As Ike, an official working at NIS headquarters outside Abuja put it: 'We are a federal agency. We look out for everybody, and sometimes we need to remind the states that it is Nigeria that we are protecting, not just Sokoto or Kano [states in Northern Nigeria]' (Field diary, 26 August 2021).

The most significant challenges to Nigerian federal authority have historically been mounted in territorial terms. The most well-known crisis of political authority in the country's history was the civil war from 1967 to 1970, fought between the federal state and the secessionist Biafran army in south-eastern Nigeria (Amao, 2019: 97). In a demonstration of the conservative bent of international norms of state sovereignty, only five states internationally recognized the Biafran secessionist movement: Côte d'Ivoire, Gabon, Haiti, Tanzania, and Zambia (Seymour, 2013: 23). Although the Nigerian federal state achieved military victory in 1970, Igbo-speaking Nigerians in the South-East have continued to press for the establishment of a Biafran state in the twenty-first century, even launching a Biafran International Passport in 2009 (Onuoha, 2011: 413). The Biafran passport initiative demonstrated the importance of specifically territorial imaginaries of political authority within the current landscape of Nigerian domestic politics.

In the North-East of the country, federal officials have faced another pressing challenge to their authority, from the Boko Haram terrorist group. Not only has this group challenged the state's monopoly on the legitimate use of force, they have specifically called into question the territorialization of the Nigerian federal state by exploiting 'the porosity of the state's borders' (Onapajo and Uzodike, 2012: 32). In NIS–IOM training sessions and project reports, this undermining of territorial authority was presented as 'the most visible challenge' to state sovereignty (Field diary, 28 July 2021), and simultaneously an opportunity for federal agencies to reaffirm their authority: 'The responsibility for border security in Nigeria rests primarily on the Nigeria Immigration Service (NIS), which is responsible for front-line inspection of those entering and departing Nigeria' (Field diary, 16 August 2021).

The challenge to federal state authority from the constituent states, secessionist and ethnic political movements, and Boko Haram have been a central factor within Nigerian domestic politics in the twenty-first century (Kayode, 2016). These challenges were explicitly conceptualized by officials from the NIS and MoJ in territorial terms. As NIS official Obi explained: 'What we are really doing, what we are responsible for, is maintaining the strong state. Yes, the police do this, the military do this too, but we are the ones policing the boundaries [of Nigeria]' (Field diary, 6 August 2021). In essence, federal state authorities were engaged in a struggle for territorialization at the national level. Whereas the discourse and practice of NIS and MoJ officials depicted 'sovereignty, territorial legitimacy, and formal control of state apparatuses from above', secessionist movements and local political groups evoked 'popular conceptions of sovereignty that are framed as the preservation of ethnic identities and achieving territorial independence from below' (Onuoha, 2011: 404). Historically, in the face of civil war, secessionist challenges, and coups d'état, the federal state has endured through the centralization of power, in particular through the military and paramilitary federal agencies such as the Nigerian Police Force, the Nigerian Customs Service, and the NIS (Olonisakin et al., 2018: 30). In the context of political liberalization since 1999, these agencies have increasingly turned outward to international partners in their efforts to exert authority over local bureaucracies and political groups.

Traversing the boundary between domestic and international: Extraversion in Africa

Analysing the political significance of African states' claims regarding territorial authority can foreground the agency of Southern actors within the broader context of postcolonial global hierarchies. The norms and practices of territorial sovereignty were historically developed in colonial contexts (Anghie, 2004; Branch, 2014; Goettlich, 2019), and these norms were subsequently promoted and upheld by Northern states and Northern-dominated international organizations. Nonetheless, this postcolonial context does not mean that 'only structure matters'; rather, political elites in the Global South have exhibited 'an autonomy of action' when leveraging the norm of territorial statehood to pursue their political goals both domestically and on the international arena (Bayart and Ellis, 2000: 220–221). The fixity of borders in Africa can certainly be partially explained with reference to the 'international normative foundations of juridical statehood' (Seymour, 2013: 21), but it also requires an account of the agency of local actors who sought to secure control over those state institutions that were internationally recognized as legitimate, and then strategically deployed this sovereign status to affirm their political authority.

Many authors have utilized the notion of extraversion to undertake such an analysis (Bayart and Ellis, 2000; Eberlein, 2006; Peiffer and Englebert, 2012; Stambøl, 2021b). Extraversion refers to local political elites' strategies of 'mobilizing resources derived from their (possibly unequal) relationship with the external environment' (Bayart, 1993: 21–22). Sandra MacLean (2001: 149) explains that 'membership in the select international club of sovereign states conferred formal privileges which leaders found useful as they attempted to consolidate their power, legitimize their regimes, and enhance the economic opportunities for their jurisdiction'. International recognition conferred legitimate authority over the state's security forces and financial resources, as well as access to international aid (Bayart and Ellis, 2000: 225). Despite the supposed arbitrariness of postcolonial borders, political elites in states such as Nigeria and Tanzania have leveraged their internationally recognized sovereign status to lay claim to lucrative national resources within state boundaries (Emel et al., 2011). The practicalities of resource extraction in places such as the oil fields of the Niger River Delta were often outsourced to transnational corporations. Although oil export revenues rarely benefit local populations (Onuoha, 2011), outsourcing constituted a deliberate strategy of extraversion by local elites. Ruben Eberlein (2006: 576) argues that '[w]hat we call the Nigerian state functions as a mighty machine tasked with the privatization of public assets in favor of an extraverted neopatrimonial state class'. In this way, the notion of extraversion is compatible with Nandita Sharma's (2020, 2022) critique of postcolonial nationalist movements as often benefiting national elites much more than delivering on promises of democratization and economic redistribution.

In Abuja, it was impossible to miss the several abandoned building sites that materially embodied dynamics of local corruption, for instance the imposing Abuja National Library building site in the city centre, located between the Abuja National Mosque and the National Ecumenical Center. The building has been in construction since 2006, with wildly fluctuating cost estimates and seemingly little progress toward completion in recent years (Essen, 2022). According to one of the local IOM drivers, Akunna, construction had stalled because 'they already pocketed all the money they could from that project' (Field diary, 3 August 2021). This and other abandoned sites brought into stark relief how the 'infrastructure of the capital Abuja is of little use to most Nigerians, but the construction of the city opened endless possibilities for the privatization of public revenues, shared between office holders, international construction businesses and their contractors' (Eberlein, 2006: 577).

Externally, local political elites have used their sovereign status to resist influence by Northern donor states and international organizations, with varying levels of success. Caryn Peiffer and Pierre Englebert (2012) have demonstrated that differences in levels of reliance on foreign aid and access to natural resources have impacted the extent to which African political elites have been able to exert autonomy within the international arena. Nigeria, as an oil-producing state, has leveraged its strong 'extraversion portfolio' to resist foreign aid conditionality and exert significant influence on regional politics in West Africa (Peiffer and Englebert, 2012: 365).

While most research into strategies of extraversion has focused on resource extraction and relationships with donor states and private companies (although see Stambøl, 2021), below I examine how Nigerian federal state authorities deployed their relationship with the IOM in the context of crimmigration control in an extraverted manner to increase their political influence domestically and within the international system.

The development of postcolonial statehood in Africa has demonstrated the centrality of the norm of territorial sovereignty in shaping global political practices independently of the extent of governing capacity possessed by state institutions. Local political practices that have ensured the fixity of borders in Africa—notwithstanding claims regarding the 'weakness' of states on the continent—can be an important source of knowledge about the nature of sovereign authority in an age of globalization. Building on existing border criminology research into the complex relationship between increased cross-border mobility and the reassertion of territorial authority through penal border control practices in the Global North (Weber and McCulloch, 2019), experiences of postcolonial statehood in the Global South can provide deeper insights into crimmigration control as a global phenomenon that operates against the backdrop of postcolonial global hierarchy, yet which Southern actors also shape in important ways.

MIDAS as extraversion

Although immigration control was established as a federal responsibility already in 1963 through the formation of the Nigerian Immigration Service (NIS), officials from the agency explained that border control in practice was previously decentralized to individual states due to the practical difficulty of coordinating at a national level. According to NIS official Ike, thanks to the deployment of MIDAS, 'this is the first time there is centralized, real-time control at NIS HQ. Before, the states had more independence, because we could not know what they are doing' (Field diary, 26 August 2021). Officials represented this control as crucial to the legitimization of federal authority over local states, comparing their strengthened centralized authority to that of the Nigerian military. Ike's colleague, Gabriel, noted: 'We invited the military to come take a look [at the MIDAS control room in NIS headquarters], and let me tell you, they were impressed! They can see that we are developing too' (Field diary, 26 August 2021). These discussions with NIS officials demonstrated that a key problem the agency attempted to tackle through the deployment of MIDAS was the perceived need to strengthen territorial political authority at the federal level.

Critical criminologists have noted that, in the context of globalization, 'digital technologies permit the organization and coordination of economic, political and cultural life without reference to national borders or the jurisdictional boundaries of legal systems' (Carrington et al., 2018: 10). Yet, in the Nigerian context, NIS officials explained that a digital border control system was crucial to their attempts at the territorialization of political authority at a federal level. The importance of MIDAS for territorial sovereignty did not arise simply from the practical affordances of the system. In fact, the extent to which the new system has actually transformed practices on the ground was still highly limited, and large swathes of Nigeria's 'borders are not monitored, patrolled or controlled' (Ifeanyi-Aneke et al., 2021: 129). At NIS headquarters, the high-tech MIDAS control room was only partly operational, and some of the key digital components of the system, in particular its connection to Interpol's international alert lists, were not yet in use. Despite its capacity for operations such as automated facial recognition, MIDAS in Nigeria did not automatically compare a live facial image to travel documents, which was instead done manually by border control agents.

Nonetheless, officials performatively deployed the system to shore up their federal authority vis-à-vis local state bureaucracies as well as other federal agencies. According to NIS official Benjamin, although the system was not yet fully operational, 'MIDAS has made it clear that it is the Federal Government, not the states, who is in charge here' (Field diary, 26th August 2021). The importance of exclusive control over MIDAS to the NIS's political authority was reflected in the difficulties that the IOM faced in setting up interagency cooperation procedures for 'secondary inspection', in other words sharing data regarding hits in alert lists with relevant law enforcement institutions and other federal agencies. These procedures were required for the system to connect to Interpol's I-24/7 alert list and to process Advance Passenger Information (API) data, but establishing such interagency cooperation was difficult due to hesitance on part of the NIS. An official from the MoJ recounted: 'setting up secondary inspection, this has been an issue for some time. We are ready, we know what are the critical agencies that are needed in secondary inspection [. . .] But this is a problem for them [NIS]' (Field diary, 28 July 2021). According to one IOM official in Abuja, 'interagency cooperation is the most political, and this is why it is also the most difficult activity to achieve' (Field diary, 28 July 2021).

When conceptualizing the adoption of MIDAS by federal authorities as a strategy of extraversion, it is important to note that the system is free to recipient states. In other words, it did not provide federal state officials with opportunities for corruption, unlike the adoption of an expensive system developed by a private vendor. Such considerations were particularly significant in the Nigerian context, where researchers have noted that paramilitary organizations including the police and the immigration service have historically been highly corrupt (Bello, 2018: 145). In a comparison of 34 African countries in 2015, the Nigerian Police Force was ranked as the least trusted and 'most corrupt' public institution among the general public (Olonisakin et al., 2018: 31). As IOM official Fabian explained, in many country contexts, when rolling out MIDAS,

> there's a corruption side. There is a complete aversion to digitizing because it interferes with daily incomes [. . .] So there's that issue, you know, that [MIDAS] really takes over the border, the border management, from provincial managers. It's not seen as a positive development at all. (Interview, 12 February 2021)

In other words, partnership with the IOM did not confer upon Nigerian federal officials the kinds of private economic rewards that often characterize extraversion. According to IOM officials in Abuja, much of the organization's success in rolling out MIDAS in Nigeria rested on the active interventions of NIS Comptroller General Muhammed Babandede, who was head of the agency from 2016 to 2021. IOM official Mia explained that the willingness of federal agencies to engage with IOM largely depended on the extent to which these agencies' directors sought private benefits from public office: 'Many agencies are very corrupted, and the IOM is poor, so they want nothing to do with us [. . .] Babandede is a nationalist, he wants what's best for Nigeria, and not just his home state, you know?' (Field diary, 6 September 2021).

The lack of private economic rewards from the NIS–IOM partnership did not mean that federal officials gained nothing from this relationship. NIS officials deployed MIDAS performatively to assert territorial authority at a national level; the key benefits of adopting a system developed by the IOM, as opposed to private vendors, were reputational and political. NIS official Obi declared that 'IOM is the chief partner of all partners' (Field diary, 6th August 2021). This reputation—which results both from the IOM's field expertise and from its affiliation with the United Nations—was highly significant in legitimizing the NIS as the key actor responsible for migration control in Nigeria. As I explore in more detail in the next chapter, the IOM actively sought to promote international 'best practices' through their operations in Nigeria, on topics such as gender sensitivity and data security. Obi explained that the NIS has allowed the IOM to reshape national border management training curricula according to such 'global standards', as 'the IOM is uniquely placed as a UN actor to get Nigeria up to speed' (Field diary, 6 August 2021). Partnership with the international organization, then, made up in reputational benefits what is lacked in private economic rewards.

The relationship between the IOM and the NIS was not always perceived as entirely free from tensions. As part of their promotion of international 'best practices'—many of which were related to the technical specifications of MIDAS—the IOM sought to strengthen interagency cooperation between federal authorities such as immigration control services, police forces, customs agencies, and ministries of justice in the Member States that adopted MIDAS. In Nigeria, IOM officials characterized interagency cooperation as 'the most difficult activity to achieve' (Field diary, 28 July 2021). An official from the MoJ, Tayo, commented that interagency cooperation with the NIS was 'always difficult [. . .] Lots of work is needed to get everyone to work together' (Field diary, 29 July 2021). Nonetheless, the NIS engaged extensively in IOM capacity-building exercises including workshops and working groups to promote interagency cooperation, to ensure continued access to the reputational benefits from working with a UN-affiliated organization. For this reason, as I explain in the next section and the following chapter, the IOM's views on the necessity of merging the legal frameworks and practices of migration control and criminal justice have begun to shape the landscape of border control in Nigeria as well.

Moments of tension between the IOM's capacity-building agenda and the NIS's attempts at affirming their political authority at a national level—ideally, unsullied by interagency cooperation and sharing responsibility with other federal actors—demonstrated the extent to which local actors shaped the roll-out of MIDAS in Nigeria. Officials from the NIS utilized the deployment of the system and their partnership with the IOM to solve perceived problems of asserting territorial sovereign authority. As I discuss in the next chapter, the IOM developed MIDAS to solve very different kinds of problems, mainly relating to the ordering of migration and the legitimization of the international states system in a context of increasing cross-border mobility. A pragmatist conception of technology as a set of rationalities and technical tools deployed to resolve particular social problems highlights how the political meaning of a biometric control system depends upon who uses it, and what problems it is meant to resolve. Remaining technical difficulties and empirical challenges to the more 'complete' roll-out of MIDAS were not always important from the perspective of NIS officials, so long as they could deploy the system performatively to enact their territorial authority domestically.

Biometric statehood, post-imperial influence, and Southern agency

If territorial sovereign authority constituted the pressing domestic social problem that federal officials have attempted to resolve through the deployment of MIDAS, the broader technological context of 'habitualized tools, artifacts, and skills' (Hickman, 2001: 12) in which the system was adopted was largely shaped by Northern-produced technical standards and 'best practices'. This section examines the external dimensions of the deployment of MIDAS in Nigeria in order to evaluate claims about the post-imperial influence of the IOM (Andrijasevic and Walters, 2010). I argue that although MIDAS in many ways materially embodied Northern logics of crimmigration control, and in this sense the deployment of the system should be analysed against the background of postcolonial global hierarchy, nonetheless the IOM was not able to impose the system on unwitting or unwilling Nigerian federal officials. The active participation of the NIS in IOM capacity-building practices was crucial to the successes of the organization in the country.

Despite the extent to which MIDAS has shaped border control practices in Nigeria, federal officials successfully utilized the system to strengthen—not undermine—their territorial sovereign authority. They did so not only through strategies of extraversion designed to reaffirm their domestic political authority, but also through performatively deploying MIDAS to demonstrate their biometric statehood to an international audience. These performances, in turn, allowed the Nigerian federal state to effectively leverage its sovereign status for influence within the international system, both regionally and vis-à-vis Northern states. This account of the agency of Nigerian federal agencies in shaping the deployment of MIDAS, and using the system to shore up their territorial sovereign authority, demonstrates how attempts to Southernize border criminology need to complicate simplistic North–South dichotomies by examining which particular actors deploy what kinds of tools and practices of border control and why. Following Nandita Sharma's (2020) critique of nationalism as a supposedly progressive decolonial force, I also argue that although territorial sovereignty in this context was used by Nigerian federal elites to resist post-imperial influence, this form of Southern agency did not necessarily empower non-elite Nigerians or increase their global mobility to any significant extent.

Nigeria and the international system

The Nigerian federal state has a long history of engagement with the international system. Among African states, the country has demonstrated particular fervour for anti-colonial political action (Amao, 2019). Its large population and economy, significant political and military strength, and abundant oil reserves have earned Nigeria the nickname 'the giant of Africa' (Fagbadebo, 2007: 29). Despite its postcolonial status and relative economic and political weakness within broader North–South global hierarchies, scholars of International Relations such as Eduard Jordaan (2003: 170) have characterized Nigeria as a 'middle power' that is 'regionally dominant and as such, benefit[s] from the rules of the hegemonic order vis-à-vis weaker states in the region, even though [it is] in turn in a weaker position vis-à-vis states in the core'. The regional influence of Nigeria is reflected in its dominance within several regional organizations (ECDPM, 2017), not least the African Union and the Economic Community of West African States (ECOWAS). Nigeria played a central role in the creation of ECOWAS, an organization which has extensively shaped border control practices in the region and conferred upon its member states the power of collective bargaining when engaging with Northern actors such as the EU (Stambøl and Solhjell, 2021).

Historically, the Nigerian federal state actively promoted anti-colonial efforts across the African continent and has resisted neo-imperial influence from wealthier Northern states as well. Following the civil war fought against the Biafran secessionist movement, the Nigerian federal state 'had developed strong resistance to interference in the domestic affairs of African states, and has subsequently pursued this objective as a matter of foreign policy' (Amao, 2019: 97). It severed diplomatic ties with Israel in 1973 over the latter's support for the Biafran political movement, although

Israel never recognized the Biafran state as legitimate. Through its active opposition to apartheid in South Africa, Nigeria 'positioned itself as a rallying point against post-colonial attempts by the West to regain dominance in Africa, electing to support the rest of Africa against any uninvited interference' (Amao, 2019: 97). Nigerian anti-colonial efforts across the continent have also resulted in diplomatic confrontations with Northern states, including the United States, but Nigerian authorities have continued to oppose Northern state interventions on the continent. In the 1980s, Bolaji Akinyemi (1982: 227–228) characterized Nigeria as 'unique' in its 'foreign policy independence' despite significant bilateral pressure from the United States.

This active engagement in anti-colonial politics across the continent does not mean that Nigeria has been free from regional criticism or attempts at external intervention. South Africa, following the end of apartheid and the beginning of democratization, actively campaigned for the suspension of Nigeria from the United Nations in the 1990s due to the autocratic nature of the military government at the time (Ebegbulem, 2013: 33). In the period of relative political liberalization since 1999, external intervention—although, as outlined above, not without the support of certain local political elites—has manifested in the form of resource extraction, capacity-building interventions by international organizations, and bilateral aid from wealthier Northern states (Ebinumo and Ikunga, 2019). The economy of Nigeria is dependent on profits from resource extraction by transnational oil corporations as well as on foreign aid: in 2022, Nigeria received $4.44 billion in development assistance and official aid (World Bank, 2024).

In short, Nigeria's engagement in the international system has been characterized by both active resistance to Northern influences across the African continent and partial dependence on external involvement and aid facilitated by domestic federal political elites. This engagement has been characterized by overt assertions of sovereign autonomy in response to external political pressures, and notions of territoriality have been central to contesting Nigerian sovereignty. Diplomatic tensions increased given challenges to Nigerian federal territorial control, in the context of international support of Biafran succession movements in the 1970s as well as after 1999 (Onuoha, 2011). In turn, Nigeria's ability to leverage its sovereign status in international politics has rested upon the robustness of its territorial authority. International engagement with ECOWAS as well as Northern donors has often stalled when other states have questioned the ability of the Nigerian federal state to properly control its borders and assert its authority in the northeastern states where Boko Haram is active (Okunade and Ogunnubi, 2021).

The international dimensions of crimmigration control

The tension between Nigerian sovereign autonomy and its external relations, combined with the perceived importance of border control to federal authority both domestically and among an international audience, focuses the analysis of MIDAS on the international dimensions of crimmigration control in Nigeria. International 'best practices', diplomatic pressures, and global technical norms provide the broader background context within which the system was deployed by Nigerian federal authorities, and in this way shaped the roll-out of MIDAS even as NIS officials deployed the system to solve problems of domestic political authority. MIDAS materially embodied both Nigerian federal authorities' contemporary attempts to strengthen and legitimize their claims to national-level territorial control, and pressures towards certain—externally produced—norms regarding border control practices in the context of globalization.

According to contemporary global norms regarding territorial sovereignty, statehood is conceptualized in terms of state agencies' ability to regularize cross-border mobility not by limiting or stopping it entirely, but rather by sorting risky from trusted travellers using biometric data (Franko Aas, 2011a; Muller, 2010). This is what I term biometric statehood. One dimension of this norm is that the expansion of biometric systems at the border has been combined with a merger of biometric migration control databases with the legal frameworks and practices of criminal justice; in short, the global trend toward crimmigration control (Šalamon et al., 2020).

In Nigeria, the responsibilities of the NIS on the one hand and the Nigerian Police Force and the MoJ on the other have historically been quite distinct. In fact, this distinction has differed markedly from practices in Nigeria's Francophone ECOWAS neighbours, in which 'border management and immigration administration are handled by the police' (Bisong, 2019: 1299). In the context of cooperation within ECOWAS, which NIS official Olayemi described as 'a key pillar of Nigeria's international relations' (Field diary, 3 August 2021), the NIS faced significant pressures to establish more extensive practical and legal frameworks for interagency cooperation between the NIS, the police force, and the MoJ. These pressures were partly regional, arising in the context of the ECOWAS Protocol on Free Movement (Okunade and Ogunnubi, 2021). However, the IOM has also played a key role in the development of crimmigration control in Nigeria by creating working groups on interagency cooperation and even drafting new legislative frameworks for data sharing between law enforcement agencies and the NIS, as I discuss in more detail in the next chapter.

Yet, crimmigration control practices were not only developed in response to international pressures to do so; they also performatively legitimized the territorial authority of Nigerian federal agencies. As with the technical components of MIDAS, from the perspective of NIS officials, the reputational benefit that resulted from outsourcing the development of crimmigration control practices to the IOM and its Northern states was at least as important as any practical benefits or changes arising from externally funded training programmes or legal frameworks. Each IOM-funded workshop, training centre, and border post was equipped with highly visible logos and flags of donor countries.

Visibly highlighting the international dimensions of crimmigration control practices in Nigeria allowed federal agencies to perform their biometric statehood not only domestically but also to an international audience. NIS officials were aware of the importance of border control to Nigeria's involvement in the international system. Gabriel, working at NIS headquarters, argued that '[before MIDAS] we had nothing, we had pen and paper. Having a modern, biometric system is needed for us to be active in the international system' (Field diary, 26 August 2021). Gabriel's colleague, Ike, added: 'Data, data, it's all about data. And showing other states that you have the tools to collect it' (Field diary, 26 August 2021).

Performing biometric statehood was not only about collecting biometric data, but also demonstrating state capacity to utilize this data in a criminal justice context. Transnational organized crime, human trafficking, and counterterrorism were key policy fields in which Nigeria performed its biometric statehood to an international audience. The deployment of MIDAS allowed Nigerian federal authorities to demonstrate their crimmigration control credentials, already resulting in a new international deal on migration with the UK in July 2022. In the context of this deal, then UK Home Secretary Priti Patel explained that these two states will 'share their expertise to take the fight to criminal people smugglers who are responsible for a wide range of criminality [. . .] This landmark agreement will increase the deportation of dangerous foreign criminals' (UK Home Office, 2022). The Nigerian MoJ is also now involved in a UN Office on Drugs and Crime

(UNODC) initiative to deploy Nigerian prosecutors as liaison magistrates in Italy and Spain which, in the words of one Nigerian prosecutor, has resulted in a network 'which enables the EU and African prosecutors and law enforcement authorities to reach out to each other not only through official channels but also informally' (UNODC, 2020). Discussions regarding interagency cooperation and the establishment of interoperability between biometric immigration and law enforcement databases have been central to Nigeria's cooperation with the UN Counter-Terrorism Implementation Task Force (UN CTITF). Shared projects between CTITF and Nigerian 'immigration, law enforcement and customs agencies' have long aimed 'to develop an integrated information-sharing system and establish a central national database linked to the national security agencies and international databases' (UN CTITF, 2012: 3, 22).

Federal officials also regularly demonstrated their biometric border control capabilities to external audiences through highly visible promotional events and visits. For instance, in 2023 Nigeria's Minister of Interior demonstrated MIDAS to a delegation of security officials from other countries, stating that 'the NIS is now better equipped with advanced technology to curtail any breach in Nigeria's borders' (Akintaro, 2023). Such statements and demonstrations have been crucial to ensuring Nigeria's active involvement in regional and global political partnerships, despite experts and researchers arguing that the country's borders remain highly permeable (Ifeanyi-Aneke et al., 2021).

Southern agency in postcolonial contexts

The domestic and international dimensions of crimmigration control in the context of the deployment of MIDAS in Nigeria complicates assessments of the IOM's role as a post-imperial organization. It is true that increasing cooperation between criminal justice and migration control agencies in Nigeria was partly driven by pressures from Northern states and from the IOM. The EU, for instance, was actively involved with ECOWAS to shape the organization's migration control agenda according to the European migration control goals, through tools such as the EU Emergency Trust Fund for Africa (Bisong, 2019: 1303). In internal IOM documents as well as discussions with IOM officials, Northern donor states' goals were often described in terms of 'curbing irregular migration flows to Europe', as IOM official Louise put it (Interview, 9 March 2021). The organization's training programmes and workshops promoted a particular conception of migration control, characterized by a focus on security, crime control, and state sovereignty, all of which were promoted under the banner of international 'best practices'.

Yet, Nigeria's crimmigration control agenda has at every step been significantly shaped by the agency of federal authorities themselves. These officials chose to deploy MIDAS rather than use alternative systems, despite the lack of private economic rewards involved in doing so, to solve perceived problems of domestic and international political authority. For these officials, partnering with the IOM accrued significant reputational benefits, and outsourcing the development of crimmigration control frameworks to the organization further strengthened the federal state by allowing it to assert its authority more effectively within Nigeria and perform biometric statehood to an international audience. Just as in other areas of transnational 'norm diffusion' (Shiffman et al., 2018), so too in the context of crimmigration control was a broader global set of norms translated into this local context through the active participation of Nigerian federal authorities.

Whenever these authorities felt that the political costs of outsourcing the development of crimmigration control practices to the IOM might outweigh the benefits—as in the context of interagency cooperation—IOM officials faced significant obstacles to their operations in the country. Given the increasing digitalization of border controls, combined with an awareness of the transnational nature of contemporary security risks, both practitioners and academics have often viewed international migration data sharing as a natural next step in the development of border management practices (Okunade and Ogunnubi, 2021: 127). In Nigeria, the IOM even produced several reports and recommendations regarding international data sharing agreements with other states. Such initiatives have thus far been unsuccessful, however, due to the concerns of federal authorities, who viewed control over migration data as a reflection of their territorial authority. As IOM official Maria explained, 'the issue of data comes up quite regularly, always in the same terms, but without any progress' (Interview, 10 March 2021). Academic researchers have also noted that 'political challenges to the successful implementation of the ECOWAS Protocol lie in what borders symbolize for some states' (Okunade and Ogunnubi, 2021: 127).

The foregoing discussion has also demonstrated that the scope of agency for Nigerian federal actors was constrained and shaped by the broader context of postcolonial global hierarchy. While federal authorities utilized MIDAS to shore up their domestic political authority, their decision to deploy the system was also underpinned by considerations regarding economic dependency on foreign aid and a perceived need to perform state capacity to an international audience as well, in terms that were mandated by the Northern-produced norm of biometric statehood. Nonetheless, just as Nigerian political elites have used strategies of extraversion in other policy areas, in the field of migration control 'externalization policies are also contested and changed at local levels by actors and institutions "from below"' (Stock et al., 2019: 4). Analysing penal aid from the EU to West African countries, Eva Stambøl (2021: 548) has noted:

> That there is power asymmetry between Africa and Europe does not mean that African governments cannot exert political agency and leverage vis-à-vis the EU. Indeed, several African countries, especially those labeled as migration 'origin' or 'transit' countries, have played on their strategic position and increased bargaining power to align EU aid objectives with their own political agenda.

In order to avoid Eurocentric analyses of digital crimmigration control, it is invaluable to examine how Southern state agencies have actively shaped these emerging global practices (Šalamon et al., 2020). Postcolonial state institutions provide a particularly interesting empirical context for understanding the relationship between globalization and sovereign penal power, as statebuilding in Africa has always 'been accompanied by the tendency toward globalization, far more often than it has been impeded or contradicted by globalization' (Bayart and Ellis, 2000: 242). As border criminologists have highlighted in the context of outsourced crimmigration control practices in the Global North, it is not always clear that globalization necessarily undermines state power (Infantino, 2019). Rather than starting with assessments of the relative weakness or strength of 'the state' in response to the pressures of globalization, it is useful instead to conceptualize 'the Nigerian state as *one* of many institutional expressions of social power relations, where hegemony, authority and sovereignty are fought over' (Eberlein, 2006: 590, original emphasis). If the pressures of globalization caused a 'deterritorialization' of state power, crimmigration control practices by several state agencies, international organizations, and private actors can be understood as 'permanent attempts at reterritorialization'

(Engel and Olsen, 2012: 58). In contrast to international and transnational actors—and notwithstanding claims about the arbitrariness or empirical porousness of Nigerian borders—federal state agencies' political performances were still distinctive due to their enactment of a national Nigerian territory in line with the norm of biometric statehood.

This analysis of the political agency of Nigerian federal elites also serves as a reminder for border criminologists engaged with the projects of Southernization and decolonization to complicate simplistic North–South dichotomies in their analyses of the relationship between crimmigration control practices and postcolonial global hierarchies. Nandita Sharma's (2020) critical analysis of postcolonial statehood and anti-colonial nationalisms is instructive in this regard. According to Sharma (2022: 644), although nationalism did 'become a main form of anti-colonial action across imperial colonies in Asia, Africa, the Caribbean, and the Pacific', struggles for national self-determination often still resulted in intensified domestic inequalities and the political capture of state institutions by local elites. Against this background, critiques of neocolonialism—used to argue that a lack of economic and political development were due primarily to continued external influence by former imperial metropoles (Nkrumah, 1965)—risk obscuring undemocratic political dominance of domestic elites by providing 'a powerful alibi to rulers of the "national liberation" states for their failures to end the very practices that anti-colonial struggles fought against' (Sharma, 2022: 645).

The case of the expansion of MIDAS in Nigeria also demonstrates the ambiguous political nature of Southern agency in shaping global practices of digital crimmigration control. Federal authorities primarily from the NIS strategically deployed the system to shore up their claims of sovereign territorial statehood vis-à-vis both domestic and international audiences. In this sense, accounting for Southern agency is a crucial corrective to simply focusing on the post-imperial influence of Northern states and Northern-funded international organizations in shaping crimmigration control practices on a global level. Yet, Southern agency does not immediately imply a democratization of these practices across political and class lines, if this agency manifested primarily as the ability of existing political elites to further strengthen their claims to political legitimacy over competing sources of domestic political authority. The strategic use of digital crimmigration control systems by Nigerian federal political elites also suggests that even when these tools are requested and deployed by Southern actors themselves, they are still likely to retain their exclusionary and securitized dynamics and unlikely to increase the global mobility of local populations.

Conclusion

This chapter has highlighted the indispensability of accounting for Southern agency when examining the global dimensions of crimmigration control. The case of MIDAS in Nigeria showed that the political significance of border control technologies depends on who is deploying the technologies and what kinds of social problems these actors are attempting to solve through their utilization of particular technical tools. Nigerian federal officials used MIDAS to reaffirm and legitimize their domestic political authority, which they conceptualized explicitly in national-level territorial terms. Simultaneously, they used this system to perform biometric statehood to an international audience in order to gain political leverage and influence within the international system. These officials exerted significant influence on how, and to what extent, crimmigration control practices were translated into local contexts.

Analysing the role of Southern actors in enacting and shaping global crimmigration control practices is not simply a matter of expanding the empirical horizons of border criminology (Brown, 2018). It can also demonstrate that the processes of globalization do not 'take their toll across the globe in the same way and to the same extent' (Walklate, 2018: 3). Nigerian federal state agencies' performative practices not only bring into view differences in how globalization and state authority are experienced and enacted in different geographical and cultural contexts, but can also generate broader theoretical insights into the nature of state penal power in the context of migration control (de Magalhães Gomes, 2021: 91). In this way, Southernizing criminology by examining crimmigration control practices in Nigeria offers 'a unique opportunity to deal with the objectives of critical criminology as closely as possible to its assumptions' by 'exercising listening, putting oneself in context, assuming the hidden provinciality in the defense of one's universal condition, [and] learning from the one who was considered alienated' (Pires, cited in de Magalhães Gomes, 2021: 99).

Notwithstanding the impact of Nigerian federal authorities' agency on the roll-out of MIDAS in Nigeria, the discussion in this chapter also highlighted that their agency was situated within the broader context of postcolonial global hierarchy as well as domestic relations of political and class hierarchy (Sharma, 2020; Singler, 2023). The IOM—funded by wealthy Northern states and mainly intervening in Southern states—is a key actor responsible for the diffusion of norms regarding crimmigration control on a global level. In the next chapter, I turn to an analysis of the deployment of MIDAS from the perspective of the organization, which seeks to 'facilitate safe, orderly and regular migration' (IOM, 2022a) through its capacity-building efforts in Nigeria.

7
'If we don't do it, it's just not going to happen': Shaping the Digital Futures of Crimmigration Control in Nigeria

> *Solutions to the problem of knowledge are solutions to the problem of social order.*
>
> —Steven Shapin and Simon Schaffer (1985: 332)

A pedagogical paradox

In Abuja, I observed several meetings, workshops, and training sessions arranged and run by the International Organization for Migration (IOM) regarding various technical, operational, and legal dimensions of the Migration Information and Data Analysis System (MIDAS). These meetings often involved Nigerian federal officials primarily from the Nigerian Immigration Service (NIS), the Federal Ministry of Justice (MoJ), and the Nigeria Police Force. Sometimes, officials would join from other agencies as well, such as the Department of State Services (DSS), the Office of the National Security Adviser (ONSA), and the National Drug Law Enforcement Agency (NDLEA). Training sessions usually focused on the practicalities of utilizing the digital tools that comprised existing MIDAS installations, while planning meetings and workshops were characterized by a distinct focus on the future development and expansion of this system. These future-oriented discussions were not only telling in terms of potential upcoming changes to the landscape of digital border control in Nigeria; they also revealed important insights about the political role of the IOM in shaping migration management and crimmigration control practices in Nigeria and beyond through the provision of MIDAS.

Outsourcing Crimmigration Control. Samuel Singler, Oxford University Press.
DOI: 10.1093/9780198927525.003.0007

Between July and September 2021, many of these planning meetings involved discussions with contracted legal experts from the United Kingdom to discuss the data protection and privacy rights implications of an expanded MIDAS installation. Nigerian federal authorities had passed the Nigeria Data Protection Regulation (NDPR) in 2019, which would eventually become the Nigeria Data Protection Act (NDPA) in 2023 (for an extended discussion, see Singler and Babalola, 2024). In 2021, the IOM closely supported Nigerian federal authorities to ensure that the NDPA would—at some point in the future—eventually allow the country to process Advance Passenger Information (API) and Passenger Name Record (PNR) data at its external borders.

These data will be collected for the purposes of crime control and countering terrorism: 'By checking the data against law enforcement watch lists, such as those of INTERPOL, border officials can know in advance whether FTFs [foreign terrorist fighters] or other suspicious individuals are attempting to enter their country' (IOM, 2022d). API and PNR data are also more sensitive and expansive forms of digital surveillance at the border (Han et al., 2017). Despite the technical affordances of MIDAS, the system will not be able to connect to international alert lists or process API and PNR data before the establishment of further operational and legal frameworks as required by the IOM, the International Civil Aviation Organization (ICAO), and Interpol. As of 2024, Nigeria had still not implemented API/PNR data collection at its digital borders. According to the Nigeria Civil Aviation Authority (NCAA) (2024: 9), the development of remaining API/PNR-related legislative frameworks and operational procedures would rely on assistance from the IOM and other UN agencies, 'in line with international standards and good practices'.

During one of these meetings in August 2021, IOM officials discussed their efforts to influence the final text of the NDPA. The organization's officials considered how to balance their attempt to shape Nigerian legislation—according to 'technical considerations' and international 'best practices'—with respecting the sovereign prerogatives of Nigerian federal authorities. On one hand, as one official stated: '[The IOM] should provide a solution that guarantees their sovereign right over the data processing that MIDAS provides them with' (Field diary, 5 August 2021). On the other hand, according to another official: 'Our recommendations on privacy and data protection laws are needed for the API law to be of an internationally acceptable standard [. . .] We have to make sure these frameworks are in line with global best practices' (Field diary, 5 August 2021). In addition to the balance between external expert guidance and sovereign authority, these officials were seemingly concerned that the future expansion of MIDAS might undermine individual rights to privacy and data protection: 'Privacy laws still apply in a law enforcement context [. . .] You don't want a situation where secondary inspection [consisting of law enforcement and security agencies] can do whatever they want' (Field diary, 5 August 2021). Despite these concerns, however, all officials in the meeting assumed that a further expansion of the data collection capabilities of MIDAS was necessary to tackle transnational crime and terrorism at the border.

The discussions and debates I observed during this meeting and others illustrate several key dynamics related to the 'technopolitics' of border control in the Global South (Müller and Richmond, 2023; Singler and Milivojevic, 2024). As demonstrated in other contexts by scholars of border criminology (Franko Aas, 2006; Milivojevic, 2021) and critical security studies (Amicelle et al., 2015), framing border control practices as central to combatting transnational crime and terrorism clearly underpinned the expansion of tools like MIDAS. Moreover, in line with existing literature on 'border externalization' and the 'post-imperial' dimensions of Northern-funded border control interventions in the Global South (Andrijasevic and Walters, 2010; Bartels, 2018; Stambøl, 2021b), IOM officials were explicitly aware of the risk of encroaching on Nigerian sovereignty in their attempt to influence the legislation of a sovereign African state. Finally, the relationship between novel technologies and new legislation was characterized by contingency and contestation. Neither law nor technology overdetermined the characteristics of the other, suggesting the need to examine 'law or regulation and data infrastructures *together* as co-emergent by empirically following their interrelations' (Sullivan, 2022: S33, original emphasis).

However, other aspects of the meetings, workshops, and training sessions I observed in Abuja were more surprising. Despite the underlying logics of crime control and countering terrorism, discussions relating to the expansion of MIDAS did not rely on exceptionalist framings of migration as a 'crisis' or 'emergency' (Aradau and Munster, 2009; Soliman, 2019). Rather, 'migration management' was largely framed as a mundane governance issue 'solvable' through technical expertise and digital technologies. Moreover, instead of a straightforward dynamic of external influence and Northern border 'externalization' (Lemberg-Pedersen, 2019), the deployment of MIDAS was significantly shaped by the political goals and interests of Nigerian federal authorities. The interplay between the IOM and local state agencies calls for a more nuanced analysis of how 'post-imperial' influence operates on the ground. Finally, in contrast to the view that human rights offer an effective political strategy for resisting the expansion of new digital border surveillance systems (see, e.g., Trauttmansdorff, 2022: 146), in Nigeria the expansion of MIDAS in fact proceeded in tandem with the development of new rights-based legal frameworks. Rights-based discourses did not appear as an obstacle to the further expansion of security and criminal justice practices at the border. Instead, rights themselves were co-opted as a mechanism 'through' which security and crime control technologies at the border were legitimized and expanded, and which reaffirmed the rights-based expertise of the UN-affiliated IOM (Sokhi-Bulley, 2019).

Below, I argue that MIDAS performed important political functions from the perspective of the IOM: it legitimized the organization's authority and depoliticized cross-border mobility by materially enacting the discourse of 'migration management'. Given the limited flexibility of border control tools at the point of their deployment, 'the conceptions, interests and values of actors who design those devices matters as well as those who operate them' (Martin-Mazé and Perret, 2021: 281). If Nigerian federal authorities used MIDAS to solve perceived problems of domestic and international political legitimacy and authority, what social problems did the IOM attempt to solve through the development and deployment of this system?

I begin by situating the IOM within contemporary postcolonial hierarchies of political and economic influence, which underpin contemporary global norms of cross-border mobility and border control. The IOM has used its 'capacity-building' interventions—which include technical, legal, and operational components—to reinforce state-centric norms according to which cross-border mobility is viewed as a potential challenge to state sovereignty unless 'ordered' according to economic and security logics. To this end, the organization both reinforced Nigeria's external borders and promoted the development of deterritorialized practices of 'migration management' and biometric statehood. Yet, the organization's extensive involvement in Nigeria—particularly when viewed against the backdrop of postcolonial global hierarchy—risked opening the organization up to postcolonial criticisms and politicizing its activities. Turning to an analysis of the IOM's capacity-building practices in Abuja, Nigeria, I show that the organization engaged in pedagogical performances to present the organization as an apolitical 'expert' of border control. These performances allowed the organization to obscure the paradoxical nature of significantly reshaping Nigerian border control practices while claiming the role of a neutral and disinterested 'teacher' of migration management. The content of these pedagogical performances focused on stressing two key sources of the IOM's authority and legitimacy: human rights standards and technical expertise that could be used to 'solve' the problem of digital border control.

These solutions, however, were not neutral. In the final section of this chapter, I show that the IOM's promotion of MIDAS manifested as the expansion of crimmigration control, that is, increased legal and operational overlap between the fields of migration control and criminal justice (Brandariz, 2022). Although the NIS remained the foremost authority in charge of border control and migration management at a federal level, MIDAS necessitated the development of historically novel interagency co-operation procedures and digital infrastructures that resulted in the expansion of crimmigration control in Nigeria.

Postcolonial hierarchy, 'migration management', and digital borders

In Chapter 6, I showed how Nigerian federal authorities shaped the roll-out of MIDAS on the ground in pursuit of their own political interests. However, they were not able to influence the initial process of technical innovation that produced the IOM's Personal Information Registration System (PIRS) in 2007, which eventually became MIDAS in 2013. The IOM, in contrast, independently developed this new in-house digital border management tool, which raises a host of important questions about the underlying social understandings and political goals that motivated this process of technological development. Answering these questions requires us to deconstruct the IOM and view it as an entity 'to be explained. By regarding IOs [international organizations] as an accomplishment needing continued maintenance and attention the focus shifts from what IOs construct to how IOs are constructed' (Srivastava, 2013: 72).

In recent decades, the IOM has moved beyond a focus on the logistics of moving migrants to a broad mandate composed of humanitarian activities, returns, data collection, and capacity-building practices in its member states (Bradley, 2024). Data-related projects have been a key driver of recent organizational growth and diversification, and the IOM has become a key player in the global 'datafication' of migration and border control (Frowd, 2024). Its data-focused projects have included the development of new indices and databases such as the Migration Governance

Indicators (MGI), the Displacement Tracking Matrix (DTM), and the Missing Migrants Project, as well as the creation of the Global Migration Data Analysis Centre (GMDAC) in Berlin in 2015 (Frowd, 2024: 11; Robinson, 2018). This focus on the datafication of migration has become a central pillar of the IOM's claims to expertise in the field of migration and border control. The organization has, since 2013, further sought to materialize its data-related expertise through the development of MIDAS (Singler, 2024a).

Why has the development of a new digital border control system, and the expansion of a wide range of data-related epistemic practices, become central to the IOM's claims to migration expertise? What political motivations and social understandings have underpinned its development of MIDAS and the deployment of the system in the Global South? A pragmatist theory of technology offers useful conceptual tools for answering these questions. Pragmatism broadly conceptualizes technology as 'the invention, development, and cognitive deployment of tools and other artifacts, brought to bear on raw materials and intermediate stock parts, with a view to the resolution of perceived problems' (Hickman, 2001: 12). This view can expand critical criminological analysis of digital technologies to include the initial steps of ideational and technical innovation that resulted in new criminal justice and border control technologies. Supplementing a performative analysis of the effects of MIDAS with a pragmatist theory of technological development provides analytical tools for responding to Martin-Mazé and Perret's (2021) call for critical researchers to uncover which actors develop what kinds of border control tools, and why.

In this view, analysing the potential political impacts of new digital border control technologies requires an understanding of the background conditions that motivated and shaped the process of technical innovation in the first place. As Larry Hickman (2001: 59) has explained, 'new forms of technological methods and artifacts tend to incorporate elements of older techniques and artifacts as their content. New technologies do not arise out of nothing, but are built on the basis of more or less reliable institutions, customs, and habits.' In other words, new technologies are created against a background context of social and material structures including political and economic hierarchies, dominant sociopolitical norms, and existing technical tools, standards, and common practices (Littoz-Monnet, 2022). Within this context, the process of technological innovation is sparked by the perceived failure of existing technologies to solve pressing social problems.

To better understand the technical affordances and political effects of MIDAS, this section situates the IOM's development of the system in relation to three relevant background conditions that shaped the process of technical innovation: first, the political and economic postcolonial hierarchies within which the organization has carved out a mediating role between Global North and South on issues relating to migration control; second, contemporary global norms of territorial statehood and mobility control, which the IOM has actively shaped and enacted by promoting a discourse of 'migration management'; finally, the technological and ideological context of the rapid digitalization of border controls, viewed as a solution to perceived failures of analogue forms of border control in response to complex contemporary problems of cross-border mobility and state security.

The 'national sovereignty project', postcolonial hierarchy, and entrepreneurialism

The IOM has become one of the largest and most influential international organizations operating in the field of migration and border control globally. Second only to the United Nations High Commissioner for Refugees (UNHCR) with its annual budget of $10.9 billion, the IOM's budget increased rapidly during the past decade from $1.55bn in 2015 to $3.34bn in 2023 (IOM, 2015b, 2023b; UNHCR, 2024b). The organization's budgetary growth was also reflected in a significant increase in total staff from 8,464 in 2013 to 22,213 in 2024. This expansion outstripped the UNHCR's budgetary and staff growth over the past decade in relative terms, and the IOM now employs more staff than the UNHCR. Overall, between 2013 and 2024, the IOM and UNHCR increased their total staff numbers by 162% and 85% respectively, while the organizations' overall budgets grew by 115% and 51% respectively (IOM, 2015a, 2024c; UNHCR, 2017, 2024a). Three considerations regarding the IOM's budget bring into view the complex relationship between the organization's capacity-building practices and postcolonial hierarchies of citizenship and mobility control.

First, the organization receives funding from its member states, who are politically invested in upholding what Fabian Georgi (2010: 64) has termed the 'national sovereignty project'. This project privileges sovereign states' political and normative authority to control cross-border mobility over alternative solutions based, for instance, on international or supranational governance solutions (Cole, 2017). IOM officials in Nigeria, both in casual conversation and during workshops and meetings, continually reaffirmed that—as an official explained during a workshop on gender sensitivity training for NIS officials—'we are here to advocate orderly, safe, regular, and responsible migration and mobility' (Field diary, 3 August 2021). The idea of 'orderly' migration was presented as a necessary safeguard for migrants' rights, which sovereign states were best placed to promote and protect. For instance, the stated goal of the gender sensitivity workshop was 'to realize the full potential of all migrants to development and to prevent exploitation', but such goals could only be pursued, according to the IOM, if migration is 'well governed' (Field diary, 3 August 2021).

IOM officials highlighted that the organization's goal was not to prevent migration, but to facilitate and promote the right kinds of migration—those that can be monitored, controlled, and ordered by state authorities. As critical researchers have argued, contemporary practices of border control aim to sort different kinds of border-crossers into 'risky' and 'trusted' individuals who can be selectively excluded or allowed to cross (Muller, 2010). In its public discourse, the IOM has regularly referred to ideas about safeguarding human rights and promoting economic exchange, while maintaining that these goals are best served by strengthening the sovereign authority of states over their borders (Ashutosh and Mountz, 2011).

Although the IOM (2024d) is publicly 'committed to the principle that humane and orderly migration benefits migrants and society', its focus on the ground seemed to be more on ordering migration rather than ensuring that border control practices were humane and non-discriminatory. IOM official José, for instance, explained that state sovereignty trumped alternative value-based considerations when rolling out systems such as MIDAS, which are potentially vulnerable to human rights violations through the misuse of personal data: 'Nobody can guarantee one hundred percent that the government will use this correctly and they will never violate any human rights. It's impossible. It's desirable, of course, but I don't think we can. [. . .] It's a sovereign state, we cannot tell the government what to do' (Interview, 17 March 2021). In Abuja, officials similarly explained that 'we of course make suggestions and include standards on human rights in our projects, but states also have rights, and we have to prioritize this sovereign right [over human rights concerns]' (Field diary, 30 August 2021).

The centrality and political sensitivity of respecting state sovereignty was closely linked to the second key consideration regarding the IOM's budget: most of its funding comes from wealthy Global North states and is used to fund capacity-building projects and other interventions in the Global South (Patz and Thorvaldsdottir, 2020). The list of top ten donors includes nine wealthy Global North states and the United Nations (IOM, 2024a). As a result, Antoine Pécoud (2020: 13) has argued that 'the IOM tends to align itself with the agenda of the Global North and is thus bound to be involved in some of the toughest measures designed to fight undocumented migration'. In a similar vein, Franck Düvell (2015) has suggested that the IOM operates within and reifies relations of postcolonial global hierarchy, aiming to export 'the European model of migration control to other parts of the world, such as West Africa'.

IOM officials were aware of mounting criticisms of the organization as 'post-imperial' (Andrijasevic and Walters, 2010), based on the claim that it 'primarily benefits the IOM's major donor states—states of the Global North who aspire to control migration, particularly by combatting irregular migration' (Hirsch and Doig, 2018: 684). In this vein, IOM official Diego explained: 'We have an under-discussed North and South relationship on migration between Europe and the rest of the world. [. . .] But I do believe our role here is not to change but to regulate migration and to prevent abuse in many places' (Interview, 16 February 2021). Similarly, Zahra pointed out how European donor states have sought to promote regional migration with the aim of reducing migration from the African continent to Europe: 'The narrative from Europe has changed considerably. There seems to be an unspoken goal, "please don't try to promote too much movement to here." Donor money is being pushed toward regional migration and regional initiatives' (Interview, 19 March 2021).

In Abuja, project documentation regularly referred to the importance of limiting 'irregular migration flows to Europe' (Field diary, 22 July 2021). Yet, in workshops and meetings, IOM officials avoided mentioning the North–South hierarchies that underpinned global migration control. Instead, they highlighted that the organization aimed to 'just provide technical support, sharing with you [Nigerian federal authorities] best practices on human rights' (Field diary, 16 August 2021). IOM official Catherine demonstrated an explicit awareness of the complex North–South hierarchies that underpinned the organization's capacity-building practices, highlighting the need to present these interventions as primarily motivated by technical considerations despite the underlying political agendas of project donors:

> Of course, the donors are maybe looking to create a relationship with the NIS to ease returns. [Another colleague] sometimes feels bad because

> she feels IOM provides tools to deport people. [...] So we need to be politically sensitive, you know? Our role is actually about global technical standards, no matter what donors want. What states do with these tools is their business. (Interview, 6 September 2021)

These statements and observations demonstrate the tension between donor and recipient state interests, which the IOM had to balance when delivering its capacity-building interventions in Nigeria. Upholding the sovereignty of recipient states in the Global South and building their capacity to control their borders also involved downplaying and neutralizing the global hierarchies that underpinned the postcolonial world order of nationally sovereign states, with its differential levels of global mobility for citizens of Northern and Southern states (Sharma, 2020).

Nonetheless, reliance on wealthy donors did not mean that the IOM simply waits to receive funding, project ideas, and requests from Northern states. The third key consideration regarding the IOM's funding model is that the organization's budget is mostly project-based and decentralized. Local officials in country offices prepare proposals in an entrepreneurial fashion, seeking to develop new projects to 'save the jobs of the mission's staff members' (Georgi, 2010: 63). New proposals must receive political support from both donors and recipient states, which requires the organization to carefully present projects as a politically desirable 'win-win-win situation' benefiting migrants, countries of origin, and receiving states (Castles and Ozkul, 2014).

According to IOM official Maria, the organization helped Southern states 'determine their needs, prioritize their needs, and then advocate for their needs in order for projects to be adapted to their own agendas, and not just coming in second compared to what the donor in that moment wants, or is willing to fund' (Interview, 10 March 2021). Officials engaged in entrepreneurial initiatives to identify projects that accorded with both donor agendas and the interests of Southern state agencies. In addition, the IOM also actively sought to shape Southern state agencies' perceptions of their own interests. As one official explained to me in Abuja, 'the biggest problem for the Nigerian government was defining what they actually want. Our responsibility is to tell them what they should want' (Field diary, 3 August 2021). Other officials agreed that the IOM should not only respond to recipient state needs, but actively 'teach' Southern states what kinds of interventions they should want in the first place: 'We can't always wait for requests to come in from the government. We have to conduct assessments, to identify possible needs. Sometimes they don't even know about them before we conduct the assessments' (Field diary, 18 August 2021).

'Migration management' and the emerging norm of biometric statehood

Critically analysing the IOM's budget highlighted how the organization's capacity-building projects—including the development of MIDAS—were underpinned by postcolonial hierarchies insofar as the IOM acted as a mediator and operational partner between its Northern donors and Southern recipient states. The organization's officials knew that their state-centric practices were heavily shaped by the political agendas of wealthy Northern donors, but sought to entrepreneurially develop project proposals that made their interventions palatable and beneficial to Southern recipient states as well. A pragmatist theory of technology suggests that these global political dynamics constitute relevant background conditions that shaped the development of MIDAS. Pragmatism also suggests that new tools are developed to resolve perceived social problems that existing technologies have been unable to adequately tackle (Hickman, 2001; Pihlström, 2021). What were these social problems from the perspective of the IOM?

Historically, the IOM has sought to achieve several goals relating to migration control, which have not always been harmonious. According to Georgi (2010: 47–48), the organization has traditionally sought to balance the aims of promoting migration, building state capacity, producing knowledge about migration, carrying out humanitarian interventions, and engaging in 'discursive practices in the struggles over hegemony in international migration policy'. We have seen above how this presentation of migration as a 'win-win-win' was crucial to smoothing over potential political tensions relating to the postcolonial dynamics that underpinned the organization's funding. In the words of official Tom, 'there is a win-win-win. There is an added value to having migrants, if the migration is orderly. And it benefits everyone' (Interview, 24 February 2021).

From the perspective of the IOM, the structure of its funding has resulted in the organizationally existential problem of how to simultaneously reaffirm a statist view of migration control while justifying and increasing its own role in migration-related capacity-building practices on a global level (Pécoud, 2018). One of the organization's key discursive strategies for self-promotion in recent decades has been the notion of 'migration management'. This discourse has allowed the organization to present migration control as a technical, managerial issue amenable to expert governance by a large international organization (Andrijasevic and Walters, 2010; Robinson, 2018).

Yann Stricker (2019) has shown how the categorization of cross-border mobility as 'international migration' has from its conception been intimately wound up both with a state-centric view of territorial sovereignty and with claims to expertise put forth by international organizations such as the International Labour Organization (ILO), which began to collect statistics on this newly categorized phenomenon in the 1920s. The conceptualization of 'international migration' as a field of transnational expertise contributed directly to 'a new national ordering of peoples and territories' as opposed to earlier 'imperial visions of governing the world' (Stricker, 2019: 471). Similarly, the concept of 'migration management' was rooted in the simultaneous enactment of migration both as an issue of sovereign authority to the member states of the IOM, and as a global field of knowledge that could only be properly grasped from 'a view from above—a God's-eye view from which all elements are related' (Dijstelbloem, 2021: 75).

In this way, the organization has been able to strike a balance between the sovereign prerogatives of its member states and affirming its own global authority. The concept of 'management' has allowed the IOM to explicitly position itself as distinct from the more rights-based and social justice-oriented UNHCR and ILO in the global migration space (Geiger, 2020). The organization's 'migration management' discourse also allowed country officials to smooth over political concerns and potential disputes between donor and recipient states, as well as between state authorities and local border communities. According to IOM official Katrina:

> [Migration management] is about changing the mindset, better understanding the importance of standardization of practices globally and the importance of having strong states. It's extremely important given the culture and politics of the [West Africa] region [. . .] They have to understand what development is being brought, why it's been brought and how they can benefit from it. That's why we are the migration management agency. (Interview, 17 February 2021)

The IOM's managerial discourse has long allowed the organization to alleviate political tensions that have resulted from its capacity-building interventions in the Global South (Fine, 2018). Yet, from the early 2000s onward, this discourse was no longer sufficient to justify the IOM's expert role in shaping the global politics of migration, or to inform the actual content of these practices. A new set of perceived social problems arose in the context of border securitization and digitalization, which the IOM set out to address through the development of MIDAS. These problems relate to the norm of biometric statehood.

IOM official José explained how the securitization of migration became a key focus for the organization's member states in the years after the 11 September terrorist attacks on the United States:

> 9/11 was a really great push in terms of new ideas about border security [. . .] So that's when the ICAO working group on new technologies started developing all these technical specifications and testing biometrics and so on. As soon as ICAO launched these technical specifications, the same technical specifications were adopted by the EU and then us. [. . .] The idea was that the use of biometrics is to have a step forward. (Interview, 17 March 2021)

In other words, the statist norms of border control which were central to the IOM's discourse of migration management now became understood in terms of sovereign states' capacity to collect biometric data at the border according to the new norm of biometric statehood (Muller, 2010).

This push for biometric border control created a need for the IOM to reconfigure its migration management discourse around a focus on the datafication of borders (Frowd, 2024), and created new opportunities for the organization to position itself as a technological intermediary between the Global North and South. Border digitalization was much quicker in the Global North than in the Global South, resulting in new hierarchies of trustworthiness on a global level. According to José:

> If there's no global interoperability, that means there's no trust, right? [. . .] Low-income countries are not able to cope and follow up with this, especially on biometrics, so for example Nigeria, Mali, you know, any other countries around Africa. And so, this is the main issue that the countries, or the international community is facing. (José, interview, 2 March 2021)

In this context, the development of MIDAS allowed the IOM to update its capacity-building interventions according to the logics of biometric statehood. The biometric capabilities of the system aligned its new project proposals with Northern policy goals, and simultaneously made these new projects palatable to Southern state agencies by presenting the system as reflection of international standards and 'best practices'.

More problematically for the IOM, the increasing securitization of migration and stricter border controls in the Global North also resulted in higher levels of awareness among Southern member states regarding the impact of postcolonial hierarchies on global cross-border movements. IOM official Luca explained: 'I must say that the public narrative [among European countries] is not so well hidden any more. [. . .] Eventually people are going to see it. And I think a number of African member states are reacting to that' (Interview, 3 March 2021). Reorienting the organization's capacity-building projects around new digital border control tools allowed the IOM to present itself as a neutral, technical service provider informed by international technical standards rather than political goals. The organization's country officials in the Global South began entrepreneurially linking recipient member state interests to the development and deployment of new digital border control tools:

> Normally we take our Member States during the project, you know, a representative of the ministry of interior [or] the head of the Immigration Department, for example, to go to technical exhibitions and conferences and say, 'Look, this is what's happening outside now. So, you can tell me that you need this, this, this and this, right?' (Aaron, interview, 2 March)

By reorienting its capacity-building practices and 'migration management' discourse around the digitalization of border controls, the IOM has also increasingly based its claims to migration expertise upon technological development and data collection, in contrast to an earlier focus on the logistics of mobility (Bradley, 2024). In doing so, the organization has drawn on broader ideological discourses regarding digitalization and technological innovation, while seeking to increase its role in shaping both contemporary practices and the future of migration management.

Technical standards, innovation, and the digital futures of border control

Technical innovation, driven by the private sector and public–private partnerships, has significantly shaped the norms and standards underpinning digitalized border control practices. In the EU, critical researchers have shown how large security technology companies such as IDEMIA and Sopra Steria have made hundreds of millions of euros from border technology contracts in response to EU research and development calls (Valdivia et al., 2022). Eleftherios Chelioudakis (2022: 94) has highlighted how the developers of new technologies have been uniquely placed to shape the digital border agenda: 'states become dependent on the technical expertise of their private partners, without having sufficient knowledge about or effective oversight over the research operations.' By engaging in the process of technological innovation, the IOM has sought to position itself as one of these technical experts with the ability to actively shape the future datafication and digitalization of borders.

Technical innovation and expertise have provided ample resources for the IOM to justify its role in migration management. Engaging in these practices has also influenced how the organization views migration as a social problem. This focus on technological development has allowed the IOM to plug into the broader ideology of the 'digital revolution' (Balbi, 2023), which presents digitalization as normatively desirable, politically neutral, and inevitable. In its public discourse, the IOM has explicitly drawn on the idea of the digital revolution as a solution to migration-related social problems while identifying moments of crisis as key windows of opportunity to implement its digitalization agenda. For instance, during the global wave of lockdowns in response to the Covid-19 pandemic in 2021, the organization stated: 'we are optimistic that we can use this crisis an opportunity to promote and further the inclusion of migrants and their families in the digital revolution and turn their current misfortune into eventual luck' (IOM, 2021d).

Plugging into ideas about the digital revolution has also positioned the IOM as a key actor shaping not only contemporary practices of migration management, but also the digital futures of border control. Gabriele Balbi (2023: 77) has demonstrated how ideas about the digital revolution temporally focus on both present and future: 'forecasting is not only a way to anticipate the future, which is full of uncertainties and competing alternative visions, but it is also (and above all) a way to shape and build that future.' In this vein, the IOM has stressed that 'digital technologies will continue to play a growing role in the provision of services', which necessitates 'global digital cooperation' on digital border management (Vassor, 2023: 3). Such cooperation should be led by the IOM, which can provide 'thought leadership on the nexus between migration, displacement, and legal identity, including their impact on the protection of migrants' (Vassor, 2023: 22).

In an interview excerpt above, IOM official José recounted how the post-9/11 securitization of migration acted as a catalyst for the rapid digitalization of border controls. José referred to the ICAO New Technologies Working Group (NTWG) as a key actor responsible for developing new technical standards for biometric border controls, which have subsequently been adopted by states and international organizations across the globe. Although the ICAO's standards are not formally binding, researchers have shown that the organization exerts a high degree of political influence through its standards and recommended practices (Sipos, 2023). International legal scholars have gone so far as to argue that in the global arena, 'political authority is giving place to bureaucratic power' (Albisinni, 2016: 229).

The ICAO's NTWG involves both member state officials and 'private sector experts', working together to outline future directions for the development of new border control tools (ICAO, n.d.). New proposals and standards are often based on speculative ideas about the future of border digitalization by private sector technology companies, who have sought to shape ICAO regulations according to their own plans for technological innovation. IOM official Fabian outlined the technological innovation pipeline, stretching from the private sector through to the ICAO NTWG and ultimately to the IOM's development of its own in-house digital border management system:

> Biometrics, 15 years ago, was still quite a young thing. And people were not very sure what biometrics were and where biometrics will lead us. [...] In ICAO, in the working groups where we [IOM] attend, there were a lot of private sector companies who really provided some good background and ideas on possibilities for border control, which are now a reality, of course. (Interview, 12 February 2021)

In recent years, the IOM has placed itself at the forefront of implementing new technological solutions originally developed and standardized by private sector companies and ICAO:

> Innovation is mainly private sector and ICAO. We have guys from the private sector, from governments, from ISO [the International Organization for Standardization] working together to have the new technologies and

> standards. What the IOM does is then develop MIDAS internally, so that we could be the ones implementing these ideas in the member states. [. . .] Our engagement and partnerships with the private sector are strategic. (Fabian, interview, 12 February 2021)

The development of a new digital border management tool emerged as a potential solution to the IOM's existential problem of justifying and expanding its role in global migration management—and to the problem of ordering migration through 'datafication'—in the material and ideational context of rapid border digitalization driven by private actors and international organizations. As the organization has stated in its public discourse, 'the innovations and potential' of private sector technology companies 'are of fundamental importance to biometrics, identity, migration and border management systems' (IOM, 2018a). The development of this system also allowed the organization to plug into broader ideological notions of digitalization as normatively desirable, politically neutral, and inevitable.

Yet, the organization's officials also recognized that MIDAS could be used for harmful ends as well. Despite the IOM's framing of MIDAS as a 'step forward' and a neutral technical tool that it uses to 'teach' states how to enact their biometric statehood, the organization's officials were aware that this system could be used for various harmful or nefarious ends: 'Even if we apply, let's say, maximum data protection, it's up to states to violate this [. . .] If something goes wrong, is IOM to be blamed? I don't think so' (Aaron, interview, 2 March 2021).

Moreover, officials were aware that, due to the postcolonial hierarchies and statist norms that underpinned its work, recipient states still needed to be convinced of the desirability of the border digitalization agenda more broadly, and of MIDAS specifically as a preferred option over competitor systems developed by private sector companies and Global North states. As IOM official Jane explained:

> Of course, with MIDAS we want to expand digital border management on a global level, but in this region [West Africa] states need to first learn what is so important about digital data before we can build our system. [. . .] Then we need to, say, explain why MIDAS and not private sector systems, because of things like profit and ownership and so on. (Interview, 13 April 2021)

Jane's account demonstrates that despite linking MIDAS to new global standards, the capacity-building practices intended to expand the collection and use of biometric data were nonetheless at risk of becoming politicized according to a general North–South divide. Migration is an inherently contentious political phenomenon, driven by complex social dynamics, globalization, and 'political factors within sending and receiving states, including conflicts of interest, structural dependence, welfare states and civil society pressures' (Anderson, 2017: 1528). These tensions suggest that more political and performative work was required on the ground in Nigeria to neutralize potential criticisms related to the IOM's capacity-building practices.

Pedagogical performances and the IOM as a 'teacher' of border control

Despite being couched in the discourse of migration management as well as the broader norms of biometric statehood and the digital revolution, the IOM's promotion of MIDAS in countries such as Nigeria put the organization at risk of being criticized as 'post-imperial' as it seeks to align Southern practices with those of its Global North donor states. The organization's officials were deeply concerned about the potential reputational damage of such criticisms. The IOM's reputation as 'a neutral go-between that does not interfere with the political orientations of the contracting states' is central to its authority in the field of global migration management (Pécoud, 2020: 7). In Chapter 5, I argued that the organization's officials engage in pedagogical performances to depoliticize their role in global migration governance. In interviews and official communications, the organization's officials repeatedly referred to the IOM's activities in pedagogical terms, describing them as 'teaching states about security' and giving 'briefings and lectures [. . .] to make people understand how you cannot possibly live in a modern world today without digitized information' (Diego, interview, 16 February 2021). How did this pedagogical discourse translate into practices on the ground in Abuja?

IOM officials in Nigeria were acutely aware of the risk of infringing on the authority Nigerian federal agencies in their attempt to digitalize the country's border control practices in line with the Northern-produced norm of biometric statehood. Discussing the development of new data protection legislation that is required for the processing of API/PNR data by MIDAS, one official remarked that 'usually it's not the role of international organizations to draft laws for countries [. . .] but if we don't do it, it's just not going to happen' (Field diary, 5 August 2021). Another official in the same meeting qualified the perceived need to shape national legislation with the importance of avoiding accusations of post-imperial intervention: 'The process of making laws is quite intensive and sensitive. We need to stress that we are only suggesting laws based on best practices [. . .] We don't want to appear politically incorrect, just promoting what Europe and the Americans want. But the UN needs to promote its own products' (Field diary, 5 August 2021).

Ulrike Krause (2021) has demonstrated that not only national boundaries, but also the legal frameworks for managing migrants and refugees globally—including the UN Refugee Convention—are rooted in colonial power imbalances that shaped the development of these frameworks. Nonetheless, Nigerian federal agencies actively favoured cooperation with the IOM over bilateral treaties and public–private partnerships. As one NIS official remarked: 'Our experience of IOM has been very positive. They do not try to build dependence. We've had some teething issues, of course, you know, but IOM has trained us in global standards very effectively' (Field diary, 3 August 2021). This response by Nigerian agencies echoes findings related to the IOM's capacity-building practices in other contexts. In Morocco and Tunisia, for instance, Inken Bartels (2018: 57–58) has argued that '[i]n contrast to the cooperation with the EU and its Member States, IOs were not perceived as external interventions that actualized a colonial past'.

Just as the organization's publicly available documentation stressed the pedagogical nature of its activities, so too were its capacity-building practices in Nigeria focused on 'teaching' federal officials 'best practices' relating to digital border management. In addition to providing the IT infrastructure, biometric identification equipment, and border control checkpoints required to operate MIDAS, several of the IOM's capacity-building projects involved building new Personnel Training Resource Centers (PTRCs). At these PTRCs, the IOM did not directly train border control officers, but rather carried out what it calls the 'Training of Trainers'. According to this model, the IOM taught NIS personnel how to teach others to operate MIDAS. These NIS personnel would then continue to train local officers according to a customized training curriculum, delivered via an online 'Learning Management System' (LMS) developed jointly by the IOM and INCERT, a Bulgarian 'management systems certification body' (INCERT, n.d.). The LMS curriculum included practical modules such as

'Logging into MIDAS' and 'Primary Control and Registration: Scanning Documents, Capturing Biometrics', as well as broader topics regarding the technical logics of digital border control, for instance 'Introduction to Facial Recognition' and 'Secondary Control: Data Management & Alert Lists' (Field diary, 9 September 2021).

These PTRCs were, in effect, the material embodiment of the IOM's claim to pedagogical expertise. The Training of Trainers approach allowed the IOM to distance itself from the actual deployment of MIDAS by stressing the accountability of local officials, in terms of both border control practices and the training of border control officers. Nonetheless, these training practices relied wholly on material infrastructure, IT equipment, training curricula, and training delivery software that were all provided by the IOM in cooperation with its Global North donors and private sector partners. Promotional materials inside PTRC training rooms prominently displayed the 'IOM: UN Migration' logo alongside flags of Global North donor states.

IOM officials acknowledged that the inclusion of significant pedagogical components in MIDAS-related capacity-building projects was crucial to presenting the organization as distinct from Global North states and potentially exploitative private sector companies. For instance, in its API/PNR planning meetings, officials contrasted how MIDAS data was owned by Nigerian federal authorities, while systems provided directly by donor states—such as PISCES, developed by the United States Department of State—would retain data ownership in the Global North: 'PISCES is owned by the US government, but MIDAS is owned by the Nigerian government [. . .] the Americans would probably like to access the MIDAS data too. Of course, this is not our [the IOM's] business. The Nigerian state can do whatever it wants with the data' (Field diary, 5 August 2021). The Training of Trainers approach was also central to distinguishing MIDAS from private sector alternatives, which could result in material dependencies when private companies retained ownership of digital infrastructures:

> We train local officers so that NIS knows we are helping them, not looking to take control here. [. . .] They still need to advance much more in being sure of their own data ownership. Some of them are starting to realize what it means to now receive a system for free and then not own completely the data. (Maria, interview, 10 March 2021)

NIS officials in Abuja also stressed the political importance of the IOM's pedagogical orientation in assuaging concerns regarding outside political influence, even while recognizing the significant extent to which the IOM's training curricula reshaped local practices of border control:

> To us, these training curricula are completely new. So yes, IOM has reshaped, revamped our border controls according to the international standards. But for us it is good to work with a partner on the training side, because we are still in control of the decisions on how we want to do border control in Nigeria. (Field diary, 24 August 2021)

IOM officials were aware of the importance of this pedagogical orientation in navigating the political sensitivity that surrounded a Global North-funded international organization shaping border digitalization in Nigeria. In training workshops and planning meetings, the organization's officials regularly emphasized their role as 'just a teacher' (Field diary, 19 August 2021). Whenever meetings turned to the question of the alignment of Nigerian border control practices with global standards and Northern-produced norms, IOM officials stressed that 'the most important thing is that the development comes from you' (Field diary, 19 August 2021). In private meetings, recognition of the organization's significant political influence was balanced with the need to 'make sure the NIS takes ownership, so that they are the ones implementing the changes' (Field diary, 5 August 2021).

Underpinning the IOM's pedagogical performances was a tension arising from its complete control over the material and pedagogical infrastructures necessary for NIS officials to 'take ownership' of the deployment of MIDAS. As Frowd (2020: 72) has argued in his analysis of transnational bordering practices in West Africa, pedagogical practices by Global North-funded actors are 'dependent on the prior existence of an unequal distribution of capital between teacher and learner, which the pedagogical act maintains or even exacerbates'.

So too, in Nigeria, the realities of global inequality that underpinned the IOM's pedagogical performances risked being uncovered by the materiality of MIDAS and MIDAS-related training infrastructures. The IOM's capacity-building practices involved the provision of expensive IT equipment that required regular maintenance, as well as software subscriptions and data plans for connecting MIDAS border control posts and storing the data collected by the system. As IOM official Diego explained: 'We can in many cases get infrastructure to a site but once the projects finish, there's a sustainability issue that comes to the fore from member states' (Interview,

16 February 2021). Although the IOM attempted to ensure that procured hardware, for instance, was under warranty even after the capacity-building projects formally ended, such arrangements were not always successful in cutting costs in the long run: 'This is the problem with warranties [. . .] our service agreements don't specify that the company has to pay for shipping costs. They'll replace the hardware, but they won't pay for return shipping' (Field diary, 6 September 2021).

Only the most recent MIDAS-related project proposals considered the long-term sustainability of projects even after the initial funding has run out. The organization's pedagogical orientation was highlighted as a solution to the risk of creating dependencies between the NIS and the IOM, even though this pedagogical relationship was itself a cause of those same dependencies. On one hand, in its planning documents the IOM argued that its Training of Trainers ensured the long-term sustainability and independence of MIDAS and related training practices:

> MIDAS training-related projects also play a key role in ensuring the sustainability of MIDAS projects. The establishment of PTRCs and the promotion of a learning culture among NIS officers, as well as training a critical mass of Training Focal Points [training officers], allow the NIS to become self-sufficient in its training of new MIDAS users and the training of trainers. (Field diary, 8 September 2021)

On the other hand, the pursuit of project sustainability also resulted involved locking in a long-term role for the IOM in shaping Nigeria's digital border control practices:

> Close contact between IOM's central MIDAS team at IOM HQ and the recipient Member State plays an important role in ensuring project sustainability. By providing long-distance support with any major issues that occur, and with system upgrades, the IOM central MIDAS team boosts project sustainability. (Field diary, 8 September 2021)

Ultimately, the IOM's pedagogical performances were made possible by precisely the same power imbalance and material dependencies that these performances were meant to obscure and neutralize. Long-term issues relating to project sustainability risked creating new dependencies that could undermine the IOM's presentation of MIDAS as a tool for Nigerian federal authorities to enact global norms of biometric statehood while remaining free from external political influence. Additional performative work was required to ensure that the IOM's pedagogical performances were viewed as politically neutral and primarily focused on the promotion of international norms and standards. To this end, the content of the organization's pedagogical interventions focused primarily on two themes, which allowed it to plug into broader discourses of universal best practices and political neutrality: human rights and technical standards.

Governing 'through' rights at the digital border

A central source of the IOM's normative authority linked to its pedagogical role in Nigeria was its claim to human rights expertise. The organization's training modules included topics on human rights, gender sensitivity training, and recognizing the 'needs of different groups and different types of vulnerability relevant to the border management context' (Field diary, 26 August 2021). Nigerian federal officials highlighted how the IOM's inclusion of human rights considerations in its training allowed the NIS to benefit from the symbolic authority of the UN system: 'They [the IOM] are the ones bringing in standards on human rights, because they are a UN agency. For us the UN is a very important international partner because we want to engage with the international community' (Field diary, 2 September 2021).

Existing research has highlighted how the IOM's staff express a 'genuine but overly formal humanitarianism' (Frowd, 2018: 1658), which often clashes with the organization's capacity-building practices that focus more on strengthening states' ability to control migration than on protecting the human rights of migrants themselves (Hirsch and Doig, 2018). In Nigeria, this tension between the discursive promotion of human rights and potentially exclusionary practices of border control was also evident. Human rights were seemingly a core concern when planning the future expansion of MIDAS to process API/PNR data, particularly in a context in which corruption at the federal and state level could undermine the rights of data subjects: 'Expanding MIDAS in this way will come with many concerns on human rights. Who will actually be on this list? [...] The relationship between agencies [required to process API/PNR data] is only starting in this country, and there is corruption in some of these agencies' (Field diary, 5 August 2021).

The IOM's preferred strategy to address human rights concerns consisted of expanding its pedagogical role to include human rights norms and shaping local legislation, because 'rights have to be institutionalized in the long run' (Field diary, 5 August 2021). Although shaping the federal-level privacy legislation, the NDPA, was viewed as potentially problematic in terms of undermining Nigerian state sovereignty, the organization's officials argued that 'we have to act in this context to make sure rights are in the legislation and to lock in who will be responsible for processing data. [. . .] It could be useful to us too, to lock in NIS as responsible for the data' (Field diary, 9 September 2021).

This statement illustrated how the promotion of human rights simultaneously emerged as a normative concern for IOM officials as well as a mechanism for justifying the organization's pedagogical expertise, empowering the organization to shape local legislation. Rights-based discourses and lawmaking practices became folded into the institutional 'expertise' of the IOM. In line with existing insights from socio-legal studies, 'rights language is itself regulated to the extent that experts and how they measure rights tell us what the "truth" about rights is (and should be) within a particular region or area, and how to properly "do" rights using the right kind of (rights-based) approach' (Sokhi-Bulley, 2019: 5).

The organization's pedagogical focus on human rights protections stood in contrast to IOM officials' statements about the undesirability and impossibility of curtailing state sovereignty to ensure that MIDAS is not used to violate human rights. Expansive forms of data collection at the border—in particular practices involving the collection and storage of sensitive biometric data—have caused serious human rights concerns even in contexts with relatively robust legislative and institutional protections (see, e.g., European Union Agency for Fundamental Rights, 2018). IOM officials were aware of the risks of expanding biometric data collection from a human rights perspective:

> Maybe in the past, we weren't paying enough attention, that we were putting a kind of ticking bomb in their hands, because biometrics and biographic information is, you know, extremely sensitive. [. . .] So now we are doing a lot of work on data protection regulation. But of course, it's also limited, what we can do in this area. (Mohammed, interview, 22 February 2021)

Despite such concerns, the centrality of respecting state sovereignty and the IOM's alignment with statist norms of biometric statehood meant that the development of human rights protections was not prioritized over the expansion of MIDAS data collection capabilities.

The IOM's inclusion of human rights as a key discursive component of its pedagogical performances in Nigeria did not result in stronger legal protections for individual migrants. In fact, IOM officials' primary concern in discussions regarding the NDPA was not that the proposed legislation would be too lax, but rather that it would create overly robust rights protections. Such legal protections could have presented an obstacle to the future expansion of MIDAS to include API/PNR data processing: 'Our recommendations on privacy and data protection laws are needed for the API law to be of an internationally acceptable standard. Otherwise, we will have a law under which could, in the worst case, even prevent API and PNR data processing in the future' (Field diary, 5 August 2021). Ultimately, the kinds of rights that were actually secured through MIDAS-related lawmaking practices were only 'minimal rights' that guard against gross privacy violations (Sokhi-Bulley, 2019: 42). As Bal Sokhi-Bulley (2019: 42 original emphasis) has argued in her critical analysis of rights discourse in the context of migration control in the European Union:

> Government through rights only adds *minimal* rights to swift return, proportionate detention or imprisonment and an unenforceable right to compassion. Far from ensuring that no one is 'left behind', the irregular migrant is actually left behind, disempowered and unable to claim the rights she wants.

In other words, a pedagogical discourse focusing on human rights was deployed to ensure the compatibility of Nigeria's future digital borders with Global North standards on expansive data collection, and to further empower the IOM as a 'teacher' of global norms on migration management and biometric statehood. One official explained that rights-based considerations should be used to strike a 'balance' between legislative protections and expanding biometric surveillance at the border: 'With these concerns about human rights, the question is really: what is the best possible balance between protections and being able to use these data for security purposes?' (Field diary, 10 September 2021).

In this context, human rights operated as a mechanism promoting the expansion—rather than the curtailment—of novel border security technologies, which resulted in the legitimization of a security-oriented framing of migration and the expansion of 'crimmigration control' in Nigeria (Amelung, 2021; Bowling and Westenra, 2018; Singler, 2023). This example demonstrates how rights themselves can be 'dangerous' (Foucault,

1991: 343). If debates about rights are engaged only by expert practitioners behind closed doors, rights can 'become technical' and non-democratic, thereby operating less as an effective safeguard against expansive security systems and more as 'mechanisms of regulation and control' (Sokhi-Bulley, 2019: 5). Conceptualizing human rights in terms of global 'best practices' was also complementary to the other key theme that characterized the IOM's MIDAS-related pedagogical performances in Nigeria: technical standards.

'Solving' the problem of border control

In addition to human rights norms, the IOM's pedagogical performances in Nigeria were characterized by a focus on technical standards. This technical expertise was reflective of a techno-solutionist attitude, demonstrated both by the organization's officials as well as in public and private documentation on MIDAS-related projects.

Technological solutionism refers to the belief that complex political problems can be 'solved' through narrow technical fixes. However, these problems, 'on careful examination, do not have to be defined in the singular and all-encompassing ways that "solutionists" have defined them; what's contentious, then, is not their proposed solution but their very definition of the problem itself' (Morozov, 2013: 6). Existing research has demonstrated that solutionist attitudes are replete both among border control professionals and within international organizations more generally (Marelli et al., 2022; Milan, 2020). Niovi Vavoula (2021: 458) has argued that the increasing proliferation of novel border control tools 'constitutes part of a broader trend of techno-solutionism, which places a tremendous amount of trust in technological tools'. IOM officials in Abuja often described their work in terms of solving technical problems, understood as an activity entirely distinct from local or global politics. In the words of one official: 'there are two kinds of people: those who pinpoint problems but never fix them, and people who solve problems. Politicians pinpoint problems. We solve problems' (Field diary, 28 July 2021).

Solutionism is a natural fit with the functionalism that international organizations embody, in other words the belief that these organizations perform specific technical functions that benefit the common good, rather than engaging in contestable political actions. In contrast to this depoliticized view, Jan Klabbers (2019: 385) has argued that in the IOM, 'functionalism is best seen not as theory, but as ideology: a more or less coherent set of thoughts with little explanatory power but strong normative appeal, and working so as to legitimize the use of power'. In the context of the increasing digitalization of border control tools, Didier Bigo (2020: 75–76) has similarly argued that 'what is at stake here is a strong political move where digital technology is depoliticizing questions and transforms who becomes in charge of security and who are the key targets of these policies'.

In the context of the IOM's MIDAS-related capacity-building practices, the organization's techno-solutionist attitude was effectively used by officials to pre-empt and neutralize potential political criticisms relating to its migration management interventions. The organization's officials presented the digitalization of borders as a politically neutral process of developing better 'tools' to solve problems relating to border control:

> We face some problems trying to convince local authorities that MIDAS serves their interests. But, from our perspective, we explain to them that the important thing is just that data is collected [. . .] In a sense our leitmotif has really been, 'nothing will change, we are just giving a tool, it will not change your work'. (Fabian, interview, 12 February 2021)

So too, in Nigeria, the IOM's deployment of MIDAS was underpinned by the belief that 'the systematic gathering, analysis, dissemination, and exchange of migration data' could solve nearly all migration-related problems in the country (IOM, 2016: 10). In training sessions, workshops, and meetings, officials argued that 'border control, today, is really just about data. Collecting the data, and sharing the data, will give you the answers you need. This is why we are here to provide you with technical support' (Field diary, 19 August 2021). This view was in line with the organization's broader contemporary focus on the 'datafication' of migration control, which allowed the IOM to lift the issue of migration control out of the arena of political contestation and into the realm of politically neutral expertise, as 'datafication is sufficiently technical as to fit within a managerial approach to migration' (Frowd, 2024: 14).

This techno-solutionist attitude was politically essential to neutralize criticisms which neither the IOM's pedagogical orientation nor its promotion of human rights could sufficiently address. When asked about the long-term sustainability of PTRCs, one official justified the creation of potential dependencies between the NIS and IOM with reference to the technical nature of migration control:

> This is a technical issue, and technical skills need to be taught over time. Sometimes developing countries are like teenagers, they want everything now, without putting in the work. But until we know they have the capacity to manage these technologies properly, we need to keep teaching them. (Field diary, 28 July 2021)

In other words, the 'solution' to migration control lies in the correct or 'proper' use of technical tools, which must be 'taught' by the IOM over a long period of time.

Of course, officials recognized that these tools could be used 'improperly' as well, for instance to undermine the very human rights protections that were another key component of the IOM's normative authority. A techno-solutionist attitude that stressed the neutrality of new technologies, however, provided ample resources for limiting the IOM's responsibility and accountability in such instances as well: 'All we can do is provide the tools and teach them to use them properly. Our projects should just focus on providing technical standards and explaining best practices. What authorities do with these tools is beyond our mandate' (Field diary, 5 August 2021).

Positioning itself as a technical expert organization through the provision of MIDAS not only depoliticized its capacity-building interventions, but also reaffirmed the IOM's authority within the field of global migration governance. Aside from its practical impact on the ground, the very provision of a technical system conferred symbolic authority on its developer, the IOM (Boswell, 2009). As explained in the previous chapter, for Nigerian federal officials the organization's adherence to international standards and 'best practices' strengthened the political legitimacy of their local partners as well. In this way, these international standards, as enacted by the IOM in Nigeria through its MIDAS-related capacity-building initiatives, simultaneously shaped local border control practices and depoliticized this influence.

Existing research has demonstrated how 'failure to meet the "international community's" standards' can exert 'significant normative or peer pressure' on the recipient states of IOM interventions (Andrijasevic and Walters, 2010: 990). In training sessions and workshops with Nigerian federal agencies, these technical standards were described by IOM officials as neutral steps toward a more sophisticated, modern technological solution to problems of border control: '[The IOM] is just here to help you, to empower you, to use data to fight crime and manage the border. Our approach is just to provide you with the technical standards that will take you to the next level' (Field diary, 19 August 2021). MIDAS-related capacity-building practices were often presented as requiring a 'three-pronged approach' consisting of legal, operational, and technical interventions in Nigeria. According to IOM officials, despite the extent to which the organization was involved in shaping new privacy legislation and establishing new interagency standard operating procedures at a federal level, 'we only lead on the technical pillar. [. . .] With the legal and operational pillars, you are the expert, and you teach us' (Field diary, 5 August 2021).

IOM officials presented the international technical standards enacted through MIDAS as entirely external to the organization, by arguing that it 'doesn't have the mandate to define any norms or to set standards' (Zahra, interview, 19 March 2021). However, researchers have shown that in practice, 'the IOM exercises a significant degree of autonomy as an expert authority with the power to define migration and how to govern it' (Robinson, 2018: 423). This view accords with a pragmatist understanding of technology, according to which the political and social impacts of new border control technologies will be influenced by the social understandings and perceptions of the developers of these tools. The IOM's development of MIDAS demonstrates how 'solutions to the problem of knowledge are solutions to the problem of social order' (Shapin and Schaffer, 1985: 332). Far from being neutral, MIDAS enacted migration as a particular kind of social problem, informed by the background conditions of global hierarchy, the post-9/11 securitization of migration, and a belief in the normative desirability of expansive digitalization, as we have seen above. Importantly, the notion of enactment highlights how the conditions in which new technologies were developed can shape their political effects in unintended ways as well: '*enactments* accomplished by data practices are not reducible to the intended outcomes of willful human action' (Scheel et al., 2019: 585 original emphasis). For this reason, it is important to examine what kinds of new practices the deployment of MIDAS generated in Nigeria, in order to better understand how the system enacted a particular—contingent and contestable—view of migration as a problem of digital surveillance, security, and crime control.

The emergence of crimmigration control in Nigeria

The IOM's pedagogical performances in Nigeria—characterized by a focus on human rights expertise and technological solutionism—neutralized politically sensitive criticisms regarding the organization's post-imperial orientation. These performances presented MIDAS as a politically neutral, technical solution to the problem of border control. This section turns to an analysis of the practical and operational effects of the IOM's MIDAS-related capacity-building practices in Nigeria, to consider whether 'behind the veil of technological solutionism lurks deeply inequitable and exploitative activities' (Taffel, 2018: 177).

'Little security nothings' and the merger of criminal justice and border control

Migration, particularly in the post-9/11 era, has become increasingly securitized through public discourse linking border control to national security measures meant to detect and prevent terrorism and other acute security threats (Bourbeau, 2011; Huysmans, 2004; Lazaridis and Skleparis, 2016). The notions of 'crisis' and 'emergency' have been used by governments globally to justify expansive border security measures, undermining the principles and protections of human rights and humanitarian law (Atak and Crépeau, 2014). In this context, border zones have been increasingly characterized by 'the imposition of exceptional security measures and suspension of normal rights. All who enter this zone are regarded as suspicious' (Zedner, 2019: 332). Both the IOM and the NIS periodically affirmed this securitized view. Until recently, the NIS described its mission in explicitly securitized terms. In an internal training strategy document from 2015, it stated that the agency sought to 'strengthen the security and prosperity of Nigeria through proactive, effective and efficient border security and migration management' (Field diary, 2 September 2021). The IOM also stressed that one of its key goals in Nigeria was to 'reduce security threats and cross-border organized crime' (IOM, 2024b).

Scholars of critical security studies have noted that border securitization has operated in more mundane registers as well, as cross-border mobility has quietly but steadily become entrenched in the institutional remits of security- and crime control-oriented agencies and subject to security technologies (Amicelle et al., 2015; Bigo, 2020; Huysmans, 2006). Even in the absence of highly exceptional and visible proclamations regarding migration as a security threat, securitization has still proceeded through 'devices, sites, practices without exceptional significance. Yet, *these little security nothings* are highly significant, since it is they rather than exceptional speech acts that create the securitizing process' (Huysmans, 2011: 377 original emphasis).

In Abuja, migration was rarely framed by IOM officials in terms of 'crisis', 'emergency', or 'exception'. Instead, the organization's capacity-building interventions framed migration control as a mundane governance issue creating the need for regularized—unexceptional—border security technologies and practices. This mundane register was, by 2024, reflected in a reconceptualized mission statement by the NIS, strikingly absent of any mention of security or crime control. Instead, the federal agency described its mission in terms of a 'march towards reformation and restructuring to be better positioned for the implementation of modern migration management' (NIS, 2024).

According to IOM officials in Abuja, deploying MIDAS in Nigeria was much more about global 'standards' and 'best practices' than about responding to exceptional security emergencies, as we have seen above in relation to human rights norms and technical standards. Yet, these standards involved the implementation of a host of new technical and operational frameworks that brought together the fields of border control and law enforcement. A key operational component relating to the standardization of MIDAS-related border control practices was the creation of 'standard operating procedures' (SOPs) that would serve as the basis for interagency cooperation between the NIS and various policing and security agencies. These SOPs, according to IOM officials, would 'innovate Nigerian border control capabilities and increase the security of the country against terrorism and transnational organized crime' (Field diary, 19 August 2021).

The IOM's focus on promoting interagency cooperation quietly reaffirmed a securitized and crime control-oriented framing of migration. In a multi-agency training workshop in Abuja, IOM officials explained to the NIS and federal law enforcement agencies that interagency cooperation would allow Nigerian officials to combine the border control capacities of MIDAS with the goals of criminal investigation by 'connecting the dots to detect suspects and carry out threat assessments' (Field diary, 26 August 2021). A document circulated in several SOP-related workshops stated that 'the application [of] domestic inter-agency cooperation postures, represents the *principal and critical key* in the fight against transnational organized crime' (Field diary, 19 August 2021, original emphasis). Developing these SOPs would allow Nigerian federal authorities to unlock the crime control capabilities built into the technical architecture of MIDAS, by paving the way for 'security, intelligence & investigation operations' (Field diary, 19 August 2021).

The IOM's SOP-related pedagogical practices can be understood in terms of 'little security nothings', as the entrenchment of border securitization proceeded as a result of several mundane practices, frameworks, and decisions based on the neutralizing discourse of 'standard' operational frameworks. The primary motivation for linking MIDAS to criminal investigation was, according to the IOM, the implementation of 'international standards and recommended practices' (Field diary, 26 August 2021). In contrast to exceptional security measures, SOPs for interagency cooperation sought to 'ensure that border management operations are performed consistently' by acting as the basis for 'coherence and quality assurance' (Field diary, 26 August 2021). The language of standardization expanded the range of law enforcement agencies involved in operating MIDAS while simultaneously undermining opportunities for contestation and critique regarding whether the system should be used to pursue goals related to security and crime control. As the IOM's workshop materials argued: 'A Standard Procedure does not need detailed explanation or description; because it is standard' (Field diary, 10 September 2021).

Interagency cooperation between border control and criminal justice officials was highly novel in the Nigerian context, which had previously been characterized by fierce disputes over the respective mandates of competing federal agencies. These disputes had periodically even escalated to violent confrontations (Abioye and Alao, 2020), and IOM officials were aware that promoting interagency cooperation was politically sensitive: 'There is no interagency cooperation, neither legal nor traditional. But MIDAS will help promote interagency cooperation and create SOPs to force cooperation' (Field diary, 12 August 2021). MIDAS allowed the organization to obscure this political sensitivity under the guise of technical standardization, as interagency cooperation SOPs were presented as 'the most immediate follow-up to the new abilities acquired through the use of [MIDAS]' (Field diary, 19 August 2021).

IOM officials periodically expressed concerns regarding the expansion of law enforcement access to the biometric and biographic data collected by MIDAS in border control contexts. In a meeting regarding API data and privacy legislation in Nigeria, one of the organization's officials stated that, in Nigeria, 'there is poor institutional culture for interagency cooperation [. . .] It is important to specify mandates, because data access by law enforcement can be problematic in terms of individual rights' (Field diary, 5 August 2021). Another official concurred: 'We trust NIS, and NIS are the ones receiving the MIDAS data. But once there is a hit [in an alert list], then suddenly four or five agencies all have access to this data. And no one will know what they do with it' (Field diary, 5 August 2021).

Critical researchers have shown that Global North actors have promoted the expansion of crimmigration control practices in the Global South in pursuit of their own goals of limiting South–North migration (Badalič, 2019). The merger of criminal justice and border control into a diverse set of 'crimmigration control' practices has criminalized an increasing number of individuals for various new migration-related offences, while also undermining due process and individual rights—enshrined in the criminal law—for those caught up in this hybrid form of punishment (Bosworth, 2008; Zedner, 2010, 2016). IOM officials were aware of these risks, but the development of SOPs to support interagency cooperation demonstrated their willingness to present MIDAS as a tool for pursuing the goals of both border control and law enforcement and criminal justice.

Border criminologists have variously pointed to the role of nationalist anti-immigration rhetoric and the instrumentalization of criminal justice practices to pursue the goals of stricter border controls as key drivers of the proliferation of crimmigration control practices globally (Bosworth et al., 2018b; Brandariz, 2022; Šalamon et al., 2020). In Abuja, however, the IOM's desire to expand the use of MIDAS to include a range of law enforcement purposes appeared less a result of an anti-immigration agenda, and more closely related to the logics of expansive digitalization and database interoperability.

Function creep, digital identity, and biometric statehood

Across several jurisdictions in the Global North, biometric identification technologies have caused the expansion of crimmigration control, in addition to political and institutional factors. In their analysis of Australia's expansive biometric border surveillance regime, Peter Chambers and Monique Mann (2019: 398, original emphasis) noted that the proliferation of interoperable biometric databases led to an expansion of crimmigration control through a process of technological function creep:

> Border security work elevates 'the border' into a politically central site where state-led surveillance and enforcement is undertaken, in

> response to the 'challenges' of globalization [. . .] a concatenation of formerly distinct powers, functions, technologies and institutions *then* becomes necessary, including, we've argued, a selective blurring and blending of criminal and immigration law.

Others have highlighted similar processes of 'function creep' driving the expansion of crimmigration control in other contexts, such as the EU and West Africa (Taylor, 2016; Tzanou, 2010; Wienroth and Amelung, 2023). According to Tim Dekkers (2020: 1852), technological function creep can contribute to the merger of criminal justice and border control practices when 'a change in the political arena [triggers] the need to use the technology for given purposes', the technology in question is 'able to do more than it is currently used for', and there is 'an absence of clear policies on how to use the technology'.

We have seen above how changes in the political field regarding global migration management motivated the IOM to develop MIDAS. In Nigeria, the deployment of MIDAS was characterized by a steady expansion of the range of practices for which this tool was used according to the technical affordances built into the system, which exceeded the remit of border control narrowly defined. Each step of the way, the IOM sought to ensure a central role for itself in developing new legislation, policies, and operational frameworks to define how MIDAS should be used to pursue the goals of both migration control and criminal justice.

Technological function creep was evident in planning meetings and workshops, in which the expansion of MIDAS to include new interoperable databases was presented as a foregone conclusion. One IOM official described this process of steady technological expansion:

> MIDAS is just the first step, which will obviously lead to API [data processing] soon. But API is really also just a foundation for PNR data, which will eventually be used for intelligence and analytics by intelligence agencies like ONSA. We will eventually move to a PIU [Passenger Information Unit] without NIS at all, and just the security and intelligence agencies. (Field diary, 5 August 2021)

In a multi-agency workshop focusing on the development of SOPs for interagency cooperation, an IOM official explained to representatives of various Nigerian law enforcement agencies that

> [d]eveloping these SOPs [is] just a start for other activities where you can all work together. But first you need the SOPs to use the MIDAS data. MIDAS will give you a huge amount of information that wasn't available to you before, and putting together that information gives you intelligence. MIDAS is [at] the technical level to support interagency cooperation, and we [IOM] are here to provide this technical support for it. (Field diary, 19 August 2021)

In other words, a key driver of the emergence of crimmigration control in Nigeria—characterized by new legal, operational, and technical frameworks for interagency cooperation between border control and law enforcement officials—was a technical process of function creep, motivated by the IOM's techno-solutionist orientation as well as the technical affordances of MIDAS itself.

The importance of function creep was illustrated by the fact that this technical expansion was not limited to a merger of border control and criminal justice. In Abuja, IOM official Catherine explained to me that MIDAS paved the way not only for interagency cooperation across the fields of border control and criminal justice, but also for a generalized expansion of the Nigerian federal state's capacity to collect and analyse digital biometric data: 'MIDAS is of course a first step here [in Nigeria] for proper intelligence and investigation for law enforcement too. But it's not just that, it's about creating a technological foundation for legal identity. Established identity was lacking in Nigeria, but now the state is developing' (Interview, 28 July 2021).

In line with the IOM's statist view of migration as a problem of sovereign territorial control, its MIDAS-related capacity-building projects prioritized strengthening state power by making mobile populations biometrically legible to federal state authorities. The organization's officials acknowledged that MIDAS was used by NIS officials to expand and legitimize their domestic political authority vis-à-vis other federal agencies and domestic state-level agencies:

> We need cooperation between the agencies, but to NIS it's important that they are the ones who own MIDAS. [. . .] We have a good relationship with NCAA as well, so we could introduce them into the MIDAS API project, because they have the sanction powers [in relation to airlines]. Let's try to befriend them and put them on the same page. But we need to

explain the roles and responsibilities, so NIS doesn't get worried. (Field diary, 5 August 2021)

The IOM sought to strike a balance between strengthening the sovereign territorial authority of its preferred federal-level partner, the NIS, and also ensuring that the agencies that are most supportive of the organization's interventions remain in control of MIDAS-related projects and the system's expansion in the near future.

This finding accords with Sabine Dini's (2018: 1692) analysis of the IOM's capacity-building interventions in Djibouti: 'IOM straddles its border practices with state-building rationality and implements projects that generate major changes in the way African states exercise their authority over their territory and population.' Migration scholars have long highlighted how a statist orientation to migration control 'reifies the framing of migration as a security issue in need of close monitoring, regulation and control. Due to the conception of societies as nationally bounded containers, migrants emerge as disruptive factors' (Scheel and Tazzioli, 2022: 6).

In Nigeria, the IOM viewed the deployment of MIDAS as one dimension of the general drive to strengthen state authority by ensuring the biometric legibility of populations. In addition to the introduction of highly novel interagency cooperation practices between the NIS and law enforcement agencies, the IOM promoted cooperation between federal agencies outside of the criminal justice system, including the National Identity Management Commission (NIMC) and the National Information Technology Development Agency (NITDA), which were engaged in the process of developing new federal-level digital biometric identity databases for citizens as well as foreign nationals. As I explain in more detail in the next chapter, these other national biometric databases were shaped by the technical architecture of MIDAS, to ensure compatibility and interoperability between various state functions including border control, law enforcement, and identity management in other contexts as well.

As Sabine Dini (2018: 1693) has argued, 'the biometric control system, and its effects in terms of hardening borders, are embedded in a larger context, characterized by the strengthening of the state [*sic*] sovereign power, understood as its capacity to exercise control over its own population'. This capacity to make both domestic and migrant populations biometrically legible reflected the international norm of 'biometric statehood' which Nigerian federal authorities sought to enact through their deployment of

MIDAS. As recounted in the previous chapter, NIS officials explicitly acknowledged the importance of biometric data for Nigeria's involvement in international politics: '[before MIDAS] we had nothing, we had pen and paper. Having a modern, biometric system is needed for us to be active in the international system' (Field diary, 26 August 2021).

Conclusion

In this chapter, I have demonstrated that MIDAS performed important political functions for the IOM in Nigeria. The system allowed the organization to present itself as a neutral, technical 'expert' of 'migration management', understood in the securitized and digitalized terms of biometric statehood. By 'teaching' Nigerian federal authorities how to control their borders in a 'proper' and 'modern' way by deploying MIDAS, the IOM simultaneously neutralized potential criticisms of its post-imperial influence and utilized discourses of human rights norms and technical standards as additional sources of its pedagogical and political legitimacy. Yet, the deployment of MIDAS resulted in the politically contingent and contestable emergence of crimmigration control in Nigeria. IOM officials recognized that such developments created new risks for human rights and the protection of individual migrants.

In addition to a securitized framing of migration control, the technical affordances of MIDAS resulted in a process of function creep. In this vein, Mark Salter (2013: 14) has argued that 'surveillance and control of circulation, then, expands to fit the space available [. . .] the dream of perfect security justifies whatever expansion technology, policy, and inattention will allow'. Such a dynamic was reflected in the development of MIDAS on the back of the organization's earlier Personal Identification and Registration System and its knowledge-production tools such as the Global Migration Flows Interactive Map, as well as the expansion of MIDAS in Nigeria from an initial focus on border management to crimmigration control and digital identity management more broadly.

IOM officials in Abuja periodically acknowledged the risks of expanding digital surveillance in Nigeria too quickly, due to concerns relating to both technical know-how and the responsible, non-exploitative use of biometric databases: 'Until we know they have the capacity to manage a simple dataset, if we give them too much, they will choke. MIDAS provides us with a pathway to the future, but there are some risks too' (Catherine, interview, 27 July 2021). These statements raised the question of how the technical components of MIDAS itself influenced the further expansion of crimmigration control in Nigeria. While this chapter has demonstrated the political effects of MIDAS from the perspective of the IOM—highlighting how the organization engaged in pedagogical performances characterized by a focus on human rights standards and technical expertise—the next chapter turns to an analysis of the technical components of the system itself.

8 A Golden Touch? MIDAS, Biometrics, and the Expansion of Crimmigration Control

> *Trust is the key referent in shaping the biometric imaginary and the wider securitization agenda.*
>
> —Krisrún Gunnarsdóttir and Kjetil Rommetveit (2017: 201)

> *Take a look at your own fingertips under a good strong light. You may see that the patterns of their ridges are different on different fingers. [. . .] The mesmerizing convolutions of these tiny ridges are sometimes called upon to determine people's fates.*
>
> —Simon Cole (2001: 1)

Friction and failure at the biometric border

Upon my arrival at Nnamdi Azikiwe International Airport in Abuja, my first order of business was to retrieve the visa that would allow me to remain in Nigeria for the duration of my fieldwork. I had been issued an approval letter for a visa on arrival, and instructed to 'proceed to Visa on Arrival section for Approval verification, biometric enrolment, and issuance of entry Visa' before going through passport control at the airport (Nigerian Immigration Service, 2022). After my forms had been verified, I was asked to enrol my fingerprints onto the NIS's national visa system by placing both of my thumbs, then the remaining four fingers on each hand, onto a Crossmatch 4+4+2 fingerprint scanner. The Crossmatch scanner was one of three models tested and approved by the International Organization for Migration (IOM) Global Procurement and Supply Unit in Manila, Philippines, for use in Migration Information and Data Analysis System

Outsourcing Crimmigration Control. Samuel Singler, Oxford University Press. © Samuel Singler 2025.
DOI: 10.1093/9780198927525.003.0008

(MIDAS) installations. In Nigeria, the IOM's MIDAS had also been configured to issue and validate travel visas.

The scanner swiftly collected and stored two viable thumb prints, flashing a green light on the computer screen as I pressed my thumbs against the glass. However, as I placed the four fingers of my right hand onto the reader the screen flashed a red light instead. An NIS officer sprayed the glass with a cleaning solution and wiped it, then asked me to place the same four fingers on the scanner. The screen flashed red again. The officer grabbed my fingers and pressed them down harder against the glass, but the computer screen still flashed a red light. The officer flipped over my hand, closely inspected my fingertips, then asked me: 'What kind of work do you do?' (Field diary, 21 July 2021). I told them I was an academic, but that in my free time I was also an avid rock climber, which had caused my fingertips to form thick callouses and my fingerprints to fade. Frustrated with the disruption that my calloused fingertips introduced to what was supposed to be a smoothly operating biometric enrolment process, the official proceeded to push my fingertips against the reader harder and at various angles, trying to find a way for the scanner to successfully enrol my fingerprints into the MIDAS visa system. Eventually, the scanner was able to enrol the fingerprints from one hand, but the officer had to manually override the enrolment process for the other hand and upload fingerprints that the automated reader would otherwise not have accepted. I was issued my visa and allowed through passport control.

This instance was my first personal encounter with MIDAS. Thanks to the pre-issued visa approval letter from senior NIS officials, a hitch in the biometric enrolment process did not prevent me from entering the country. Nonetheless, the problematic enrolment process made concrete the potential fallibility of a system that, in the IOM and NIS's official communications, was presented as extremely trustworthy and accurate. As IOM official José argued: 'the level of accuracy [of biometrics], it's amazing. And the level of certainty and integrity of the passport or visa, and the data inside the passport, is almost one hundred percent' (Interview, 2 March 2021). Yet, existing research has pointed out that the 'theoretical matching accuracy' of biometric systems has often ignored 'real-world accuracy challenges and related but extraneous factors' (Israel, 2020: xv). Olwig and colleagues (2020: 10–11) have highlighted potential issues related specifically to fingerprinting: 'Some individuals cannot be registered by fingerprint scanners as a consequence of problems such as skin disease, erosion of the ridges due to physical labor, intentional erasure of the fingerprints, or various dry skin- or age-related problems.' The discrepancy between a perceived infallibility of technical tools on one hand and practical challenges to their deployment on the other hand highlights that the impact of novel border control technologies is not always entirely predictable, suggesting the need for a critical appraisal of the political effects of these technical tools.

The analysis below draws on recent technologically focused research in border criminology (Côté-Boucher, 2020; Ferraris, 2022; Milivojevic, 2021), Science and Technology Studies (STS) (Jacobsen, 2015; Lemberg-Pedersen and Haioty, 2020; Scheel et al., 2019), and critical security studies (Amicelle et al., 2015; Aradau and Tazzioli, 2020; Bigo, 2020). The central claim of this chapter is that the material components of MIDAS—including fingerprint scanners, facial recognition cameras, passport readers, centralized databases, data processing and exchange mechanisms, and other devices—had political impacts that were not reducible to the motivations of their human developers in the IOM or their operators in the NIS. As Mareile Kaufmann (2019: 144) has argued, in order to understand the impact of material objects within broader socio-technical networks, '[o]ne literally has to follow the object in order to trace its workings. Such mapping exercises can include historical developments to document the life stories of objects, as well as participant observation and other (digital) cartographic methods.'

This chapter proceeds in four sections. First, I argue that MIDAS is one of many biometric tools that have become key components of contemporary global crimmigration control practices, particularly in the post-9/11 era. I then turn to the theoretical implications of examining the independent political effects of material tools, expanding the discussion of materiality and agency from Chapter 3 by empirically substantiating those arguments with reference to MIDAS in Nigeria. I demonstrate the analytical benefits of conceptualizing technology with reference to performativity and pragmatism, as distinct from other popular theoretical frameworks such as instrumentalist and assemblage perspectives. I then turn to the mechanisms through which the technical components of MIDAS shaped crimmigration control practices in Nigeria. These technical tools did not act alone, but interacted with their human designers and operators. Nonetheless, I show how their political effects were irreducible to the motivations and intentions of humans, foregrounding the importance of accounting for the agency of technical tools when analysing crimmigration control practices. I argue that MIDAS expanded what Valeria Ferraris (2022: 10) has called 'the digital version of crimmigration, where immigration and criminal law converge via the processing of data collected'. In addition to the intentions of Nigerian federal authorities, discussed in Chapter 6, and those of the IOM, discussed in Chapter 7, the technical components of the system enacted a particular conception of migration. Through these devices, migration was recast as a governable problem amenable to security- and criminal justice-oriented interventions in which 'migrants of all different "types" are then exposed in a generalized form to the suspicion of the "crimmigrant other"' (Amelung, 2021: 157).

Biometric recognition and suspicious bodies

Biometric identification refers to the recognition of humans based on their physical or behavioural attributes; the term 'biometric' etymologically derives from the Greek *bios* and *metron*, 'life' and 'measure' (Maguire, 2009). More recently, this kind of recognition has been increasingly carried out by automated technologies instead of humans (Olwig et al., 2020: 7). Historically, the problem of individual identity arose in the context of modern states' efforts to make their populations legible, that is, individually knowable and 'targetable for many basic governmental operations such as taxation, enrolment into military service, or criminal investigations' (Leese, 2022: 116; Scott, 1998). Several authors have noted how the history of biometric recognition is also underpinned by colonial and racial logics of making the racialized 'other' more easily identifiable, and allowing more rigorous social sorting between populations (Browne, 2009; Lyon, 2009; Sengoopta, 2003).

The relationship between the problem of accurate identification and criminality was already apparent in the branding of convicted criminals, in order to recognize repeat offenders, in early modern European and American criminal justice contexts (Cole, 2001: 7). The practice of automated biometric recognition has now spread far beyond the context of criminal identification, as biometric passports and ID cards are common, and many of our digital devices use automated biometric recognition tools on an everyday basis (Milivojevic, 2021). Although in everyday contexts our use of biometrically capable digital devices is mainly motivated by considerations of efficiency and ease of use, the deployment of biometric technologies in both migration control and criminal justice contexts has been driven by a belief in the importance of these tools to more accurately identify potentially risky individuals. With this ubiquity of automated biometric registration, it is no longer the individual criminal who is biometrically identified and therefore rendered suspect; instead, a condition of 'categorical suspicion' is attached to all those whose identities have not yet been biometrically verified (Maguire, 2009: 13).

Territorial borders have been a key site for the development and expansion of biometric technologies. In the twentieth century, with the intensification of international economic production and cross-border mobility, European states sought to monitor and inspect border crossers more closely. In this context, 'the passport became a standard part of the travel/mobility assemblage that helped concretize identity certification, affirmed state capacity for both identification and border policing, and expanded the domain of action in which the state could act' (Salter, 2015: 24). Earlier passports only included written descriptions of their owners and were not always issued exclusively to a single person (Torpey, 2000). From 1915, the introduction of an analogue biometric recognition technology—the passport photograph—allowed the individualization of these identity documents (Salter, 2015). The incorporation of automated biometric technologies into passports, including facial recognition and fingerprint matching, received a significant boost in the wake of the 9/11 attacks in the United States, as these tools became perceived as a way to prevent such national security disasters in the future (Epstein, 2008).

In the post-9/11 world, from a statist perspective, border security has essentially been conceptualized as a problem of overcoming ambiguous or inaccurate identification, which can be solved through the deployment of biometric recognition technologies (Gates, 2011). In this view, according to Charlotte Epstein (2008: 180), 'registering the intimate details of every single body on this planet is the solution to the problem of risk'. IOM officials expressed this view when discussing the role of biometrics in border management:

> The use of biometrics is definitely driven by all the challenges [. . .] you know, there's a lot of civil wars going on, there's people on the move, there's foreign fighters, terrorist fighters, there is guys from ISIS, there is a lot of people that are on the Interpol database for example. So, the use of biometrics is more to be certain that when you look for somebody, you get the right person rather than the wrong person. So, the level of accuracy, it's higher [. . .] the use of biometrics is a step forward. (José, interview, 2 March 2021)

So too, the organization's pedagogical materials in Nigeria distinguished between pre- and 'post-9/11 borders', the latter of which were characterized by 'new threats; securitization of borders; less emphasis on borderless border; high profiling of movement of persons/goods; insurgency/terrorism/cybercrimes/TOCs [transnational organized crimes]' (Field diary, 14 August 2021). In this context, the IOM (2018: 1) conceptualized biometrics as 'a vital part of migration management'. Its official brochures focused on facilitating travel and using these technologies for humanitarian work, with only fleeting mention of how 'biometrics enhances security in migration and border management processes' (IOM, 2018a: 3). In Nigeria, however, the organization's officials spoke of these tools in more openly securitized terms. As one official explained: 'Yes, biometrics can do many things, but usually it's all about security' (Field diary, 17 August 2021).

Presenting biometric identification tools as a technical fix to the risks of globalization rested on an assumption about the fixity of individual identity and the physical body as an 'indisputable anchor to which data can be safely secured' (Amoore and Goede, 2005: 163–164). Identity, in this view, was conceptualized as 'detached from one's self, having an objective and thing-like quality' (Franko Aas, 2006: 147). This logic was reflected in the IOM's description of unidentified migrants as 'lacking' an identity altogether (Henrikson, 2021). The organization framed the issuance of legal identity to migrants—through their biometric verification—as a human rights issue, and presented those lacking biometric identity documents as 'more susceptible to risky, irregular migration—often at the hands of human traffickers and criminal smuggling groups' (Henrikson, 2021; IOM, 2021b). Border criminologists, however, have demonstrated that it is most often migrants and refugees themselves who are viewed as suspicious and untrustworthy until they have been enrolled into biometric databases. Katja Franko (Franko Aas, 2006: 144–145), for instance, has argued that the ubiquity of automated biometric recognition systems reflects an assumption about the 'inability to establish trust through speech and linguistic communication [. . .] Biological tokens of identification are therefore becoming vital in identifying the undesirable populations in the new global order.' In criminal justice and border control contexts, our biometric identifiers are increasingly 'called upon to determine people's fates' (Cole, 2001: 1).

The personalization of mobility control via biometric identity means that the border itself—and suspicion of the 'crimmigrant other' (Franko, 2020)—is now 'imprinted' onto the bodies of border crossers (Aliverti et al.,

2019). Rather than being tied to a particular location, whether border control checkpoints or more diffuse sites of border control within and beyond the territory of the state (Infantino, 2016; Leerkes et al., 2013), borders now 'materialize when biometric technologies, such as facial scans and fingerprints, are matched with existing digitally coded body images and fingerprints' (Olwig et al., 2020: 8). These technical tools shape how migrants are viewed, namely as suspicious until digitally verified. In this context, as Kristrún Gunnarsdóttir and Kjetil Rommetveit (2017: 201) have argued, 'trust is the key referent in shaping the biometric imaginary and the wider securitization agenda'.

The flipside of Nigerian federal agencies' performances of 'biometric statehood', discussed in Chapter 6, was the introduction of a new form of digitalized citizenship that sorted border crossers according to their trustworthiness: 'citizenship is (re)designed as "safe" to the extent that the citizen is "becoming digital" and thus "knowable" to the state and non-state authorities allied with the state. [. . .] Oddly, this notion of "safe citizenship" is potentially terribly unsafe for the citizen herself' (Muller, 2010: 77). IOM officials explicitly referred to this logic of social sorting when discussing biometric registration: 'There is always the need for the government to make sure that, you know, to let the good guys in and keep the bad guys out, something like that. So, this is what the use of biometrics is all about' (José, interview, 2 March 2021). NIS officers working with MIDAS at the agency's headquarters in Abuja also shared the IOM's belief that biometrics could solve the problem of ambiguous identity at the border. As officer Gabriel explained: 'How can we know, when someone arrives at the border, if they are lying to us? Biometrics and MIDAS shows us, you see, "this is who I am, and this is what proves I'm telling the truth"' (Field diary, 26 August 2021).

Against this general background of the proliferation of biometric border control tools, differences between local contexts have also shaped the political impacts of introducing a system like MIDAS. Authors focusing on the Global North have argued that the proliferation of biometric borders 'attempts to transform citizenship into a quest for verifying/authenticating "identity" for the purpose of access to rights, bodies, spaces, and so forth, thus (purportedly) stripping away the cultural and ethnic attributes of citizenship' (Muller, 2004: 280). Matthias Leese (2022: 126) has examined the effects of new biometric databases while arguing that 'the European citizenry has already been biometrically fixed through the incorporation of biometric templates in passports and ID cards'. However, in Nigeria the existence of shared attributes of citizenship across the entire national population and the use of biometric identification tools were historically very limited. To borrow Leese's terminology, the Nigerian citizenry had not yet been 'biometrically fixed' when the IOM began its MIDAS-related capacity-building practices in the country. The introduction of MIDAS coincided with, and was technically linked to, the introduction of a National Biometric Identity Card (NBIC) and the establishment of an incipient national biometric database. In other words, biometric identification at the border did not transform earlier identity management practices, which had elsewhere been linked to other aspects of state governance, such as taxation and welfare provision (Scott, 1998). Rather, these practices were from the outset shaped by the logics of crimmigration control and the surveillance of mobility, as well as the attendant condition of 'categorical suspicion' (Maguire, 2009: 13) of those not yet biometrically verified.

If, as various authors have argued, there is something distinct about contemporary biometric border control tools compared to their earlier analogue equivalents (Epstein, 2008; Gates, 2011; Gunnarsdóttir and Rommetveit, 2017; Muller, 2010), it is analytically significant that the generalization of biometric identity in Nigeria was grounded in the use of automated biometric recognition technologies in a crimmigration control context. Compared to less complex methods of recognition, the contestability and potential fallibility of automated biometric identification tools were obscured beneath a veneer of technical complexity and neutrality. These tools represented 'a binary language of ones and zeroes which radically reduces possibilities for negotiations and therefore also resistance' (Franko Aas, 2006: 150). In this context of binary digital verification, 'an identification error can deny and exclude individuals' (Jacobsen and Rao, 2018: 27), yet acknowledgement of such errors was noticeably absent from official discourses relating to the rollout of MIDAS.

The previous chapter demonstrated how, through its capacity-building interventions in Nigeria, the IOM contributed to the expansion of crimmigration control by supporting the technical, operational, and legal merger of migration control and criminal justice. This expansion was underpinned and justified with reference to a techno-solutionist view of border control, 'which places a tremendous amount of trust in technological tools' (Vavoula, 2021: 458). But in what way did these technical components of MIDAS shape crimmigration control practices distinctly from the intentions and motivations of either the IOM or Nigerian federal officials? What was the impact of introducing widespread biometric identification tools for the first time in the context of border control and migration management, and how did these devices shape the logics of state power, criminal justice, and migration control in Nigeria?

Technology, agency, and the politics of crimmigration control

Addressing these questions regarding the impact of the technical tools that composed MIDAS requires a framework for conceptualizing the relationship between humans and non-humans in shaping crimmigration control practices. In Chapter 3, I suggested that synthesizing insights from the framework of performativity and the tradition of pragmatism provides a useful avenue for evaluating the development and deployment of new border control technologies in the Global South. In this section, I apply this framework to the technical components of MIDAS in Nigeria.

Instrumentalism and the impact of MIDAS on the ground

An instrumentalist view of border control technologies would focus primarily on the political motivations of the Nigerian federal agencies that have deployed MIDAS. In this view, 'technology is neutral, a tool that can be turned to whatever use a user desired' (McCarthy, 2018: 6). Accordingly, understanding the deployment of MIDAS in Nigeria would require an empirical assessment of the extent to which the system has achieved its stated goals as outlined by the NIS and IOM, namely an 'enhanced capacity to process migrants at [Nigeria's] international borders' (Field diary, 23 August 2021).

The extensive rollout of MIDAS across various air, land, and sea border posts undoubtedly increased the NIS's capacity to biometrically process border crossers, although, as one IOM official explained, 'the Nigerian authorities will absolutely not share the data with us' (Field diary, 28 July 2021), which complicated empirically assessing the system's impact. Both NIS and IOM officials were aware of the remaining limitations of the system, not least the fact that 'MIDAS only tracks entries at legal border crossing points [. . .] but there are thousands of migrants and foreigners who can cross by irregular means' (Luca, interview, 3 March 2021). NIS training workshop materials stated that in Nigeria, there remain 'well over 1400 illegal routes

. . . 84 legal???' (Field diary, 14 August 2021). Moreover, due to difficult environmental and political conditions in the border zones of the country, border control checkpoints required ongoing maintenance and repeated repairs. Occasionally, in Nigeria and elsewhere, existing MIDAS installations fell into disuse due to a lack of electricity or internet connection once IOM project funding ran out:

> Now, the problem that we had, and that I'm facing now, you know, three, four years after is that the government didn't foresee maintenance costs in its budget. So, for as long as IOM supported, for example, the internet connection, MIDAS was working. But since the project period ended [. . .] the government simply didn't have resources to continue paying the internet connection. (Louise, interview, 9 March 2021)

According to an instrumentalist conception, the deployment of MIDAS can be understood as highly limited in terms of its impact on Nigerian border control practices. However, despite these material limitations, the discussion in Chapters 6 and 7 demonstrated that from the perspective of both NIS and IOM officials, the rollout of the system nonetheless had several desirable effects that were not reducible to its practical impacts at border control checkpoints. For instance, it legitimized the political authority of the Nigerian federal state vis-à-vis other domestic actors and demonstrated the technical expertise and neutrality of the IOM within the field of global migration management. These effects were distinct from the extent to which MIDAS actually transformed border control practices on the ground, suggesting that the effects of material technologies reached beyond their immediate failures or successes. Foucault (1995: 272) highlighted a similar dynamic when examining the continued maintenance and expansion of the prison system despite frequent proclamations of the failure of that institution: 'perhaps one should reverse the problem and ask oneself what is served by the failure of the prison; what is the use of these different phenomena that are continually being criticized.'

Assemblage theories and MIDAS as a socio-technical network

Critical interdisciplinary research into new border control tools has sought to overcome this focus on their instrumental uses by highlighting that they 'can also have unintended consequences and side-effects. Although they may be implemented with certain effects in mind, in practice other previously unthought-of effects may materialize [. . .] technology can initiate changes to the social environment' (Dekkers, 2020: 1852–1853). Rather than simply focusing on the extent to which the operators of a system such as MIDAS successfully deployed the system to achieve their goals at border control checkpoints, critical perspectives have sought to examine the impact that new technologies have had on their human users, whether intended or not (Wood, 2021). As outlined in Chapter 3, claims about the independent effects of technologies require a theoretical reorientation away from conceptualizing agency solely as an attribute of humans, towards what Anna Leander (2021: 162) has called 'relational ontologies' that focus on the agency of both human and non-human 'actants' in the socio-technical networks within which they are situated. In their analysis of EU biometric border controls, Nina Amelung and colleagues (2021: 44–45) have argued that a critical analysis of bordering practices requires accounting for the effects on regulative frameworks, developments in biometric technologies, technical database infrastructures, and organizational imperatives and principles. Applying this framework to the Nigerian context, NIS officers, IOM officials, and the technical components of MIDAS—as well as border crossers, technology vendors, and other infrastructures—entered into a border control 'assemblage', and agency within this 'heterogeneous network of activities' was 'distributed' among these various actors (Amelung et al., 2021: 36–37).

The metaphor of the assemblage can productively highlight how the NIS and IOM's practices of border control were concretely shaped by the materiality of MIDAS and the environments within which the system operates. The materiality of the technical components of the system intervened in official plans to construct sustainable and smoothly operating MIDAS border control checkpoints and disrupted the intentional actions of humans. In this way, technologies and their limitations contributed to 'a diminished agency of humans' (Milivojevic and Radulski, 2020: 202). IOM officials lamented how the materiality of MIDAS occasionally disrupted the organization's plans for the smooth operation of the system after installation:

> There is definitely a sub-use of the system because of all these technical problems [. . .] The material, the equipment is not just written off. So, if a computer is used for four years, every day of the week, sometimes you find that there is no communication between the MIDAS systems

> between different ports. This is terrible, because we are putting in an IT system and a BMIS system that is relatively sophisticated [. . .] but eventually they were transmitting data by just charging it on a flash disk and bringing it together maybe once a month. (Maria, interview, 10 March 2021)

Georgios Glouftsios (2021: 454) has argued that it is in these moments of disruption and failure that technical systems exert their independent effects on human practices most forcefully: 'information systems materialize in the process of operational management as unruly, unstable and failing infrastructures.' To account for these effects, Glouftsios (2021: 463) has suggested that critical research into large-scale border management systems should focus on how these technologies require ongoing 'corrective maintenance' to ensure their continued operation, as well as 'adaptation to emerging technologies and service needs'.

The account above demonstrated how IOM officials were aware of how the maintenance needs of MIDAS impacted the rollout of the organization's capacity-building projects on the ground. New project proposals increasingly factored in long-term maintenance costs, and officials in Abuja explained 'we have realized that we've created a monster, and the monster is very expensive' (Field diary, 6 September 2021). Conceptualizing MIDAS in Nigeria as a socio-technical assemblage also brings into view how not only the materiality of digital tools, but also other human actors, shaped these maintenance processes. When seeking to replace worn and broken equipment in the field, the organization's officials were forced to engage in tough negotiations with technology vendors regarding the scope of warranties. One official in Abuja explained that the complicated warranty policies sometimes introduced additional unpredictability into project costs: 'Sometimes the SLAs [Service Level Agreements] don't specify that the company has to pay for shipping costs. They'll replace the hardware, but they won't pay for the return shipping. So then we have to go and find that money somewhere' (Field diary, 6 September 2021).

Continued adaptation of the MIDAS infrastructure to emerging technical systems and service needs was also apparent in the Nigerian context. From its inception within the IOM's Immigration and Border Management (IBM) division as the Personal Identification and Registration System (PIRS) in 2007, the system underwent several significant updates and a name change to MIDAS in 2013 (Aaron, interview, 2 March 2021). It continually adapted to newly emerging technologies, for instance those that allowed real-time internet connectivity and better automated biometric matching. The organization's officials identified broader technical developments as key drivers continually transforming MIDAS:

> Originally, there was no dynamic things, everything was on the screen, and then somehow the technologies changed. Now, when you open the system, you will see dynamic things going on the other side [. . .] It's a bit strange waiting for the new technologies, but we attempt to consume them quickly. So, we immediately leave old products and move to new products and new technologies. (Aaron, interview, 2 March 2021)

The technical infrastructure of MIDAS not only adapted to streamline existing functionalities, but also incorporated an increasing number of border control-related functions. The organization proudly tweeted a quote from the Head of the Border and Identity Solutions Unit, stating that 'innovation is at the core of IOM's MIDAS programme which has evolved to cover the whole travellers' journey'.[1]

The technical functionality of the system was also configured to meet the technological and service needs of specific Member States. As the IOM's (2018b: 2) official brochure explained, under a section titled 'MIDAS interoperability and adaptability', the system 'is completely customizable and can be tailored to the specific requirements of governments'. Possible functionalities included checking API data, issuing E-Visas, connecting to other border management systems, and transferring data between border management contexts and national identity databases.

In Nigeria, the system was adapted to the broader technological environment of the federal government's efforts to expand biometric identification in the country. As outlined in the previous chapter, since 2021 the IOM has been engaged in establishing the technical, legal, and operational frameworks that will allow MIDAS to process API/PNR data at air borders in the future. In addition, the system was already interoperable with the newly established NBIC and Foreigner Registration (FR) systems run by Nigerian federal authorities. These systems were mandated by an ECOWAS Decision (A/DEC-01/12/14) in 2014, aimed to facilitate intra-ECOWAS travel. Conceptualizing these discrete systems as part of a broader

[1] IOM Immigration and Border Management Twitter account, 1 July 2021. Available at: https://x.com/IOM_IBM_HQ/status/1410600036510035976 [Accessed 29 September 2024].

'biometric assemblage' (Madianou, 2019) highlights how the materiality of each system shaped the others. MIDAS was adapted specifically to allow for interoperability with the other incipient biometric databases, and in turn exerted a kind of technical agency of its own on them. Although the NBIC and FR systems were initially established independently of MIDAS, they were eventually reconfigured to accord with the technical standards of the latter system, including international 'best practices' relating to ICAO standards on biometric portrait quality (ICAO, 2018). In this way, technical tools and standards developed in the risk- and security-focused context of contemporary border control (Muller, 2009) reshaped Nigerian national identification systems as well.

Performativity, pragmatism, and the risk of depoliticization

Assemblage theories can be helpful in illuminating how the technical components of MIDAS exerted independent effects on border control practices and other information systems in Nigeria. These impacts were distinct from the intended effects of the system in the instrumentalist sense, suggesting that socio-technical assemblages can have emergent outcomes that are irreducible to the intentions of any single actor within the broader network. Of course, the expansion of MIDAS was underpinned by the political motivations of Nigerian federal authorities as well as the IOM's solutionism, demonstrating that 'the biometric assemblage is not just the result of technological convergence; it equally depends on the social, political, and economic factors in which technologies are developed and used' (Madianou, 2019: 585). Nonetheless, assemblage theories can highlight how the socio-technical network as a whole had important emergent effects—such as importing technical standards and logics from crimmigration control technologies to other areas of governance—that were irreducible to the intentions of any specific actor. In short, technological assemblages are more than the sum of their parts (Franko Aas, 2012a).

In Chapter 3 I argued that synthesizing literature on performativity and pragmatism provides a useful perspective for a critical appraisal of contemporary digital crimmigration control tools. Incorporating the insights of performativity is central to grasping the kinds of aggregate effects that assemblage theories bring into view. The notion of performativity illuminates how the technical components of MIDAS not only constrained or allowed humans to engage in particular kinds of border control practices in an instrumental sense, but also performatively enacted both biometrics and migration as particular kinds of social problems and contributed to the creation of 'new, technologically mediated forms of subjectivity' (Franko Aas et al., 2009b: 5). Critical researchers such as Stephan Scheel and Funda Ustek-Spilda (2019: 668) have utilized the notion of enactment to challenge perspectives that ontologically treat migration as an already existing phenomenon which digital border control tools can measure, instead arguing that new technologies 'help enact the object they set out to measure as an intelligible reality'.

In the Nigerian context, MIDAS enacted migration as a problem of risk and criminal justice by contributing to the merger of legal, technical, and operational frameworks of migration control and law enforcement. As one IOM official explained in Abuja: 'MIDAS is helping the [Nigerian] agencies understand what a migrant is' (Field diary, 17 August 2021). The processing of API/PNR data, interoperability with Interpol's I-24/7 alert lists, and requiring standard operating procedures between the NIS and law enforcement agencies all performatively enacted migration as a problem of crimmigration control. The expansion and interoperability of biometric identification tools was also a key component in recent cooperative efforts by Nigerian federal authorities and UN organizations to combat transnational organized crime, human trafficking, and terrorism (UN CTITF, 2012; UNODC, 2020). These efforts materially embodied logics of crimmigration control by representing migration control and criminal justice-related databases as essentially dealing with similar kinds of policy issues. The technical logics embedded in the MIDAS architecture merged previously disparate fields of governance, and not always as a result of intentional actions on behalf of either the NIS or the IOM. These technical tools, by collecting, verifying, and sharing biometric data, also brought 'migration into being as an object of governance and perform[ed] it as a *global reality* to manage in technical and pragmatic ways' (Robinson, 2018: 421, original emphasis). From the perspective of individual border crossers, MIDAS shaped individual identities by recasting them in digital biometric terms. As 'without biometrics, there is no lawful mobility' (Ferraris, 2022: 11), the identity of border crossers became dependent on their biometric verifiability. This is why the IOM characterized 'irregular' migrants as lacking an identity entirely (Henrikson, 2021).

Performativity is useful in grasping the political impacts of technical objects in shaping human practices, understandings, and identities, and I return to the performative effects of MIDAS in Nigeria in the next section. This perspective does not necessarily imply the kind of ontological levelling that proponents of assemblage perspectives presuppose when attempting to discard analytical distinctions between '[h]uman and non-human, meaning and materiality, big and small, macro and micro, social and technical, nature and culture' (Law, 2009: 147). Flattening these ontological distinctions risks inadvertently depoliticizing crimmigration control technologies by obscuring the political responsibility of the human designers and operators of these tools underneath a detailed examination of various technical 'actants'. Existing analyses of border control assemblages have provided extremely detailed accounts of the technical systems and networks that enact contemporary circuits of crimmigration control (Amelung et al., 2021; Ferraris, 2022; Madianou, 2019; Olwig et al., 2020). MIDAS in Nigeria would also lend itself handily to a detailed exploration of the various technical components of the system. However, such an endeavour would risk overlooking or obscuring the epistemic hierarchies and postcolonial power relations that underpinned the IOM's capacity-building practices, including its development of MIDAS.

When analysing MIDAS, it is crucial to grasp its performative effects without losing sight of the relationship between system and broader relations of global hierarchy. Focusing excessively on the agentic powers of biometric technologies themselves risks unwittingly reaffirming the techno-solutionist view of the developers of crimmigration control technologies, who elide personal responsibility for these systems and trust 'other people to determine whether the tools [they are] developing become problematic' (Olwig et al., 2020: 51). Throughout my research, IOM officials in Nigeria repeatedly abrogated responsibility for the effects of MIDAS by shifting accountability on to either Nigerian federal authorities or the systems themselves. On one hand, potential misuses of the system were presented as unavoidable 'because when a member state wants to intentionally violate some rules, you cannot do anything because they have full ownership of the system' (Aaron, interview, 2 March 2021). On the other hand, the continued expansion of MIDAS was presented as a result of the technical requirements of the system itself, based on contemporary international standards that were presented as politically neutral: 'We add new components to the system because this is what's required to make sure everything is working properly [. . .] This is not a political choice. That choice has been made somewhere else. We are here making sure everything works properly' (Field diary, 17 August 2021).

In order to challenge such depoliticizing statements regarding MIDAS, this book has drawn upon the pragmatist conception of technology as 'the invention, development, and cognitive deployment of tools and other artifacts, brought to bear on raw materials and intermediate stock parts, with a view to the resolution of perceived problems' (Hickman, 2001: 12). By focusing on what kinds of social problems humans were trying to solve by developing and deploying new technologies, the pragmatist conception of technology can temper the agentic claims of assemblage theories by highlighting the unique capacity of humans to deliberate about possible political alternatives and intentionally choose between them, particularly in times of crisis, dislocation, and innovation (Hickman, 2007; Howarth, 2013; Pihlström, 2021).

Such moderation is important when analysing the underlying politics of MIDAS in Nigeria. As Gunnarsdóttir and Rommetveit (2017: 198) have explained, technical experts are particularly powerful in determining 'who the relevant stakeholders are and which societal problems need consultation', and shaping 'the framing of issues and how to address them'. Petra Molnar (2021: 70) has similarly argued that

> [i]nternational organizations such as the IOM and UNHCR are major players and driving forces in the development and deployment of migration management technologies. Often, they are the first on the ground following a humanitarian disaster and they set the agenda in terms of prioritization when it comes to humanitarian innovation and technological development. As such, powerful international organizations like IOM and UNHCR get to designate spaces of technological experimentation such as iris scanning and other biometrics in grey zones of accountability such as forced migration situations or humanitarian catastrophes, in order to appease states that they may be beholden to and to cement their presence in various locations.

The IOM played an influential role in shaping dominant problematizations of border control, by designing technologies that enacted a particular view of migration as a governable problem amenable to security- and criminal justice-oriented interventions. By focusing on these moments of technological design and social problematization, pragmatism complements a performative analysis of MIDAS in Nigeria by highlighting the uniquely human capacity to deliberate upon what kinds of social or political 'problems' technical tools should address, even as material objects and technologies shape these discussions (Pihlström, 2021). The pragmatist focus on the practical effects of (technical) knowledge also helps to reorient critical analysis away from ontological debates about the 'agency' (or lack thereof) of human and non-human 'actants' towards the practical impacts of a new technology such as MIDAS on the ground.

MIDAS and the technical logics of crimmigration control in Nigeria

The previous section illustrated how a synthesis of performativity and pragmatism offers a productive avenue for critically analysing the political effects of the technical components of MIDAS in Nigeria, while also foregrounding the unique political accountability of humans within these broader socio-technical networks. This section picks up the discussion of the performative effects of the system by analysing the mechanisms through which MIDAS exerted these effects in Nigeria. The key mechanisms were perceptions of the infallibility of biometric recognition, the introduction of technical feedback loops, and technological affordances that tended towards increasing expansion and interoperability.

Biometric borders, truthful bodies?

Trust in the accuracy of biometric recognition technologies was a ubiquitous theme in discussions with both IOM officials and NIS officers. These individuals presented analogue forms of identity verification as inherently untrustworthy and arbitrary. As an NIS officer explained at the agency's headquarters:

> Before MIDAS, the officers were forced to write down information of passengers, or migrants, by hand on paper. And they will look at the photo, and look at the face, and say 'yes' or 'no' [. . .] The officer has very limited time for each passenger, so the comparison must be done in an instant, so this is not always very accurate. [. . .] MIDAS never gets tired. (Field diary, 3 August 2021)

Public IOM documents similarly stated that 'biometrics considerably improves the quality and accuracy of registration processes' of migrants (IOM, 2018a: 3). The technical architecture of MIDAS continually reaffirmed the reliability of automated recognition technologies as opposed to manual alternatives, not only in the verification of border crossers' identities but also for NIS officers themselves, who had to log in to the system using a fingerprint scanner. IOM official Mohammed explained that:

> People will forget a password. They will share their password. Then the agency will not know who is doing what in the system [. . .] So, basically, that's why we initiated the connectivity of the session with fingerprint [identification], because at least we know that the border officers will not forget their fingerprint. (Interview, 22 February 2021)

Trust in the infallibility of automated identification and verification technologies permeated the MIDAS-related capacity-building practices, even as officers—such as the one I encountered upon my arrival in Abuja—periodically overrode the system manually whenever automated technologies failed.

The use of biometrics in the context of border management has mirrored how these tools have become viewed as providing 'unambiguous evidence of identity' in a criminal justice context (Lynch et al., 2008: 11). Such trust, however, belies the probabilistic and imperfect nature of automated verification based on fingerprint matching and facial recognition. Fingerprint matching, for instance, is often regarded as producing a 'binary either-or judgement' of identity, yet in fact relies on 'probability calculations' to declare whether two prints match (Amelung, 2021: 158). Facial recognition, in turn, has been shown to produce much higher error rates for darker-skinned individuals and for women. Joy Buolamwini and Timnit Gebru (2018: 11) calculated that among the most popular facial recognition systems, white men have error rates between 0.0% and 0.3%, while 'darker females have the highest error rates for all gender classifiers ranging from 20.8%–34.7%.' In the context of a system such as MIDAS, an erroneous facial recognition match could have grave consequences, preventing travel and even resulting in a false positive match in international criminal alert lists; racial disparities in the reliability of these technologies were particularly concerning for a system rolled out primarily in African states. Yet, a binary understanding of identity contributed to the expansion of crimmigration control measures by enacting bodies as suspicious until verified by an automated matching system. In this vein, NIS officer Ike argued that 'MIDAS is not just about what the officers are doing anyway: checking the photo and checking the passenger's face. MIDAS connects to other systems like Interpol [. . .] In this way, we know who someone really is before letting them through the border' (Field diary, 26 August 2021).

IOM officials did occasionally acknowledge the limitations of biometric technologies. José, for instance, explained: 'Facial recognition is by far the least accurate of all the systems of biometrics. [. . .] Facial is not the most accurate one. Yes, everyone knows that, this is common sense. But the problem is, it's the only biometric which is standard, which is mandatory to be on the [passport] chip' (Interview, 2 March 2021).[2] Officials recognized the potential shortcomings of biometrics on the one hand, while on the other hand advocating expansion of their use due to their technical superiority over manual alternatives. This dynamic mirrored developments at the EU external border, where Leese (2022: 114) has shown that EU officials have recognized that large-scale biometric databases are 'not always complete, accurate and reliable', yet they have continued to expand and proliferate. In Nigeria, IOM and NIS officers mainly compared biometric technologies to analogue recognition practices and presented the former as a leap forward in terms of accuracy and reliability, as exemplified by NIS officer Gabriel's remarks earlier in this chapter. IOM official José also followed up his critical remarks regarding facial recognition by arguing:

> The reliability, it's probably not one hundred percent, nothing is. [. . .] Is it possible that people cross the border with the wrong passport, or that there is a false alert? Yes, of course this is possible. Everything is possible. [. . .] But otherwise, we'll still be on, you know, what we were doing twenty or thirty years ago when we had a manual system. And my question is: would that be more efficient? (Interview, 2 March 2021)

José's question of whether a manual system is preferable to automated facial recognition is an important and relevant one. Highlighting the potential fallibility of biometrics does not necessarily imply a Luddite rejection of digital technologies at the border. The point is rather to demonstrate how automated biometric systems exerted performative effects through their

[2] Developers of biometric technologies agree that out of the three most popular biometric technologies—facial recognition, fingerprinting, and iris scans—facial recognition is the least accurate (Murad, 2020).

perceived infallibility, complexity, and ubiquity within the technical architecture of MIDAS. In contrast to manual facial recognition, which IOM and NIS officials recognized as inherently contestable, the identification and verification processes of automated systems were presented in binary terms and as largely trustworthy, notwithstanding the occasional critical remark.

One immediate political effect of this perceived infallibility was to reduce 'possibilities for negotiations and therefore also resistance' (Franko Aas, 2006: 150). More broadly, the focus on the increased matching accuracy of MIDAS compared to analogue practices served to enact migration control primarily as an issue of accuracy, data quality, and technical sophistication. This focus sidestepped broader questions about the politics of migration control, and the potential contestability of merging migration control databases with those of law enforcement and national identity. The IOM presented the merging of MIDAS with the NBIC and FR databases as a technical exercise, in which the main considerations were to 'assess the quality and integrity of biometric and other data in national databases' (Field diary, 1 September 2021). The relevant stakeholders and independent evaluators of new biometric initiatives were not local political actors or migrants, but rather 'a biometrics expert' who assessed compliance of all databases with ICAO standards and the data quality of the MIDAS database (Field diary, 1 September 2021). Once data quality was assessed, the expansion of biometric recognition practices and the merging of databases was a foregone conclusion.

While biometric systems turned migration control into an issue of data quality and matching accuracy, humans were nonetheless politically responsible for the initial development and deployment of these technologies. This political responsibility would be obscured by focusing only on the emergent effects of 'biometric assemblages' once they were operational (Madianou, 2019). As outlined above, the expansion of biometric technologies in a border control context was underpinned by the logics of risk and security. Despite the IOM's focus on facilitating migration in its official brochures, officers in the field still repeatedly referred to the deployment of biometrics in securitized terms. Pragmatism highlights how biometric systems only exerted their performative effects once the prior choice was made to deploy these systems in the field. This perspective foregrounds the political responsibility that organizations such as the IOM accrued by making decisions about what kinds of biometric technologies to deploy in the context of migration management. Discourses regarding the infallibility of biometrics rested upon a prior choice to problematize migration control as a social problem relating to the risk- and security-based context in which biometric technologies have proliferated in recent decades.

Interoperability, evidence, and feedback loops

The merger of border control and law enforcement databases points to another mechanism through which MIDAS exerted its performative effects upon the field of crimmigration control in Nigeria: the introduction of technical feedback loops that justified the continued expansion of the system (O'Neil, 2016). In Chapter 5, IOM official Diego presented MIDAS as a 'foundational building system' that subsequently 'facilitates newer systems' (Interview, 16 February 2021). With such terms, the IOM presented the expansion of the system as a natural response to previously identified information gaps. In Nigeria, a lack of communication between MIDAS and law enforcement databases was similarly presented as a technical problem resulting in information gaps that had to be addressed. One IOM official explained in an NIS training workshop that 'MIDAS fills information gaps between your systems. Combining this information with other databases results in intelligence, and you can act on intelligence' (Field diary, 19 August 2021).

The notion of a feedback loop (O'Neil, 2016) highlights how biometric databases and surveillance technologies can proliferate even when their developers and operators do not initially intend for these systems to expand beyond narrow use cases. In recasting migration control as a matter of data collection and accurate recognition, MIDAS simultaneously transformed a lack of data—including a lack of interoperability between various biometric databases—into an 'information gap', in other words a technical problem that had to be overcome to ensure the smooth operation of the system. This feedback loop was situated within the broader solutionist attitude of the IOM and other developers of border control technologies. Techno-solutionism is reflected in the dominant 'paradigm of migration management', which 'fuels—in tandem with the turn toward evidence-based policy-making—a quest for more and better knowledge on migration, especially in terms of its quantification' (Scheel and Ustek-Spilda, 2019: 665). IOM officials expressed this approach to migration management when arguing that the collection of more, and increasingly accurate, data at the border was a key goal of MIDAS-related capacity-building projects:

> We cannot do anything, if the data are not clear. The data has to be the first thing. And the policy has to be evidence-based [. . .] And in order to do analysis, there must be data sharing also within a country. We have tried in West Africa to support on improving migration data, but it is difficult sometimes, not because they don't want to improve their own sector, but because they don't want to share with other agencies [. . .] So we try to show them that by sharing data between sectors, between migration and police, and other systems, there are much more huge benefits that the country can achieve beyond just controlling a physical border. (Maria, interview, 10 March 2021)

The technical components of MIDAS continually represented migration control in terms of data collection and interoperability. Whenever the system successfully matched an individual border crosser to domestic law enforcement alert lists, for instance, these technologies materially enacted the border as a site of crimmigration control. In other geographical contexts, critical researchers have already demonstrated that the performative effects of new digital border control technologies have limited opportunities for politically challenging the logics of crimmigration control. By repeatedly representing migration as a matter of calculable risks and their mitigation through ever-expansive data collection practices (Amoore, 2014), this calculability itself is no longer called into question. Instead, criticisms of these systems have focused on the adequacy of existing tools to carry out adequate matching processes or sufficiently sophisticated risk calculations (Scheel and Ustek-Spilda, 2019: 675). The potential fallibility of digital border control technologies has also reinforced the feedback loop that promotes the expansion of systems like MIDAS; failure itself has been reconceptualized as a reason for further expansion, rather than opening up spaces for political contestation (Lisle, 2018).

The establishment of technical feedback loops related to the data collection capacities of MIDAS, and its interoperability with other systems, reinforced the merger of migration control and criminal justice. Meneses Queiroz (2019) has argued that the establishment of interoperability between the European asylum database EURODAC and law enforcement systems resulted in the conflation of the purposes of migration and crime control, an increase in the amount of personal data that was stored in these systems, and broader law enforcement access to data originally collected for migration control and asylum purposes. In Nigeria, IOM officials recognized that the establishment of interoperability between MIDAS and law enforcement databases came with a risk of eroding data retention limits and the principles of purpose limitation. In a workshop regarding the processing of API data—and the establishment of related interagency cooperation mechanisms—one official expressed concern regarding data privacy when allowing law enforcement access to MIDAS data:

> Nigeria doesn't have a clear framework for data protection specifically for law enforcement agencies [. . .] Even though data should be deleted if there is not an API hit, I think we need to worry about data protection for innocent people. Who will actually be on these watchlists? Nigerian terrorism laws are very broad. (Field diary, 5 August 2021)

Despite this moment of concern, however, deliberations in the workshop were shaped by the technical feedback loop that demanded more data in order to ensure that MIDAS was working properly. Another official argued:

> Yes, the law should give them guidelines on what should be done. But what's most important is to make sure the systems are working properly. The data need to be globally interoperable. The national watchlist used to be printed on a piece of paper, but biometric data will give certainty that the person is the one you're looking for, so they can be used for arrest or preventing that person from leaving or entering. So, we need to find a way to outline procedures for data interoperability. (Field diary, 5 August 2021)

These moments demonstrate how the technical logics of MIDAS contributed to a feedback loop that expanded crimmigration control in Nigeria. Yet, despite the impact of technical logics in shaping human perceptions and practices, pragmatism is again helpful in tempering claims about technological agency and locating political responsibility for the impacts of the system in the humans that developed and deployed it. While technologies exert their agency most forcefully in the context of 'habitualized tools, artifacts, and skills' (Hickman, 2001: 12), pragmatism and other humanist perspectives on technological structures differentiate between 'decisions taken *within* a structure and decisions taken *about* a structure' (Howarth, 2013: 185, original emphasis).

As Molly Cochran (2002: 527) has argued, '[t]o establish a truth pragmatically is to settle a controversial or complex issue for the time being, until something comes along to dislodge the comfort and reassurance that has thereby been achieved, forcing inquiry to begin again'. Workshops such as the one in which IOM officials raised potential concerns about data privacy—which were then overridden by a logic of technical necessity relating to expanded data collection—constituted moments of rupture and uncertainty, in which humans engaged in normative deliberation and decided how to conceptualize migration as a particular kind of social problem. Although the deployment of digital migration control technologies has become widespread enough to constitute a condition of habitualized technical action, the pragmatist perspective is useful in reminding us that 'policymaking is considerably broader than technical decision-making, which means that policymakers often compromise on critical issues and act on public perceptions or fears' (Beduschi, 2021: 584). In other words, by raising concerns about whether expansive biometric tools were suitable and safe in a migration control context, and then answering such questions in the affirmative, IOM officials actively made decisions about the structure of crimmigration control in Nigeria and engaged in a uniquely human process of moral deliberation: 'Only humans can consider whether the normative system they have constructed is righteous or if it requires corrections'[3] (Pihlström, 2021: 53).

MIDAS, modernization, and teleological progress

In Abuja, I was surrounded by talk of facial recognition, positive hits between interoperable migration databases, and secondary inspection of incoming API data for risk assessment purposes. However, when I asked an official whether the Logitech webcams utilized in MIDAS installations were really accurate enough to reliably carry out automated facial recognition, they seemed slightly surprised by my question:

> MIDAS doesn't currently do any automated facial recognition. The live pic is just manually compared to the photo in the document. MIDAS does automatically match the photo in the document and the picture in the passport chip. But the officer compares the live image to the document. (Field diary, 3 September 2021)

[3] Author's translation from Finnish.

At NIS headquarters, I was shown a state-of-the-art control room where the entirety of Nigeria's digital borders could be monitored at once. One computer could be used to search the MIDAS visa system and another to view positive hits between migration and law enforcement databases, and an entire corner of workstations was dedicated to the interaction between MIDAS and the Interpol I-24/7 alert list. These latter workstations, however, were unmanned in 2021. The connection to Interpol alert lists was dependent on the establishment of interagency cooperation mechanisms—as outlined in the previous chapter—and was not yet online even in late 2024.

Despite the significant remaining technical, operational, and legal obstacles to fully unlocking the remaining potential of MIDAS, training workshops and meetings often proceeded as though future additions to the system's functionality were foregone conclusions. In discussions about drafting data privacy legislation relating to the processing of API data, one IOM official asserted that not all details needed to be ironed out at that stage, as 'they'll need to amend things when PNR is introduced anyway' (Field diary, 5 August 2021). Used primarily for automated risk profiling at the border, PNR data is much more detailed and sensitive than API, and even more explicitly related to law enforcement purposes (Leese, 2014; Vavoula, 2021). As 'PNR data infringes more on individuals' privacy than API data' (Han et al., 2017: 1056), processing it requires more stringent legal frameworks for data privacy and rights protections, according to the ICAO (2010). Although it was unlikely that Nigerian federal authorities would have the capacity to process PNR data any time soon, IOM officials assumed that MIDAS data processing capabilities would expand in the future.

These examples highlight how perceptions about technical neutrality and teleological progress, as expressed by IOM officials in Chapter 5, were translated into practices in the field. Both IOM and NIS officials routinely referred to the deployment of MIDAS as 'a step forward' and 'the beginning of modern border control in Nigeria', as NIS officer Ike explained (Field diary, 26 August 2021). Border control technologies were conceptualized in terms of a linear developmental path from earlier 'pen and paper' practices still commonly deployed in the Global South, towards the kind of 'modern, biometric system' utilized by states in the Global North (Field diary, 26 August 2021). This view was exemplified by one IOM official's metaphor of MIDAS as a rudimentary automobile compared to the more advanced cars of the Global North:

> Of course, we need to explain to NIS that they can't jump straight to a Ferrari. Europe and the US can drive a Ferrari, but here we need to start from a slow car, and build the roads and teach them how to drive first. And then, in the future, they can drive the Ferrari too. (Field diary, 3 September 2021)

The material infrastructure of MIDAS underpinned these teleological views. The technical architecture of the system, developed by the IBM division of the IOM in Geneva, was set up to support the kinds of data collection and interoperability mechanisms that were used at the external borders of Northern states. These included API and PNR data processing, Interpol alert list connectivity, and transnational biometric data sharing between the immigration authorities of different states. Moreover, the IBM team at IOM headquarters continually searched for new ways to expand the technical capacities of the system, for instance by introducing a 'MIDAS health module' in response to the 2014–2016 Ebola outbreak in West Africa and further expanding this module following the onset of the Covid-19 pandemic (Katrina, interview, 17 February 2021). Such capacities were beyond what most MIDAS-operating states required, and indeed these states sometimes resisted further expansion of the system. IOM officials argued that in the African context, 'it's important for systems to all eventually move towards one system. An integrated region needs an integrated system' (Diego, interview, 16 February 2021). However, as outlined in Chapter 6, Nigerian federal authorities viewed MIDAS as a cornerstone of their territorial sovereignty. For this reason, states such as Nigeria were loath to give up what they viewed as their sovereign prerogative to exclusive ownership of MIDAS data: 'the issue of data comes up quite regularly, always in the same terms, but without any progress' (Maria, interview, 10 March 2021).

The seeming contradiction between NIS officers' portrayal of MIDAS as a natural next step in modern border management on the one hand, and the federal government's resistance to international data-sharing agreements on the other hand, again highlighted the underlying politics of the technical mechanisms that contributed to the expansion of crimmigration control in Nigeria. As was the case with the debates regarding privacy legislation and API data above, disagreements between the IOM and the Nigerian federal authorities represented moments of uncertainty and ambiguity about the desirability and suitability of deploying specific technical components of MIDAS in response to the perceived social problem of migration control. The pragmatist conception of technology focuses on these moments of contingency. In doing so, it foregrounds the uniquely human capacity to engage in normative deliberation and distinguishes between conditions of habitualized action, in which technical objects are more influential upon human practices, and conditions of deliberation and innovation, which are 'characterized by organized and deliberate transformations of existing situations in ways that generate new outcomes, or products' (Hickman, 2001: 17).

This perspective is helpful in challenging teleological conceptions of crimmigration control. As Kelly Gates has argued: 'Understanding the experimental status of the technology is critical, because the prevalent myth of inevitability surrounding [biometrics] and other new forms of surveillance itself performs an important role in their institutionalization.' The contingent political pressures and decisions—and their relation to the post-colonial hierarchies that underpinned the IOM's capacity-building practices more broadly—that drove the expansion of MIDAS were implicitly reflected in the continuation of the Ferrari metaphor by the IOM official above. Although, on one hand, the desire of Global South countries to eventually 'upgrade' to using the 'Ferrari' of border control systems was viewed as a foregone conclusion, on the other hand the benefits of using such a system were uncertain: 'These people don't need a Ferrari right now [. . .] It's actually working against their best interest. They don't have roads, gas stations, a garage. They don't know how to drive. We shouldn't really be advocating things like PNR data collection here yet' (Field diary, 3 September 2021). Nonetheless, the IOM and its Global North donor states had to ensure that states such as Nigeria followed this path of technological development: 'After a few years, we will go and get angry if they are not using the Ferrari. MIDAS, and API, is politically relevant to get through our plans for modernizing the border eventually' (Field diary, 3 September 2021).

Conclusion

This chapter examined the technical components of MIDAS in Nigeria and uncovered the mechanisms through which these tools exerted performative effects that expanded practices of crimmigration control in the country. Conceptualizing MIDAS as a socio-technical network, in which both humans and non-human technologies had performative agency, was useful in highlighting that the political impacts of the system were not always reducible directly to the motivations of the IOM or the NIS. The technical components of MIDAS themselves had several political effects: they enacted migration as a matter of data collection and recognition accuracy; they introduced feedback loops that tended toward the expansion of the system beyond a focus on migration control into a law enforcement context; and they performed crimmigration control as the 'Ferrari' of migration management, in other words a modern and desirable 'next step' in modern border control practices for states in the Global South.

Examining the independent effects of technical tools on human practices was crucial to properly grasping the reasons why, and the mechanisms through which, crimmigration control expanded and was depoliticized underneath a veneer of technical neutrality and complexity. Nonetheless, a pragmatist conception of technology—which recognizes that only humans can engage in normative deliberation and choose between political alternatives for competing technological futures—was useful in contesting these mechanisms of depoliticization by focusing on moments of rupture, uncertainty, and debate in which the contingency of Nigerian border control practices was momentarily apparent. It was in these moments that the politics of crimmigration control in the Global South was most visible, and in which competing visions of what 'migration' is were decided. The result of these contingent political decisions was the merger of not only the legal and operational frameworks of criminal justice and border control, but also the establishment and expansion of interoperable digital infrastructures that materially enacted the logics of crimmigration control in Nigeria.

In 2024, at the time of writing this book, the technical architecture of MIDAS had become sufficiently entrenched in the landscape of border control in Nigeria to form part of the 'habitualized tools, artifacts, and skills' (Hickman, 2001: 12) that shaped perceptions about the social problems that digital technologies are meant to solve. This technology had introduced social and technical logics that caused the emergence and expansion of crimmigration control practices in Nigeria. Nonetheless, the future of digital crimmigration control in the country is not predetermined, but will be shaped by moments of contingent normative deliberation and political practices by international organizations and Nigerian federal officials.

Yet, recent developments suggest that the fields of criminal justice and border control will continue to merge in the near future. The IOM has continued to promote more extensive interagency cooperation between the NIS and law enforcement agencies to allow the future collection of PNR data through MIDAS, 'to enhance the capacity of the Federal Government of Nigeria in border security and strengthening their counterterrorism efforts across the country' (IOM, 2023a). The IOM has also signed a series of agreements 'on API/PNR technical assistance' with the UN Office of Counter-Terrorism (UNOCT), explicitly linking the border surveillance capabilities of MIDAS with enhancing recipient states' 'national capacities to detect, prevent, and investigate terrorist offences and related travels' (IOM, 2022c). The implementation of API/PNR data collection and the integration of MIDAS with international alert lists was planned for late 2024. Minister of Interior Olubunmi Tunji-Ojo explained that with such technical capabilities, the NIS would be able to 'pre-profile anybody before the person gets into Nigeria' (Obiowo, 2024). These developments have only increased the importance of critically analysing the social, political, and technical logics that have underpinned the deployment and expansion of MIDAS.

9
Conclusion: Enacting the 'Crimmigrant Other' in the Global South

> *'What? Did I not grant your wish for the golden touch?'*
> *'Yes, but it is a curse to me now', Midas wept.*
>
> —Exchange between Dionysus and King Midas (Craft, 1999)

A critical juncture for digital borders

After I decided to embark on research examining the International Organization for Migration (IOM) and its Migration Information and Data Analysis System (MIDAS), I came across several journalistic and activist accounts of the deployment of this system in countries such as Nigeria and Niger. These accounts were highly critical of MIDAS and the IOM, presenting this technology as a component within a wider network of policing and surveillance systems meant to ease deportations from the European Union and North America to African states (Privacy International, 2019; Zandonini, 2019). Civil society organizations raised concerns regarding interoperability between MIDAS and various law enforcement agencies, paving the way for intrusive and expansive biometric surveillance that begins at the border but extends far beyond border zones through domestic and transnational policing practices (Privacy International, 2024). I was intrigued by how Orwellian this system appeared in such accounts. The idea of a global surveillance network raised the questions of why exactly states in Africa agreed to deploy a system supposedly aimed at facilitating forced deportations from the Global North, and why MIDAS was still largely overlooked in academic research.

Outsourcing Crimmigration Control. Samuel Singler, Oxford University Press. © Samuel Singler 2025.
DOI: 10.1093/9780198927525.003.0009

When delving further into the empirical material, and later interviewing IOM officials and observing their capacity-building practices in Nigeria, it became clear that presenting the system as a globally interoperable surveillance network did not reflect the empirical realities of how MIDAS operated. Far from my initial conception of an exceptionally pervasive and technologically advanced surveillant assemblage, the everyday operation of MIDAS instead appeared exceedingly mundane. IOM officials' accounts of developing and deploying the system were often highly technical and seemingly devoid of politics. Yet, as I have argued throughout this book, the lack of spectacle surrounding MIDAS was precisely why this system exerted such significant social and political effects, and why a critical appraisal of its role in shaping global crimmigration control practices was so important. I have endeavoured to show that representations and conceptualizations of novel digital border control tools as politically neutral, due to their technical nature, were themselves some of the key mechanisms driving the increasing merger of the logics and practices of migration control and criminal justice on a global level.

In this book, I examined the development and deployment of MIDAS in Nigeria as a case study of the broader global phenomenon of the increasing digitalization of border controls. As outlined in Chapter 2, this research addressed remaining research lacunae in the field of border criminology relating to the role of Southern actors in shaping global practices of crimmigration control, the postcolonial dimensions of migration control interventions carried out by international organizations such as the IOM, and the impact of novel digital technologies in contributing to the merging of migration control and criminal justice. To address these research gaps, I developed a theoretical framework synthesizing the literature on performativity and pragmatism in Chapter 3, which I then utilized to analyse primary empirical data in Chapters 5–8. Below, I outline the key findings of this research, and in so doing highlight the contributions of this book to the existing literature and future research on border criminology.

I have carried out this research amid a critical juncture in the digitalization of border controls. As I write this conclusion, the emerging global architecture of digital crimmigration control is still in flux. Novel technologies—including various biometric systems, blockchain, and artificial intelligence—are reshaping the landscape of migration control as well as the governance of refugees and asylum (Cheesman, 2022). The United Nations (UN) has established a 'UN Legal Identity Agenda' aiming to 'provide legal identity for all' by the year 2030 (UNSD, 2022). Actors such as the

IOM have already argued that the expansion of biometric border control technologies will be a crucial component in this endeavour, which has created a 'nexus between migration, displacement, the protection of migrants, and universal access to legal identity' (IOM, 2021b: 7). Although framed in terms of human rights and access to social services, the findings of this book suggest that biometric and other surveillance technologies rolled out in the name of legal identity will also come with significant risks and may result in the subjection of migrants to increasing levels of scrutiny and suspicion.

Although large institutional actors and states have often focused on the capacity of novel digital tools to increase the efficiency and speed of border control and refugee management practices, activists and non-governmental organizations have urged governments around the world to more carefully weigh the risks and benefits of new biometric technologies (The Engine Room and Oxfam, 2018). The expansion of biometric recognition systems in the context of surveillance and policing is also currently the subject of much political contestation in the United States and in Europe (ACLU, 2021; Ragazzi et al., 2021). In a 2022 report, the Office of the UN High Commissioner on Human Rights (OHCHR) called for a moratorium on the use of automated biometric recognition technologies in public spaces (OHCHR, 2022).

How and to what extent these technologies will be used to expand crimmigration control in the future are still open questions. Engaging in debates regarding the risks, benefits, and broader political implications of these technologies requires a critical appraisal of how they have been developed and how they have influenced human practices once deployed on the ground. A key finding of this book is that we need to be attentive to the political significance of decisions that are made by technical experts out of view from the public. As technologies are always designed by someone and for some purpose, these experts also implicitly rely on a socially specific conception of migration as a particular kind of social problem, which is then subjected to their technical 'solutions'. Once these decisions have been made, and new digital tools become normalized, 'it becomes difficult to rediscover the contested assumptions that were freely in play before stability was effected' (Jasanoff, 2004a: 278–279). The technical tools developed to 'solve' or 'manage' migration will in turn determine what kind of social problem global mobility really is. Katja Franko (2020: 83–84) has argued that

> [t]he construction of the crimmigrant other thus has a number of productive effects. These include the daily reinstatement of an unequal global order and its hierarchies of citizenship [. . .] The crimmigrant other is a 'failed citizen' who does not belong to the national 'community of value'.

In this book, I have suggested that the 'crimmigrant other' is not only socially constructed through discourses about criminality, deviance, and difference, but also materially enacted through mundane technologies that quietly merge the fields of migration control and criminal justice. These tools represent border crossers as inherently suspicious until biometrically verified. Reminiscent of the mythical King Midas transforming all he touched into gold, the IOM's MIDAS also transforms the people it touches into a particular type of potentially risky and suspicious political subject, who can be selectively included or excluded through mechanisms of crimmigration control.

I have argued that given the global political dynamics underpinning the current deployment of biometric control technologies—in short, postcolonial political, economic, and epistemic hierarchies—these debates must be inclusive of voices and experiences from the Global South as well. In this book, I have advocated the democratization of border criminology through an examination of the role of Southern actors in shaping crimmigration control practices. I have also promoted the decolonization of this field by mounting an epistemic challenge to Northern-produced discourses regarding the political neutrality of border control technologies. These two considerations underpin the key findings of this research.

Performing biometric statehood

I have sought to demonstrate the analytical value of highlighting the role of Southern actors in shaping contemporary practices of crimmigration control on a global level. Border criminologists have demonstrated in other contexts that 'criminalizing mobility is not simply taught or imposed in a top-down fashion by global agencies concerned with migration dynamics and problems' (Vigneswaran, 2013: 123). So too, the case of MIDAS in Nigeria demonstrated that digital crimmigration control practices could not be fully grasped without accounting for the political motivations of the

Southern actors that translated systems such as MIDAS into specific local contexts.

This research contributes to the literature on the externalization of border control practices (Stock et al., 2019; Ford and Lyons, 2013; Martin, 2017; Badalič, 2019) by demonstrating that Southern state agencies are not only actors to which Northern states outsource border controls (Frelick et al., 2016; Lavenex, 2016), but also themselves externalize the development of border control technologies and training curricula to international organizations such as the IOM. In Nigeria, federal authorities had good political reasons for doing so. Domestically, partnership with the IOM conferred symbolic authority upon the Nigerian Immigration Service (NIS), which reaffirmed the political power of the organization vis-à-vis other federal and local state agencies. As one IOM official put it, 'whoever has MIDAS has the power' (Field diary, 5 August 2021). The technical infrastructure of the system—all border crossing points were connected to the central server at NIS headquarters, and all data had to pass through the server in Abuja—reaffirmed the legitimacy of the NIS within the broader ongoing struggle for territorialization at the national level. In the words of NIS official Benjamin, 'MIDAS has made it clear that it is the Federal Government, not the states, who is in charge here' (Field diary, 26 August 2021).

Internationally, the deployment of MIDAS constituted a performance of 'biometric statehood' by Nigerian federal officials. Federal state agencies demonstrated their governing capacity and political legitimacy through the collection of biometric data at borders, and the use of this data for law enforcement purposes. These performances allowed Nigerian federal authorities to 'be active in the international system' (NIS officer Gabriel, field diary, 26 August 2021) by entering into international partnerships together with actors such as the UK Home Office, the UN Office on Drugs and Crime, and the UN Counter-Terrorism Implementation Task Force. Regionally, the deployment of MIDAS and its role in expanding Nigeria's National Biometric Identity Card and Foreigner Registration systems allowed the NIS to fulfil Nigeria's obligations as a member state of the Economic Community of West African States (ECOWAS). The system demonstrated to other ECOWAS states that Nigerian authorities 'can control their borders too' (IOM official Jayden, interview, 6 April 2021).

The agency of Nigerian federal agencies was crucial in shaping the deployment and expansion of MIDAS in Nigeria, but this does not mean that MIDAS empowered regular Nigerian migrants or resulted in more robust protections of their rights. The findings of this book accord with Nandita

Sharma's (2020) critical insights into how the agency of national elites in postcolonial contexts has not always been deployed to deliver on promises of democratization and economic redistribution. While increasing the political authority of federal agencies, MIDAS has not increased the global mobility of regular Nigerians and other mobile populations of the Global South but instead subjected these populations to increased scrutiny at the border. This scrutiny is imbued with the exclusionary logics of crime control and countering terrorism, as demonstrated by the increasing influence of the UN Office of Counter-Terrorism (UNOCT) in shaping the IOM's capacity-building practices regarding the collection and analysis of PNR data at the border. On one hand, MIDAS has allowed Southern state agencies to enact their biometric statehood and join the international community of sovereign states. On the other hand, this system can end up having the same kinds of unforeseen, adverse consequences as the golden touch of King Midas—who lamented that his magical power 'is a curse to me now' (Craft, 1999)—from the perspective of would-be border crossers in the Global South.

Pedagogical authority, human rights, and technical expertise in the IOM

Analysing Nigerian federal agencies' deployment of MIDAS as a performance of 'biometric statehood' foregrounded the agency of these authorities while situating this agency within the scripts and standards of global crimmigration control. These standards, as outlined in Chapters 7 and 8, were developed primarily in the Global North, and have been transmitted into the Global South by organizations such as the IOM. Conceptualizing crimmigration control as a global phenomenon highlighted the agency of Southern actors, and demonstrated how this agency was shaped and constrained by contemporary postcolonial hierarchies.

These hierarchies were partly socioeconomic, as they related to material inequalities as well as a dependence on natural resource incomes and foreign aid. As Philippe Frowd (2020: 72) has argued, Northern-funded capacity-building interventions have been 'dependent on the prior existence of an unequal distribution of capital between teacher and learner', and indeed the policy goals of Northern donor states significantly shaped the IOM's project proposal process. In addition, the nature of postcolonial hierarchy was epistemic, as the architecture of MIDAS was decisively shaped by operational 'best practices' and international technical standards that were largely produced by Northern states and by Northern-dominated organizations such as the IOM. By providing Southern states with new digital border control systems, the organization not only helped these states achieve pre-existing goals related to migration management, but also introduced new norms regarding how exactly migration should be governed. In other words, built into the technical infrastructure of MIDAS was a particular conception of 'what is a migrant' (IOM official Tom, interview, 24 February 2021). In Nigeria, the system enacted migration as a matter of law enforcement and criminal justice by expanding the technical, operational, and legal overlap between these fields of governance.

The postcolonial hierarchies that underpinned the IOM's capacity-building practices periodically risked being politicized and contested due to the extent to which the organization infringed on the sovereign prerogatives of Nigerian federal authorities. The IOM significantly reshaped Nigerian border control practices, helped draft new security-related privacy legislation, and introduced material dependencies that locked Nigerian authorities into a long-term relationship with the organization. To neutralize potential criticisms regarding these post-imperial dynamics, IOM officials actively engaged in pedagogical performances that enacted an organizational identity focused on 'teaching' Southern states global 'best practices' on human rights and the technical standards of digital border control. These pedagogical performances were highly effective in assuaging concerns regarding the infringement of Nigerian sovereignty. As one NIS official put it: 'The IOM has made big changes to how we do things here [in Nigeria]. But we are not concerned because these changes are necessary for us to implement modern practices. Every step of the way, we are reassured IOM will not undermine us, but teach us how to do things properly' (Field diary, 24 August 2021).

Yet, the IOM's expertise regarding human rights and technical standards was not neutral. The technical tools that composed MIDAS, despite their mundanity, reinforced the expansion of 'the digital version of crimmigration, where immigration and criminal law converge via the processing of data collected' on a global level (Ferraris, 2022: 10). The standardization of automated biometric border control technologies globally has contributed to a standardized view of the inherent suspiciousness of those not yet biometrically verified. This suspicion has been underpinned by the desire to 'protect spaces of privileged sociality against unwanted entrants' within the contemporary context of postcolonial inequality (Jacobsen and

Rao, 2018: 26). Southern actors themselves have actively participated in the expansion of this global phenomenon, yet it is important to avoid unitary notions of 'the Global South' and instead examine which actors specifically have participated in, resisted, and reshaped the global dynamics of crimmigration control, and for what political reasons.

The technopolitics of border control

This book also contributed to the burgeoning literature on novel technologies of border control (Amicelle et al., 2015; Aradau and Tazzioli, 2020; Jeandesboz, 2016; Molnar, 2021; Scheel et al., 2019), by focusing specifically on the role of these technologies in strengthening interconnections between the fields of migration control and criminal justice (Amelung, 2021; Milivojevic, 2019a). By examining MIDAS through a framework that synthesized performativity and pragmatism, I argued that the system had both symbolic and practical political effects. The IOM's officials were aware of the material limitations of MIDAS and recognized that biometric technologies were not always necessarily the best tool for governing migration: 'I think in many states where we have MIDAS projects, I'm not sure if it really lacks biometric data collection at the borders [. . .] I don't think biometrics are the way to go for migration' (Zahra, interview, 19 March 2021). Yet, the effects of MIDAS reached beyond their immediate impact or practical utility on the ground. Their political significance arose from how they recast migration specifically as a problem of data accuracy, expanded biometric data collection, and neutral technical expertise. These performative effects were less about whether biometric border controls were 'actually' more efficient, reliable, and secure, and more about the extent to which perceptions of their neutrality and necessity were widely accepted. The proliferation of these tools was not necessarily dependent on their practical successes; even their failure could be recast as a reason for their further expansion such that 'there is no opt-out, whether or not biometry works' (Gunnarsdóttir and Rommetveit, 2017: 200).

By highlighting the performative effects of technical tools themselves, I sought to highlight that these devices are not neutral. Their symbolic political effects reached beyond their practical effects on the ground, as both the IOM and Nigerian federal authorities performatively used the system to pursue various organizational and political goals. Although many contemporary digital border control tools—such as those deployed at the

US–Mexican and EU external borders—have been met with political controversy, the technical components of MIDAS have resulted in much less political resistance due to their mundane nature. These tools were presented by the IOM as a neutral, technical solution to the social 'problem' of ordering migration by making it legible to states. MIDAS did not reduce migrants to 'bare life' and its deployment could be characterized as spectacular or exceptional. Rather, the system was constitutive of the normal, everyday operation of crimmigration control on a global level. As Valeria Ferraris (2022: 11) has argued: 'There is no state of exception or extra-legality here [. . .] Massive data collection and the subsequent data interoperability are instruments which not only define who is or can be legal, but also who is a potential criminal'. MIDAS reinforced a technological solutionism that shifted 'accountability away from governments and human actors towards digital databases and algorithms' by enacting migration as a governable problem—devoid of politics and postcolonial hierarchy—that can be efficiently managed by neutral technical tools (Metcalfe and Dencik, 2019: 13).

By conceptualizing MIDAS in pragmatist terms as a set of tools developed in view of solving specific kinds of social problems, I sought to sidestep tricky ontological debates regarding agency in sociotechnical 'assemblages' by focusing on the practical impact of this system in expanding crimmigration control in Nigeria. I argued that while the system exerted political impacts independently of the intentions of its designers and operators, nonetheless its initial development was contingent upon the uniquely human process of normative deliberation between several alternative courses of action. Migration is not an objectively knowable, neutral problem that can be dispassionately assessed and governed by technical experts. As Stephan Scheel, Evelyn Ruppert, and Funda Ustek-Spilda (2019: 579) have argued: 'what is known, negotiated and targeted as migration is mediated by a plethora of data practices [. . .] These data practices, while often framed as matters of technocratic expertise, are of course political.' Behind each new digital border control tool are moments of deliberation, debate, and negotiation regarding the utility and desirability of these new technologies, as well as discussions regarding the kinds of social problems they are supposedly meant to solve. Once these tools proliferate and recede into the mundane background of everyday life, however, their contingency becomes increasingly difficult to uncover. MIDAS was also the product of contingent normative deliberation by its human designers and operators, whose problem formulations and social understandings resulted in a system that has contributed to the merger of criminal justice and border control in Nigeria.

The kind of expertise that is currently seen as relevant to the management of migration has been decisively shaped by the epistemic assumptions and social attitudes of influential political actors in the Global North. Contemporary digital border control tools have primarily been funded and developed by Northern states and non-state organizations. These actors have been motivated by a specific conception of migration as a problem of risk management, solutions to which must balance the needs of state security with those of facilitating economic cross-border movement. Contesting this view—and unveiling the postcolonial politics that underpins contemporary global crimmigration control practices—requires decolonizing the field of border criminology by challenging the epistemological and ontological assumptions that have underpinned dominant conceptions of the nature of technology in human societies. One avenue for mounting this challenge is to conceptualize technologies themselves as reshaping practices of crimmigration control in ways that are irreducible to their human designers, yet contingent upon the postcolonial social conditions in which these humans deliberated upon the utility of these new tools.

The upshot of this view is that it undermines the supposed neutrality of technical experts, and reconceptualizes their role in the politics of migration control. These experts cannot be neutral, as their preferred 'solutions' to migration management presuppose socially and historically specific conceptions of what kind of problem migration really is. Their role should not be to act as the ultimate authority who decides what constitutes 'proper' migration management, but rather to engage with all relevant publics to better understand what kinds of political alternatives are available to them. In this view,

> the role of the expert in democratic societies is not to make policy or to tell people what to think, but to alert people to possible ways in which their thinking about matters of importance may be improved [. . .] all affected parties [should] be heard from not only during the planning stages of significant public projects, but during the stages of their implementation as well. (Hickman, 2001: 6, 61)

Hearing from all parties affected by migration requires 'an awareness of the various aspects of global inter-connectedness and inter-dependence' (Franko Aas, 2012b: 10). The 'technical experts' of global crimmigration control technologies should aim to better understand the relationship between these tools and the divisions, hierarchies, and mechanisms of exclusions upon which they are based and which they enact.

Shaping the digital futures of crimmigration control

In addition to the empirical findings presented in this book, I have attempted to develop theoretical and empirical foundations for future research. Thus far, I have conducted empirical research into the deployment of MIDAS only in a single country, Nigeria. As I write this conclusion, the system is operational in 29 states, raising the question of how local political dynamics have impacted the technical, operational, and legal configuration of a supposedly standardized system across differing country contexts. The IOM itself has presented MIDAS as 'completely customizable' (IOM, 2018b: 2), yet in Nigeria at least, the technical architecture of the system was repeatedly determined by international standards and 'best practices'. To further develop the analysis presented in this book, it would be productive to examine how customizable MIDAS really is by comparing its deployment in several country contexts.

The theoretical framework set out in this book also provides a basis for examining other global technologies of border control. MIDAS is not the only technical tool operational in several countries and developed by UN agencies. For instance, the UNOCT and the UN Office on Information and Communications Technology (UNOICT) have developed the goTravel 'software solution', which enhances interoperability between border control and law enforcement databases and allows 'law enforcement to obtain passenger data from (airline) carriers and conduct targeted analysis as well as share the findings of their data assessment' (UNOCT, n.d.). The emergent UN Legal Identity agenda has also brought together a host of UN organizations, governmental agencies, non-governmental organizations, and private companies to identify avenues for the development of new digital identity technologies and the expansion of existing ones (UNSD, 2022). Such initiatives raise questions regarding their relationship to postcolonial hierarchies, and the ways in which legal identity—within specific practical contexts for collecting biometric data, such as border control and criminal justice—is framed as a social problem to which digital technologies are the preferred solution.

Theorizing how processes of technological development and innovation can reshape the content and boundaries of criminal justice provides productive avenues for critical research into how technical experts seek to shape not only contemporary practices of surveillance and security, but also the digital futures of crimmigration control. The rapid digitalization of law enforcement, surveillance, and border control is situated within broader ideological notions of the normative desirability and inevitability of the 'digital revolution' (Balbi, 2023). Because of the future-oriented nature of contemporary ideological visions regarding digitalization, processes of technological innovation demonstrate that 'the future is "already here," with imaginaries and claims about different futures acted on through investments, policies and everyday decisions that make some futures more likely and others less so' (Halford and Southerton, 2023: 273). This book has shown that politically contingent processes of technological development can later become forgotten beneath the mundane, everyday operation of surveillance technologies. Once new tools become banal, 'security slips beyond the boundaries of democratic politics—not through speech-acts, or claim-making, but in their absence' (Goold et al., 2013: 988). For these reasons, it is crucial to ask who gets to develop new technical standards and digital crimmigration control tools, which contingent political and normative ideas these new technologies affirm, and which alternative views, experiences, and understandings they marginalize. Doing so will allow critical criminologists to not only critique and contest new surveillance and security technologies once they have been deployed, but also engage in social struggles to reshape the digital futures of criminal justice and border control.

Technical expertise, criminal justice, and critique

IOM official José told me in an interview that the organization was often critically interrogated by academics and activists who are suspicious of its political motivations:

> One gentleman from an international NGO was once saying that IOM is setting up or trying to have global domination through a database of biometrics in all its member states [. . .] Everybody is thinking that we're aiming for global domination on biometrics. I said, 'Are you serious? We are IOM, and we don't own anything!' There's this idea about us, you

> know, having some strange objectives and dark objectives to achieve global domination through biometrics. So, this is really interesting. (Interview, 2 March 2021)

In this book, I have not argued that the organization's activities and discourses conceal a hidden agenda to establish a global surveillant assemblage, or that its officials self-consciously seek to subject all migrants to increased levels of scrutiny and suspicion. Through my interactions with dozens of IOM officials, I agree with Philippe Frowd's (2018: 1658) assessment that the work of the IOM is partly underpinned—whatever its other political dimensions—by a 'genuine humanitarianism' as well.

Nonetheless, I have demonstrated that the political impacts of MIDAS, including its contribution to the expansion of crimmigration control practices, are not reliant on its human designers being motivated by a hidden agenda or nefarious intentions. The contemporary digital tools that are used to control borders are not neutral. Through their mundane everyday operation, they quietly reaffirm hierarchies of trustworthiness between the privileged few and the suspicious many at the border. The reification of such hierarchies is an emergent effect of a complex combination of political motivations and performative effects of the Southern actors that deploy systems such as MIDAS, organizations such as the IOM that develop these tools, and the technical components of the technologies themselves.

Due to the ubiquity and complexity of the digital tools that shape our everyday lives, it has become increasingly difficult to locate responsibility for these technologies in any particular individual or organization, or to hold these human actors accountable for the political effects of technical devices. To critique the exclusionary effects of digital border control technologies and achieve epistemic justice in the context of migration and criminal justice, the disparate and intersecting agencies of these various actors must be carefully disaggregated and empirically examined. In this way, we can avoid resorting to polemical attacks that ignore the unintended and unforeseen impacts of new digital technologies. Simultaneously, we can develop critical arguments that locate responsibility for the harmful effects of new technologies in their developers and users, while rejecting technosolutionist views that blame the tools themselves and view these harmful effects merely as temporary speed bumps on the road to more inclusive digital utopias. My hope is that this book contributes—however slightly—to more productive dialogue and critical discussion about the risks, benefits, and political implications of digital technologies at the border.

Bibliography

Aas KF (2007) *Globalization & Crime*. London: SAGE Publications.

Aas KF and Gundhus H (2015) Policing humanitarian borderlands: Frontex, human rights and the precariousness of life. *The British Journal of Criminology* 55(1): 1–18.

Abboud S and Muller B (2013) Geopolitics, insecurity and neocolonial exceptionalism: A critical appraisal of the UN Special Tribunal for Lebanon. *Security Dialogue* 44(5–6): 467–484.

Abioye O and Alao D (2020) Inter-agency conflict and its implication on national security in Nigeria. *KIU Journal of Social Sciences* 6(2): 47–53.

Abrahamsen R (2000) *Disciplining Democracy: Development Discourse and Good Governance in Africa*. London: Zed Books.

Abrahamsen R (2004) The power of partnerships in global governance. *Third World Quarterly* 25(8): 1453–1467.

Abrahamsen R (2017) Africa and International Relations: Assembling Africa, studying the world. *African Affairs* 116(462): 125–139.

Abrahamsen R and Williams MC (2009) Security beyond the state: Global security assemblages in international politics. *International Political Sociology* 3(1): 1–17.

Access Now (2024) The EU AI Act: A failure for human rights, a victory for industry and law enforcement. Available at: https://www.accessnow.org/press-release/ai-act-failure-for-human-rights-victory-for-industry-and-law-enforcement/ (accessed 25 July 2024).

Acharya A (2014) Global International Relations (IR) and regional worlds. *International Studies Quarterly* 58(4): 647–659.

Achiume T (2020) Report of the Special Rapporteur on contemporary forms of racism, racial discrimination, xenophobia and related intolerance. *United Nations General Assembly A/75/50289*.

ACLU (2021) ACLU comment on facial recognition and biometric technology moratorium act. Available at: https://www.aclu.org/press-releases/aclu-comment-facial-recognition-and-biometric-technology-moratorium-act (accessed 27 July 2022).

Adamson FB (2016) Spaces of global security: Beyond methodological nationalism. *Journal of Global Security Studies* 1(1): 19–35.

Aden H (2018) Information sharing, secrecy and trust among law enforcement and secret service institutions in the European Union. *West European Politics* 41(4): 981–1002.

Agamben G (1998) *Homo Sacer: Sovereign Power and Bare Life*. Stanford, CA: Stanford University Press.

Agbiboa D (2013) Protectors or predators? The embedded problem of police corruption and deviance in Nigeria. *Administration & Society* 47(3): 244–281.

Agnew J (1994) The territorial trap: The geographical assumptions of International Relations theory. *Review of International Political Economy* 1(1): 53–80.

Agnew J (2015) Revisiting the territorial trap. *Nordia Geographical Publications* 44(4): 43–48.

Agnew J (2017) *Globalization and Sovereignty: Beyond the Territorial Trap*. 2nd ed. Lanham, MD: Rowman & Littlefield.

Agozino B (2004) Imperialism, crime and criminology: Towards the decolonisation of criminology. *Crime, Law and Social Change* 41(4): 343–358.

Agozino B (2019) Humanifesto of the decolonization of criminology and justice. *Decolonization of Criminology and Justice* 1(1): 5–28.

Aguilera R (2020) *The Glass Half-Empty: Debunking the Myth of Progress in the Twenty-First Century*. London: Repeater Books.

Ahmed K and Tondo L (2021) Fortress Europe: The millions spent on military-grade tech to deter refugees. *The Guardian*, 12 June. Available at: https://www.theguardian.com/global-development/2021/dec/06/fortress-europe-the-millions-spent-on-military-grade-tech-to-deter-refugees (accessed 29 September 2024).

Ahmed S (2017) *Living a Feminist Life*. Durham, NC: Duke University Press.

Ahram A (2017) Territory, sovereignty, and new statehood in the Middle East and North Africa. *Middle East Journal* 71(3): 345–362.

Aitken D (2019) *Responses to Deaths in Custody: The Politics of Prisons and Immigration Removal Centres*. Doctoral dissertation. University of Oxford, Oxford.

Ajana B (2013) Asylum, identity management and biometric control. *Journal of Refugee Studies* 26(4): 576–595.

Akintaro S (2023) FG says Nigerian Immigration Service is now better equipped with technology. Available at: https://nairametrics.com/2023/03/10/fg-says-nigerian-immigration-service-now-better-equipped-with-technology/ (accessed 20 July 2023).

Akinyemi B (1982) The emergence of Nigeria as a regional power in International Relations. *Studia Diplomatica* 35(3): 227–243.

Albisinni FG (2016) ICAO's standards and recommended practices. *Italian Journal of Public Law* 8(1): 203–231.

Aliverti A, Milivojevic S, and Weber L (2019) Tracing imprints of the border in the territorial, justice and welfare domains: A multi-site ethnography. *The Howard Journal of Crime and Justice* 58(2): 240–259.

Aliverti A, Carvalho H, Chamberlen A, et al. (2021) Decolonizing the criminal question. *Punishment & Society* 23(3): 297–316.

Altheide D and Schneider C (2013) *Qualitative Media Analysis*. 2nd ed. London: SAGE Publications.

Amao O (2019) The foreign policy and intervention behaviour of Nigeria and South Africa in Africa: A structural realist analysis. *South African Journal of International Affairs* 26(1): 93–112.

Amelung N (2021) 'Crimmigration control' across borders. *Historical Social Research* 46(3): 151–177.

Amelung N, Granja R, and Machado H (2021) *Modes of Bio-Bordering: The Hidden (Dis)Integration of Europe*. Singapore: Palgrave Macmillan.

Amicelle A, Aradau C, and Jeandesboz J (2015) Questioning security devices: Performativity, resistance, politics. *Security Dialogue* 46(4): 293–306.

Amoore L (2014) Security and the incalculable. *Security Dialogue* 45(5): 423–439.

Amoore L and Goede MD (2005) Governance, risk and dataveillance in the war on terror. *Crime, Law and Social Change* 43(2–3): 149–173.

Anctil Avoine P and Tillman R (2015) Demobilized women in Colombia: Embodiment, performativity and social reconciliation. In: Shekhawat S (ed.) *Female Combatants in Conflict and Peace*. Basingstoke: Palgrave Macmillan, pp. 216–231.

Anderson B (2017) Towards a new politics of migration? *Ethnic and Racial Studies* 40(9): 1527–1537.

Andersson R (2014) *Illegality, Inc.: Clandestine Migration and the Business of Bordering Europe*. Oakland, CA: University of California Press.

Andreessen M (2023) The techno-optimist manifesto. Available at: https://a16z.com/the-techno-optimist-manifesto/ (accessed 26 May 2024).

Andrijasevic R and Walters W (2010) The International Organization for Migration and the international government of borders. *Environment and Planning D: Society and Space* 28(6): 977–999.

Anghie A (1999) Finding the peripheries: Sovereignty and colonialism in ninetheenth-century international law. *Harvard International Law Journal* 40(1): 1–80.

Anghie A (2004) *Imperialism, Sovereignty and the Making of International Law*. Cambridge: Cambridge University Press.

Appiah KA (1992) *In My Father's House: Africa in the Philosophy of Culture*. Oxford: Oxford University Press.

Aradau C and Munster R van (2009) Exceptionalism and the 'war on terror': Criminology meets International Relations. *The British Journal of Criminology* 49: 686–701.

Aradau C and Tazzioli M (2020) Biopolitics multiple: Migration, extraction, subtraction. *Millennium: Journal of International Studies* 48(2): 198–220.

Armenta A (2017) Racializing crimmigration: Structural racism, colorblindness, and the institutional production of immigrant criminality. *Sociology of Race and Ethnicity* 3: 82–95.

Ashutosh I and Mountz A (2011) Migration management for the benefit of whom? Interrogating the work of the International Organization for Migration. *Citizenship Studies* 15(1): 21–38.

Atak I and Crépeau F (2014) National security, terrorism and the securitization of migration. In: Chetail V and Bauloz C (eds) *Research Handbook on International Law and Migration*. Cheltenham: Edward Elgar, pp. 93–112.

Austin JL (1955) *How to Do Things with Words*. Cambridge, MA: Harvard University Press.

Autesserre S (2010) *The Trouble with the Congo: Local Violence and the Failure of International Peacebuilding*. Cambridge: Cambridge University Press.

Awolowo O (1947) *Path to Nigerian Freedom*. London: Faber and Faber.

Babatola J (2012) Nigeria–Cameroon boundary dispute: The quest for Bakassi Peninsular. *International Affairs and Global Strategy* 4: 81–95.

Bacon M (2012) *Pragmatism: An Introduction*. Cambridge: Polity Press.

Badalič V (2019) Tunisia's role in the EU external migration policy: Crimmigration law, illegal practices, and their impact on human rights. *Journal of International Migration and Integration* 20(1): 85–100.

Badmington N (2003) Theorizing posthumanism. *Social Critique* 53: 10–27.

Baird T (2019) *Human Smuggling in the Eastern Mediterranean*. Abingdon: Routledge.

Balbi G (2023) *The Digital Revolution: A Short History of an Ideology*. Oxford: Oxford University Press.

Banerjee A (2012) Dynamic borders, dynamic identities: A pragmatist ontology of 'groups' for critical multicultural transnational feminisms. In: Hamington M and Bardwell-Jones C (eds) *Contemporary Feminist Pragmatism*. Abingdon: Routledge, pp. 71–89.

Barber PG and Bryan C (2018) International Organization for Migration in the field: 'Walking the talk' of global migration management in Manila. *Journal of Ethnic and Migration Studies* 44(10): 1725–1742.

Barker V (2017) Penal power at the border: Realigning state and nation. *Theoretical Criminology* 21(4): 441–457.

Barker V (2018) *Nordic Nationalism and Penal Order: Walling the Welfare State*. Abingdon: Routledge.

Barnett M and Coleman L (2005) Designing police: Interpol and the study of change in international organizations. *International Studies Quarterly* 49(4): 593–619.

Barnsley I and Bleiker R (2008) Self-determination: From decolonization to deterritorialization. *Global Change, Peace & Security* 20(2): 121–136.

Bartels I (2018) Practices and power of knowledge dissemination: International organizations in the externalization of migration management in Morocco and Tunisia. *Movements* 4(1): 47–66.

Basaran T and Guild E (2017) Mobilities, ruptures, transitions. In: Basaran T, Bigo D, Guittet E-P, et al. (eds) *International Political Sociology: Transveral Lines*. Abingdon: Routledge, pp. 272–285.

Basaran T, Bigo D, Guittet E-P, et al. (2017) Transversal Lines: An Introduction. In: Basaran T, Bigo D, Guittet E-P, et al. (eds) *International Political Sociology: Transversal Lines*. Abingdon: Routledge, pp. 1–9.

Bayart J-F (1993) *The State in Africa: The Politics of the Belly*. London: Longman Publishing.

Bayart J-F and Ellis S (2000) Africa in the world: A history of extraversion. *African Affairs* 99(395): 217–267.

Beaulac S (2000) The Westphalian legal orthodoxy—myth or reality? *Journal of the History of International Law* 2: 148–177.

Beck U (2007) The cosmopolitan condition: Why methodological nationalism fails. *Theory, Culture & Society* 24(7–8): 286–290.

Beckett K and Evans H (2015) Crimmigration at the local level: Criminal justice processes in the shadow of deportation. *Law & Society Review* 49(1): 241–277.

Beduschi A (2021) International migration management in the age of artificial intelligence. *Migration Studies* 9(3): 576–596.

Beighton C (2019) Reasoning with qualitative data: Using retroduction with transcript data. Available at: https://doi.org/10.4135/9781526477378 (accessed 26 May 2024).

Beirne P (1983) Cultural relativism and comparative criminology. *Contemporary Crises* 7: 371–391.

Bello PO (2018) Criminal justice response to human trafficking in Nigeria and South Africa: suggestions for better performance. *Contemporary Justice Review* 21(2): 140–158.

Benjamin R (2019) Introduction: Discriminatory design, liberating imagination. In: Benjamin R (ed.) *Captivating Technology: Race, Carceral Technoscience, and Liberatory Imagination in Everyday Life*. Durham, NC: Duke University Press, pp. 1–22.

Benjamin W (2002) The task of the translator. In: Marcus Bullock MWJ (ed.) *Walter Benjamin: Selected Writings, Volume 1, 1913–1926*. Cambridge, MA: The Belknap Press of Harvard University Press, pp. 253–263.

Bennett J (2010) *Vibrant Matter: A Political Ecology of Things*. Durham, NC: Duke University Press.

Berg J (2021) Criminology: Some lines of flight. *Journal of Criminology* 54(1): 21–33.

Bhatia M and Canning V (2020) Misery as business: How immigration detention became a cash cow in Britain's borders. In: Albertson K, Corcoran M, and Phillips J (eds) *Marketisation and Privatisation in Criminal Justice*. Bristol: Bristol University Press, pp. 257–271.

Bhui HS (2013) Introduction: Humanizing migration control and detention. In: Franko Aas K and Bosworth M (eds) *The Borders of Punishment: Migration, Citizenship, and Social Exclusion*. Oxford: Oxford University Press, pp. 1–17.

Bigo D (2016) Rethinking security at the crossroad of international relations and criminology. *British Journal of Criminology* 56(6): 1068–1086.

Bigo D (2020) The socio-genesis of a guild of 'digital technologies' justifying transnational interoperable databases in the name of security and border purposes: A reframing of the field of security professionals? *International Journal of Migration and Border Studies* 6(1–2): 74–92.

Bilgen A, Nasir A, and Schöneberg J (2021) Why positionalities matter: Reflections on power, hierarchy, and knowledges in 'development' research. *Canadian Journal of Development Studies* 42(4): 519–536.

Bisong A (2019) Trans-regional institutional cooperation as multilevel governance: ECOWAS migration policy and the EU. *Journal of Ethnic and Migration Studies* 45(8): 1294–1309.

Bøås M (2021) EU migration management in the Sahel: Unintended consequences on the ground in Niger? *Third World Quarterly* 42(1): 52–67.

Bohman J (2002) How to make social science practical: Pragmatism, critical social science and multiperspectival theory. *Millennium: Journal of International Studies* 31(3): 499–524.

Boswell C (2009) *The Political Uses of Expert Knowledge: Immigration Policy and Social Research*. Cambridge: Cambridge University Press.

Bosworth M (2008) Border control and the limits of the sovereign state. *Social & Legal Studies* 17(2): 199–215.

Bosworth M (2011) Deportation, detention and foreign national prisoners in England and Wales. *Citizenship Studies* 15 (5): 583–595.

Bosworth M (2017a) Border criminology and the changing nature of penal power. In: Liebling A, Maruna S, and McAra L (eds) *The Oxford Handbook of Criminology*. 6th ed. Oxford: Oxford University Press, pp. 373–390.

Bosworth M (2017b) Penal humanitarianism? Sovereign power in an era of mass migration. *New Criminal Law Review* 20(1): 39–65.

Bosworth M and Flavin J (2007) Race, control, and punishment: From colonialism to the global war on crime. In: Bosworth M and Flavin J (eds) *Race, Gender, & Punishment: From Colonialism to the War on Terror*. New Brunswick, NJ: Rutgers University Press, pp. 1–10.

Bosworth M and Hoyle C (2011) What is criminology? An introduction. In: *What Is Criminology?* Oxford: Oxford University Press, pp. 1–12.

Bosworth M and Singler S (2022) A mundane spectacle? (In)visibility, normalisation and state power in the UK's migrant escorting contract. In: Bosworth M and Zedner L (eds) *Privatising Border Control: Law at the Limits of the Sovereign State*. Oxford: Oxford University Press, pp. 179–189.

Bosworth M, Franko K, and Pickering S (2018a) Criminal justice research in an era of mass mobility: A brief introduction. In: Fili A, Jahnsen S, and Powell R (eds) *Criminal Justice Research in an Era of Mass Mobility*. London: Routledge, pp. 1–11.

Bosworth M, Franko K, and Pickering S (2018b) Punishment, globalization and migration control: 'Get them the hell out of here'. *Punishment & Society* 20(1): 34–53.

Bourbeau P (2011) *The Securitization of Migration: A Study of Movement and Order*. London: Routledge.

Bowling B (2013) Epilogue: The borders of punishment: Towards a criminology of mobility. In: Aas KF and Bosworth M (eds) *The Borders of Punishment: Migration, Citizenship, and Social Exclusion*. Oxford: Oxford University Press, pp. 291–306.

Bowling B and Westenra S (2018) 'A really hostile environment': Adiaphorization, global policing and the crimmigration control system. *Theoretical Criminology* 24(2): 163–183.

Bradley M (2024) 'We're an organization that does stuff': The International Organization for Migration, logistics and expert authority in migration governance. *Geopolitics*. DOI: 10.1080/14650045.2024.2318589.

Braidotti R (2006) Posthuman, all too human. *Theory, Culture & Society* 23(7–8): 197–208.

Braidotti R (2010) Nomadism: Against methodological nationalism. *Policy Futures in Education* 8(3–4): 408–418.

Braidotti R (2013) *The Posthuman*. Cambridge: Polity Press.

Branch J (2010) 'Colonial reflection' and territoriality: The peripheral origins of sovereign statehood. *European Journal of International Relations* 18(2): 277–297.

Branch J (2014) *The Cartographic State: Maps, Territory, and the Origins of Sovereignty*. Cambridge: Cambridge University Press.

Brandariz JA (2022) Criminalization or instrumentalism? New trends in the field of border criminology. *Theoretical Criminology* 26(2): 285–303.

Brenner N and Elden S (2009) Henri Lefebvre on state, space, territory. *International Political Sociology* 3(4): 353–377.

Brinkmann S (2017) Humanism after posthumanism: Or qualitative psychology after the 'posts'. *Qualitative Research in Psychology* 14(2): 109–130.

Brown M (2018) Southern criminology in the post-colony: More than a 'derivative discourse'? In: Carrington K, Hogg R, Scott J, et al. (eds) *The Palgrave Handbook of Criminology and the Global South*. Cham: Palgrave Macmillan, pp. 83–104.

Brown S (2006) The criminology of hybrids: Rethinking crime and law in technosocial networks. *Theoretical Criminology* 10(2): 223–244.

Brown W (2013) Sovereignty matters: Africa, donors, and the aid relationship. *African Affairs* 112(447): 262–282.

Brown W (2017a) Climate change, democracy and crises of humanism. In: Baldwin A and Bettini G (eds) *Life Adrift: Climate Change, Migration, Critique*. London: Rowman & Littlefield International, pp. 25–40.

Brown W (2017b) *Walled States, Waning Sovereignty*. 2nd ed. Brooklyn, NY: Zone Books.

Browne S (2009) Digital epidermalization: Race, identity and biometrics. *Critical Sociology* 26(1): 131–150.

Bull H (1977) *The Anarchical Society: A Study of Order in World Politics*. Basingstoke: The Macmillan Press.

Buolamwini J and Gebru T (2018) Gender shades: Intersectional accuracy disparities in commercial gender classification. *Proceedings of Machine Learning Research* 81: 1–15.

Bush B (2013) Colonial research and the social sciences at the end of empire: The West Indian social survey, 1944–57. *The Journal of Imperial and Commonwealth History* 41(3): 451–474.

Butler J (2007) *Gender Trouble*. 2nd ed. Abingdon: Routledge.

Butler J (2010) Performative agency. *Journal of Cultural Economy* 3(2): 147–161.

Cable V (1995) The diminished nation-state: A study in the loss of economic power. *Daedalus* 124(2). The MIT Press: 23–53.

Campbell D (2005) Beyond choice: The onto-politics of critique. *International Relations* 19(1): 127–134.

Campbell J and Page M (2018) *Nigeria: What Everyone Needs to Know*. Oxford: Oxford University Press.

Campos-Delgado A (2021) Abnormal bordering: Control, punishment and deterrence in Mexico's migrant detention centres. *The British Journal of Criminology* 61(2): 476–496.

Canning V (2020) Corrosive control: State-corporate and gendered harm in bordered Britain. *Critical Criminology* 28: 259–275.

Carrier N (2011) Critical criminology meets radical constructivism. *Critical Criminology* 19(4): 331–350.

Carrington K, Hogg R, Scott J, et al. (2018) Criminology, Southern theory and cognitive justice. In: Carrington K, Hogg R, Scott J, et al. (eds) *The Palgrave Handbook of Criminology and the Global South*. Cham: Palgrave Macmillan, pp. 3–17.

Castles S and Ozkul D (2014) Circular migration: Triple win, or a new label for temporary migration? In: Battistella G (ed.) *Global and Asian Perspectives on Migration*. Cham: Springer, pp. 27–49.

Césaire A (2000) Discourse on colonialism. In: *Discourse on Colonialism*. NYU Press, pp. 29–78.

Chacón J (2009) Managing migration through crime. *Columbia Law Review Sidebar* 109: 135–148.

Chakrabarty D (2008) *Provincializing Europe: Postcolonial Thought and Historical Difference*. New ed. Princeton, NJ: Princeton University Press.

Chambers P and Mann M (2019) Crimmigration in border security? Sorting crossing through biometric identification at Australia's international airports. In: Billings P (ed.) *Crimmigration in Australia: Law, Politics, and Society*. Singapore: Springer, pp. 381–404.

Chan J (2000) Globalisation, reflexivity and the practice of criminology. *Journal of Criminology* 33(2): 118–135.

Chance the Rapper (2016) Blessings (Reprise). *Coloring Book*. Chicago: Chicago Recording Company.

Chandler D (2007) The security–development nexus and the rise of 'anti-foreign policy'. *Journal of International Relations and Development* 10(4): 362–386.

Chang H (2022) *Realism for Realistic People*. Cambridge: Cambridge University Press.

Charbonneau L (2009) NGO expelled from Darfur considered ICC cooperation. *Reuters*, 16 March. Available at: https://www.reuters.com/article/us-sudan-warcrimes-ngo-idUSTRE52F6SX20090316 (accessed 28 May 2022).

Cheesman M (2022) Self-sovereignty for refugees? The contested horizons of digital identity. *Geopolitics* 27(1): 134–159.

Chelioudakis E (2022) Privatization of security, border management, and defense in the EU: Does reliance on tech companies erode states' sovereignty? In: Hudson G and Atak I (eds) *Migration, Security, and Resistance*. London: Routledge, pp. 83–103.

Chernilo D (2006) Social theory's methodological nationalism: Myth and reality. *European Journal of Social Theory* 9(1): 5–22.

Christie N (1997) Four blocks against insight: Notes on the oversocialization of criminologists. *Theoretical Criminology* 1(1): 13–23.

Cielemęcka O and Daigle C (2019) Posthuman sustainability: An ethos for our Anthropocenic future. *Theory, Culture & Society* 36(7–8): 67–87.

Clapham C (1996) *Africa and the International System: The Politics of State Survival*. Cambridge: Cambridge University Press.

Cochran M (2002) Deweyan pragmatism and post-positivist social science in IR. *Millennium: Journal of International Studies* 31(3): 525–548.

Cohen S (2011) *Folk Devils and Moral Panics: The Creation of the Mods and Rockers*. 3rd ed. Abingdon: Routledge.

Cold-Ravnkilde SM (2021) Borderwork in the grey zone: Everyday resistance within European border control initiatives in Mali. *Geopolitics* 27(5): 1450–1469.

Cole SA (2001) *Suspect Identities: A History of Fingerprinting and Criminal Identification*. Cambridge, MA: Harvard University Press.

Cole WM (2017) World polity or world society? Delineating the statist and societal dimensions of the global institutional system. *International Sociology* 32(1): 86–104.

Comaroff J and Comaroff JL (eds) (2006) *Law and Disorder in the Postcolony*. Chicago, IL: The University of Chicago Press.

Corcoran MS (2020) Spectacular suffering: Transgressive performance in penal activism. *Theoretical Criminology* 24(4): 651–668.

Côté-Boucher K (2020) *Border Frictions: Gender, Generation and Technology on the Frontline*. Abingdon: Routledge.

Craft C (1999) *King Midas and the Golden Touch*. New York, NY: William Morrow.

Cunneen C (2011) Postcolonial perspectives for criminology. In: Bosworth M and Hoyle C (eds) *What Is Criminology?* Oxford: Oxford University Press, pp. 249–266.

Dal Santo L and Sepúlveda Penna C (eds) (2024) *Southernising Criminology: Challenges, Horizons and Praxis*. London: Routledge.

Dauchy A (2023) Dreaming biometrics in Niger: The security techniques of migration control in West Africa. *Security Dialogue* 54(3): 213–230.

Dauvergne C (2008) *Making People Illegal: What Globalization Means for Migration and Law*. Cambridge: Cambridge University Press.

Davidson D (2001) *Subjective, Intersubjective, Objective*. Oxford: Oxford University Press.

Davies PHJ (2001) Spies as informants: Triangulation and the interpretation of elite interview data in the study of the intelligence and security services. *Politics* 21(1): 73–80.

De Genova N (2013) Spectacles of migrant 'illegality': the scene of exclusion, the obscene of inclusion. *Ethnic and Racial Studies* 36(7): 1180–1198.

de Magalhães Gomes C (2021) Notes on gender, race and punishment from a decolonial perspective to a Southern criminology agenda. *International Journal for Crime, Justice and Social Democracy* 10(4): 90–101.

de Noronha L (2019) Deportation, racism and multi-status Britain: Immigration control and the production of race in the present. *Ethnic and Racial Studies* 42(14): 2413–2430.

de Sousa Santos B (2016) *Epistemologies of the South: Justice Against Epistemicide*. Abingdon: Routledge.

Death C (2014) Legitimacy and governmentality in Tanzania: Environmental mainstreaming in the developing world. In: Gabay C and Death C (eds) *Critical Perspectives on African Politics: Liberal Interventions, State-Building and Civil Society*. Abingdon: Routledge, pp. 67–88.

Degenhardt T and Bourne M (2020) When risks meet: The dance of experience, professional expertise and science in border security technology development. *Criminology & Criminal Justice* 20(2): 207–225.

Dekkers T (2020) Technology driven crimmigration? Function creep and mission creep in Dutch migration control. *Journal of Ethnic and Migration Studies* 46(9): 1849–1864.

Dekkers T, van der Woude M, and Koulish R (2018) Objectivity and accountability in migration control using risk assessment tools. *European Journal of Criminology* 16(2): 237–254.

Delamont S (2004) Ethnography and participant observation. In: Seale C, Gobo G, Gubrium J, et al. (eds) *Qualitative Research Practice*. London: SAGE Publications, pp. 205–217.

Deleuze G and Guattari F (1987) *A Thousand Plateaus: Capitalism and Schizophrenia*. Minneapolis, MN: University of Minnesota Press.

Devetak R and True J (2006) Diplomatic divergence in the Antipodes: Globalisation, foreign policy and state identity in Australia and New Zealand. *Australian Journal of Political Science* 41(2): 241–256.

Dewey J (1929) *Experience and Nature*. London: George Allen & Unwin.

Dewey J (1938) *Logic: The Theory of Inquiry*. New York, NY: Henry Holt and Co.

Dewsbury J-D (2011) The Deleuze-Guattarian assemblage: Plastic habits. *Area* 43(2): 148–153.

Dijstelbloem H (2021) *Borders as Infrastructure: The Technopolitics of Border Control*. Cambridge, MA: The MIT Press.

Dini S (2018) Migration management, capacity building and the sovereignty of an African State: International Organization for Migration in Djibouti. *Journal of Ethnic and Migration Studies* 44(10): 1691–1705.

Dittmer J (2014) Geopolitical assemblages and complexity. *Progress in Human Geography* 38(3): 385–401.

Duffield M (2001) *Global Governance and the New Wars: The Merging of Development and Security*. London: Zed Books.

Düvell F (2015) The globalisation of migration control. Available at: https://www.opendemocracy.net/en/globalisation-of-migration-control/ (accessed 20 June 2022).

Ebegbulem J (2013) An evaluation of Nigeria–South Africa bilateral relations. *Journal of International Relations and Foreign Policy* 1(1): 32–40.

Eberlein R (2006) On the road to the state's perdition? Authority and sovereignty in the Niger Delta, Nigeria. *The Journal of Modern African Studies* 44(4): 573–596.

Ebinumo S and Ikunga SA (2019) The dynamics of foreign aid and the dependency theory: The Nigeria's experience. *KIU Journal of Humanities* 4(2): 87–94.

ECDPM (2017) Regional organisations in Africa. Available at: https://indd.adobe.com/view/f49ac87d-7aa3-4cf7-822e-841d674bbc92 (accessed 28 July 2022).

Edwards A and Hughes G (2008) Inventing community safety. In: Carlen P (ed.) *Imaginary Penalities*. Cullompton: Willan Publishing, pp. 64–83.

El Khiyari H and Wechsler H (2016) Face verification subject to varying (age, ethnicity, and gender) demographics using deep learning. *Journal of Biometrics & Biostatistics* 7(4): 1000323.

Elden S (2010) Thinking territory historically. *Geopolitics* 15(4): 757–761.

Emel J, Huber M, and Makene M (2011) Extracting sovereignty: Capital, territory, and gold mining in Tanzania. *Political Geography* 30(2): 70–79.

Engel U and Olsen GR (2012) Authority, sovereignty and Africa's changing regimes of territorialization. In: Cornelissen S, Cheru F, and Shaw T (eds) *Africa and International Relations in the 21st Century*. Basingstoke: Palgrave Macmillan, pp. 51–65.

Enloe C (2016) Being reflexively feminist shouldn't be easy. In: Wibben A (ed.) *Researching War: Feminist Methods, Ethics and Politics*. London: Routledge, pp. 258–259.

Epstein C (2008) Embodying risk: Using biometrics to protect the borders. In: Amoore L and De Goede M (eds) *Risk and the War on Terror*. Abingdon: Routledge, pp. 178–193.

Ericson R (2007) *Crime in an Insecure World*. Cambridge: Polity Press.

Essen C (2022) Abandoned Abuja National Library project completion cost climbs to N100b, from N8.59b. *The Guardian*, 2 May. Available at: https://guardian.ng/property/abandoned-abuja-national-library-project-completion-cost-climbs-to-n100b-from-n8-59b/ (accessed 28 May 2022).

EU Agency for Fundamental Rights (2018) Interoperability and fundamental rights implications: Opinion of the European Union Agency for Fundamental Rights. Available at: https://fra.europa.eu/sites/default/files/fra_uploads/fra-2018-opinion-01-2018-interoperability_en.pdf (accessed 31 July 2024).

Eubanks V (2018) *Automating Inequality: How High-Tech Tools Profile, Police, and Punish the Poor*. New York, NY: St Martin's Press.

European Commission (2022) Smart Borders. Available at: https://ec.europa.eu/home-affairs/policies/schengen-borders-and-visa/smart-borders_en (accessed 1 May 2021).

European Union Agency for Fundamental Rights (2018) *Under Watchful Eyes: Biometrics, EU IT Systems and Fundamental Rights*. Luxembourg: Publications Office of the European Union.

Evans P (1997) The eclipse of the state? Reflections on stateness in an era of globalization. *World Politics* 50(1): 62–87.

Eze RC (2016) Nigeria as a geo-political entity and sovereign actor in International Relations: Interrogating its emergence. *Academic Journal of Interdisciplinary Studies* 5(1): 59–64.

Fabini G (2019) Internal bordering in the context of undeportability: Border performances in italy. *Theoretical Criminology* 23(2): 175–193.

Fagbadebo O (2007) Corruption, governance and political instability in Nigeria. *African Journal of Political Science and International Relations* 1(2): 28–37.

Falola T and Heaton M (2014) *A History of Nigeria*. Cambridge: Cambridge University Press.

Fan M (2013) The case for crimmigration reform. *North Carolina Law Review* 92(1): 75–148.

Fanon F (2001) *The Wretched of the Earth*. London: Penguin.

Fearon J (2017) Civil war and the current international system. *Daedalus* 146(2): 18–32.

Fearon J and Laitin D (2003) Ethnicity, insurgency, and civil war. *American Political Science Review* 91(1): 75–90.

Ferguson J (1994) *The Anti-Politics Machine: 'Development', Depoliticization, and Bureaucratic Power in Lesotho*. Minneapolis, MN: University of Minnesota Press.

Ferguson J (2006) *Global Shadows: Africa in the Neoliberal World Order*. Durham, NC: Duke University Press.

Ferraris V (2022) Entangled in the technology-driven borderscape: Border crossers rendered to their digital self. *European Journal of Criminology*. DOI: 10.1177/14773708221086717.

Fine S (2018) Liaisons, labelling and laws: International Organization for Migration bordercratic interventions in Turkey. *Journal of Ethnic and Migration Studies* 44(10): 1743–1755.

Fitzpatrick J (2002) Sovereignty, territoriality, and the rule of law. *Hastings International and Comparative Law Review* 25(3): 303–340.

Flanagan S, Frost E, and Kugler R (2001) *Challenges of the Global Century: Report of the Project on Globalization and National Security*. Washington, DC: Institute for National Strategic Studies.

Flynn M and Cannon C (2009) The privatization of immigration detention: Towards a global view. *Global Detention Project Working Paper*.

Ford M and Lyons L (2013) Outsourcing border security: NGO involvement in the monitoring, processing and assistance of Indonesian nationals returning illegally by sea. *Contemporary Southeast Asia* 35(2). ISEAS—Yosuf Ishak Institute: 215–234.

Forster M (2022) Refugee protection in the artificial intelligence era: A test case for rights. *Chatham House International Law Programme Research Paper*. Available at: https://www.chathamhouse.org/sites/default/files/2022-09/2022-09-07-refugee-protection-artificial-intelligence-era-forster.pdf (accessed 29 September 2024).

Fossey E, Harvey C, McDermott F, et al. (2002) Understanding and evaluating qualitative research. *Australian and New Zealand Journal of Psychiatry* 36(6): 717–732.

Foucault M (1991) On the genealogy of ethics: An overview of work in progress. In: Rabinow P (ed.) *The Foucault Reader: An Introduction to Foucault's Thought*. London: Penguin, pp. 340–372.

Foucault M (1995) *Discipline and Punish: The Birth of the Prison*. 2nd ed. New York, NY: Vintage Books.

Franck A and Vigneswaran D (2021) Hacking migration control: Repurposing and reprogramming deportability. *Security Dialogue*. DOI: 10.1177/0967010621996938.

Franko Aas K (2006) 'The body does not lie': Identity, risk and trust in technoculture. *Crime, Media, Culture: An International Journal* 2(2): 143–158.

Franko Aas K (2007) Analysing a world in motion. *Theoretical Criminology* 11(2): 283–303.

Franko Aas K (2011a) 'Crimmigrant' bodies and bona fide travelers: Surveillance, citizenship and global governance. *Theoretical Criminology* 15(3): 331–346.

Franko Aas K (2011b) Visions of global control: Cosmopolitan aspirations in a world of friction. In: Bosworth M and Hoyle C (eds) *What Is Criminology?* Oxford: Oxford University Press, pp. 406–419.

Franko Aas K (2012a) (In)security-at-a-distance: Rescaling justice, risk and warfare in a transnational age. *Global Crime* 13(4): 235–253.

Franko Aas K (2012b) 'The Earth is one but the world is not': Criminological theory and its geopolitical divisions. *Theoretical Criminology* 16(1): 5–20.

Franko Aas K and Bosworth M (2013) *The Borders of Punishment: Migration, Citizenship, and Social Exclusion*. Oxford: Oxford University Press.

Franko Aas K, Gundhus HO and Lomell HM (2009a) Introduction: Technologies of (in)security. In: Franko Aas K, Gundhus H, and Lomell H (eds) *Technologies of Insecurity: The Surveillance of Everyday Life*. Abingdon: Routledge, pp. 1–17.

Franko Aas K, Gundhus H, and Lomell H (eds) (2009b) *Technologies of Insecurity: The Surveillance of Everyday Life*. Abingdon: Routledge.

Franko K (2020) *The Crimmigrant Other: Migration and Penal Power*. Abingdon: Routledge.

Franko K (2021) The two-sided spectacle at the border: Frontext, NGOs and the theatres of sovereignty. *Theoretical Criminology* 25(3): 379–399.

Freedom House (2022) Nigeria. Available at: https://freedomhouse.org/country/nigeria (accessed 28 May 2022).

Frelick B, Kysel I, and Podkul J (2016) The impact of externalization of migration controls on the rights of asylum seekers and other migrants. *Journal on Migration and Human Security* 4(4): 190–220.

Friedman S (2020) *The Class Ceiling: Why It Pays to Be Privileged*. Bristol: Policy Press.

Frontex (2022) EU-wide picture. Available at: https://frontex.europa.eu/we-know/eu-wide-picture/ (accessed 29 September 2024).

Frowd PM (2018) Developmental borderwork and the International Organization for Migration. *Journal of Ethnic and Migration Studies* 44(10): 1656–1672.

Frowd PM (2020) *Security at the Borders: Transnational Practices and Technologies in West Africa*. Cambridge: Cambridge University Press.

Frowd PM (2024) The 'datafication' of borders in global context: The role of the International Organization for Migration. *Geopolitics*. DOI: 10.1080/14650045.2024.2318580.

Fussey P and Sandhu A (2022) Surveillance arbitration in the era of digital policing. *Theoretical Criminology* 26(1): 3–22.

Fussey P, Davies B, and Innes M (2020) 'Assisted' facial recognition and the reinvention of suspicion and discretion in digital policing. *British Journal of Criminology* 61(2): 325–344.

Gabbidon SL (1996) An argument for including W.E.B. DuBois in the criminology/criminal justice literature. *Journal of Criminal Justice Education* 7(1): 99–112.

Gadd D (2012) In-depth interviewing and psychosocial case study analysis. In: Gadd D, Karstedt S, and Messner S (eds) *The SAGE Handbook of Criminological Research Methods*. London: SAGE Publications, pp. 36–48.

Gadd D, Karstedt S, and Messner S (2012) Editorial introduction. In: Gadd D, Karstedt S, and Messner S (eds) *The SAGE Handbook of Criminological Research Methods*. London: SAGE Publications, pp. 1–8.

Gahima G (2012) *Transitional Justice in Rwanda: Accountability for Atrocity*. Abingdon: Routledge.

Gallagher J (2016) Interviews as catastrophic encounters: An object relations methodology for IR research. *International Studies Perspectives* 17(4): 445–461.

Gammeltoft-Hansen T (2011) *Access to Asylum: International Refugee Law and the Globalisation of Migration Control*. Cambridge: Cambridge University Press.

Gani J and Khan R (2024) Positionality statements as a function of coloniality: Interrogating reflexive methodologies. *International Studies Quarterly* 68(2): sqae038.

Garland D (1996) The limits of the sovereign state: Strategies of crime control in contemporary society. *The British Journal of Criminology* 36(4): 445–471.

Garland D (2001) *The Culture of Control: Crime and Social Order in Contemporary Society*. Chicago, IL: The University of Chicago Press.

Garland D (2002) Of crimes and criminals: The development of criminology in Britain. In: *The Oxford Handbook of Criminology*. 3rd ed. Oxford: Oxford University Press, pp. 7–50.

Garland D and Sparks R (2000) Criminology, social theory and the challenge of our times. *The British Journal of Criminology* 40(2): 189–204.

Gates K (2011) *Our Biometric Future: Facial Recognition Technology and the Culture of Surveillance*. New York, NY: New York University Press.

Geiger M (2020) Possible futures? The new 'UN Migration Agency' and the shifting global order. In: Geiger M and Pécoud A (eds) *The International Organization for Migration: The New 'UN Migration Agency' in Critical Perspective*. Cham: Palgrave Macmillan, pp. 293–306.

Geiger M and Pécoud A (2014) International organisations and the politics of migration. *Journal of Ethnic and Migration Studies* 40(6): 865–887.

Georgi F (2010) For the benefit of some: The International Organization for Migration and its global migration management. In: Geiger M and Pécoud A (eds) *The Politics of International Migration Management*. Basingstoke: Palgrave Macmillan, pp. 45–72.

Gerard A and Pickering S (2013) Crimmigration: criminal justice, refugee protection and the securitisation of migration. In: Bruce Arrigo H (ed.) *The Routledge Handbook of International Crime and Justice Studies*. Abingdon: Routledge, pp. 587–611.

Giese D and Schnapp K-U (2021) Deductive, inductive, and retroductive reasoning. In: Morin J-F, Olsson C, and Atickan EÖ (eds) *Research Methods in the Social Sciences: An A–Z of Key Concepts*. Oxford: Oxford University Press, pp. 77–81.

Gillior H (2018) Digitalisation—an unstoppable mega trend. Available at: https://www.institutefordigitaltransformation.org/digitalisation-an-unstoppable-mega-trend/ (accessed 29 July 2024).

Glouftsios G (2021) Governing border security infrastructures: Maintaining large-scale information systems. *Security Dialogue* 52(5): 452–470.

Goettlich K (2019) The rise of linear borders in world politics. *European Journal of International Relations* 25(1): 203–228.

Goldstein K (2002) Getting in the door: Sampling and completing elite interviews. *PS: Political Science & Politics* 35(4): 669–672.

Goode E and Ben-Yehuda N (2009) *Moral Panics: The Social Construction of Deviance*. 2nd ed. Chichester: Wiley-Blackwell.

Goold B, Loader I, and Thumala A (2013) The banality of security: The curious case of surveillance cameras. *British Journal of Criminology* 53(6): 977–996.

Greenfield A (2016) *Radical Technologies: The Design of Everyday Life*. London: Verso.

Greer E (2019) More border surveillance tech could be worse for human rights than a wall. *The Washington Post*, 13 February. Available at: https://www.washingtonpost.com/outlook/2019/02/13/more-border-surveillance-tech-could-be-worse-human-rights-than-wall/ (accessed 26 July 2022).

Griffiths M and Yeo C (2021) The UK's hostile environment: Deputising immigration control. *Critical Social Policy* 41(4): 521–544.

Grovogui S (2001) Sovereignty in Africa: Quasi-statehood and other myths in international theory. In: Dunn K and Shaw T (eds) *Africa's Challenge to International Relations Theory*. Basingstoke: Palgrave, pp. 29–45.

Grovogui S (2002) Regimes of sovereignty: International morality and the African condition. *European Journal of International Relations* 8(3): 315–338.

Gundhus H (2021) Shaping migrants as threats: Multilayered discretion, criminalization, and risk assessment tools. *International Journal for Crime, Justice and Social Democracy* 10(3): 56–71.

Gunnarsdóttir K and Rommetveit K (2017) The biometric imaginary: (Dis)trust in a policy vacuum. *Public Understanding of Science* 26(2): 195–211.

Haggerty K and Ericson R (2000) The surveillant assemblage. *The British Journal of Sociology* 51(4): 605–622.

Halford S and Southerton D (2023) What future for the sociology of futures? Visions, concepts and methods. *Sociology* 57(2): 263–278.

Han C-R, McGauran R, and Nelen H (2017) API and PNR data in use for border control authorities. *Security Journal* 30(4): 1045–1063.

Hannah-Moffat K (2019) Algorithmic risk governance: Big data analytics, race and information activism in criminal justice debates. *Theoretical Criminology* 23(4): 453–470.

Hanson L (2015) *Cartographic Criminology: An Assessment and Proposal for an Integrated Approach to Crime Mapping*. Doctoral dissertation. University of Kent, Kent. Available at: https://kar.kent.ac.uk/49514/ (accessed 4 September 2020).

Haraway D (1988) Situated knowledges: The science question in feminism and the privilege of partial perspective. *Feminist Studies* 14(3): 575–599.

Hardie-Bick J, Sheptycki J, and Wardak A (2005) Introduction: Transnational and comparative criminology in a global perspective. In: James Sheptycki AW (ed.) *Transnational and Comparative Criminology*. London: GlassHouse Press, pp. 1–16.

Hardyns W and Pauwels LJR (2018) The Chicago School and criminology. In: Triplett RA (ed.) *The Wiley Handbook of the History and Philosophy of Criminology*. Oxford: John Wiley & Sons, pp. 123–139.

Harman S (2012) *Global Health Governance*. Abingdon: Routledge.

Harrison P (2000) Making sense: Embodiment and the sensibilities of the everyday. *Environment and Planning D: Society and Space* 18(4): 497–517.

Hartry A (2012) Gendering crimmigration: The intersection of gender, immigration, and the criminal justice system. *Berkeley Journal of Gender, Immigration, and the Criminal Justice System* 1: 1–27.

Harvey WS (2011) Strategies for conducting elite interviews. *Qualitative Research* 11(4): 431–441.

Haukio J (ed.) (2017) *Katso pohjoista taivasta*. Helsinki: Otava.

Hayles NK (1999) *How We Became Posthuman: Virtual Bodies in Cybernetics, Literature, and Informatics*. Chicago, IL: The University of Chicago Press.

Heidegger M (1993) *Basic Writings* (ed. D Farrell Krell). New York, NY: HarperCollins.

Hellerstein E (2021) Between the US and Mexico, a corridor of surveillance becomes lethal. *.coda*, 14 July. Available at: https://www.codastory.com/authoritarian-tech/us-border-surveillance/ (accessed 26 July 2022).

Henrikson O (2021) Access to legal identity is crucial for safe, orderly and regular migration. Available at: https://eea.iom.int/news/access-legal-identity-crucial-safe-orderly-and-regular-migration (accessed 20 July 2022).

Hernández CCG (2017) What is crimmigration law? *Insights on Law and Society* 17(3): 22–25.

Hernández CCG (2018) Deconstructing crimmigration. *University of California, Davis Law Review* 52: 197–253.

Hickel J (2017) *The Divide: A Brief Guide to Global Inequality and Its Solutions.* London: Windmill Books.

Hickman L (2001) *Philosophical Tools for Technological Culture.* Bloomington, IN: Indiana University Press.

Hickman L (2007) *Pragmatism as Post-Modernism.* New York, NY: Fordham University Press.

Hiemstra N and Conlon D (2017) Beyond privatization: Bureaucratization and the spatialities of immigration detention expansion. *Territory, Politics, Governance* 5(3): 252–268.

Hirsch A (2018) *Brit(Ish): On Race, Identity and Belonging.* London: Vintage.

Hirsch AL and Doig C (2018) Outsourcing control: The International Organization for Migration in Indonesia. *The International Journal of Human Rights* 22(5): 681–708.

Holden M (2020) Ecological crisis, action and pragmatic humanism. In: Wills J and Lake R (eds) *The Power of Pragmatism: Knowledge Production and Social Inquiry.* Manchester: Manchester University Press, pp. 195–209.

Holsti K (2018) Change in international politics: The view from high altitude. *International Studies Review* 20(2): 186–194.

Howarth D (2013) *Poststructuralism and After: Structure, Subjectivity and Power.* Basingstoke: Palgrave Macmillan.

Howden D, Fotiadis A, and Loewenstein A (2019) Once migrants on Mediterranean were saved by naval patrols. Now they have to watch as drones fly over. *The Guardian*, 4 August. Available at: https://www.theguardian.com/world/2019/aug/04/drones-replace-patrol-ships-mediterranean-fears-more-migrant-deaths-eu (accessed 26 July 2022).

Hughes G and McLaughlin E (2003) Towards a new paradigm of sovereign power? Community governance, preventative safety and the Crime and Disorder Reduction Partnerships. *The British Criminology Conferences: Selected Proceedings* 6: 1–14.

Huysmans J (2004) Minding exceptions: The politics of insecurity and liberal democracy. *Contemporary Political Theory* 3(3): 321–341.

Huysmans J (2006) *The Politics of Insecurity: Fear, Migration and Asylum in the EU.* Abingdon: Routledge.

Huysmans J (2011) What's in an act? On security speech acts and little security nothings. *Security Dialogue* 42(4–5): 371–383.

Huysmans J and Nogueira JP (2016) Ten years of IPS: Fracturing IR. *International Political Sociology* 10(4): 299–319.

ICAO (2010) *Guidelines on Passenger Name Record (PNR) Data*. Montreal: ICAO.

ICAO (2017) *ICAO Trip Guide on Border Control Management*. Montreal: ICAO.

ICAO (2018) *Technical Report: Portrait Quality (Reference Facial Images for MRTD)*. Montreal: ICAO. Available at: https://www.icao.int/Security/FAL/TRIP/Documents/TR%20-%20Portrait%20Quality%20v1.0.pdf (accessed 20 July 2022).

ICAO (n.d.) Technical Advisory Group on the Traveller Identification Programme (TAG/TRIP). Available at: https://www.icao.int/Security/FAL/TRIP/Pages/Panels.aspx (accessed 29 September 2024).

Ifeanyi-Aneke F, Ifedi F, and Aga S (2021) Nigeria immigration service and the challenge of cross border human trafficking in Nigeria 2011–2019. *University of Nigeria Journal of Political Economy* 11(1): 124–134.

IMF (2023) IMF and good governance. Available at: https://www.imf.org/en/About/Factsheets/Sheets/2023/The-IMF-and-Good-Governance#:~:text=The%20IMF%20promotes%20good%20governance,to%20access%20available%20viewer%20actions. (accessed 29 September 2024).

INCERT (n.d.) About us. Available at: https://incert.bg/en/za-nas/ (accessed 29 September 2024).

Infantino F (2016) *Outsourcing Border Control: Politics and Practice of Contracted Visa Policy in Morocco*. Basingstoke: Palgrave Macmillan.

Infantino F (2019) *Schengen Visa Implementation and Transnational Policymaking: Bordering Europe*. Cham: Palgrave Macmillan.

Innovatrics (2023) 'Exceptional' biometrics: Solving local peculiarities of biometric identity projects. Available at: https://id4africa.com/wp-content/uploads/2023/06/PS3-3-Jan-Lunter-Innovatrics.pdf (accessed 12 June 2024).

Interpol (2022) Databases. Available at: https://www.interpol.int/en/How-we-work/Databases (accessed 28 July 2022).

IOM (2011) PIRS, the International Organization for Migration's Personal Identification and Registration System. Available at: https://www.iom.int/sites/g/files/tmzbdl486/files/jahia/webdav/shared/shared/mainsite/activities/ibm/09-IOM-IBM-FACT-SHEET-Personal-Identification-and-Registration-System-PIRS.pdf (accessed 28 July 2022).

IOM (2015a) IOM snapshot 2015. Available at: https://www.iom.int/sites/g/files/tmzbdl486/files/documents/iom_snap_en%202015.pdf (accessed 29 September 2024).

IOM (2015b) Summary update on the programme and budget for 2015 C/106/17. Available at: https://governingbodies.iom.int/system/files/en/council/106/C-106-17-Summary-Update-of-the-PB-2015.pdf (accessed 29 September 2024).

IOM (2016) *Migration in Nigeria: A Country Profile 2014*. Geneva: IOM.

IOM (2018a) IOM and biometrics. Available at: https://www.iom.int/sites/g/files/tmzbdl486/files/our_work/DMM/IBM/iom_and_biometrics_external_info_sheet_november_2018.pdf (accessed 29 September 2024).

IOM (2018b) MIDAS: A comprehensive and affordable Border Management Information System. Available at: https://acbc.iom.int/sites/default/files/2019-11/midas-brochure18-v7-en_digital-2606_1.pdf (accessed 29 September 2024).

IOM (2019) *World Migration Report*. Geneva: IOM.

IOM (2021a) About IOM. Available at: https://www.iom.int/about-iom (accessed 29 September 2024).

IOM (2021b) *IOM Institutional Strategy on Legal Identity*. Geneva: IOM.

IOM (2021c) IOM snapshot: Dignified, orderly and safe migration for the benefit of all. Available at: https://www.iom.int/sites/default/files/about-iom/iom_snapshot_a4_en.pdf (accessed 29 September 2024).

IOM (2021d) The future of development is digital. Available at: https://medium.com/@UNmigration/the-future-of-development-is-digital-384b66eac912 (accessed 29 September 2024).

IOM (2022a) Global compact for migration. Available at: https://www.iom.int/global-compact-migration (accessed 28 July 2022).

IOM (2022b) Immigration and border management. Available at: https://www.iom.int/immigration-and-border-management (accessed 26 July 2022).

IOM (2022c) IOM and UNOCT sign agreement to collaborate on API/PNR technical assistance. Available at: https://www.iom.int/news/iom-and-unoct-sign-agreement-collaborate-api/pnr-technical-assistance (accessed 29 September 2024).

IOM (2022d) The United Nations partners with the Federal Government of Nigeria on the establishment of an Advance Passenger Information and Passenger Name Record system. Available at: https://nigeria.iom.int/news/united-nations-partners-federal-government-nigeria-establishment-advance-passenger-information (accessed 10 March 2023).

IOM (2023a) IOM and UNOCT hold border governance workshop for law enforcement agencies in Nigeria. Available at: https://rodakar.iom.int/news/iom-and-unoct-hold-border-governance-workshop-law-enforcement-agencies-nigeria (accessed 29 September 2024).

IOM (2023b) Summary update on the programme and budget for 2023 C/114/7. Available at: https://governingbodies.iom.int/system/files/en/council/114/c-114-7-summary-update-on-programme-and-budget-2023.pdf (accessed 29 September 2024).

IOM (2024a) Donor relations. Available at: https://www.iom.int/donor-relations (accessed 9 January 2024).

IOM (2024b) Immigration and border governance in Nigeria. Available at: https://nigeria.iom.int/sites/g/files/tmzbdl1856/files/documents/2024-07/062024_ibg-nigeria-briefer.pdf (accessed 29 September 2024).

IOM (2024c) IOM staff data report. Available at: https://www.iom.int/sites/g/files/tmzbdl486/files/documents/2024-10/iom-staff-data-q3-2024.pdf (accessed 29 September 2024).

IOM (2024d) Mission. Available at: https://www.iom.int/mission (accessed 29 September 2024).

iProov (2024) Border control. Available at: https://www.iproov.com/what-we-do/use-cases/border-control (accessed 12 June 2024).

Israel M and Hay I (2012) Research ethics in criminology. In: Gadd D, Karstedt S, and Messner S (eds) *The SAGE Handbook of Criminological Research Methods*. London: SAGE Publications, pp. 500–515.

Israel T (2020) *Facial Recognition at a Crossroads: Transformation at Our Borders & Beyond*. Ottawa: Samuelson-Glushko Canadian Internet Policy & Public Interest Clinic.

Jackson R (2007) *Sovereignty: Evolution of an Idea*. Cambridge: Polity Press.

Jackson RH (1986) Negative sovereignty in Sub-Saharan Africa. *Review of International Studies* 12(4). Cambridge University Press: 247–264.

Jackson R and Rosberg C (1986) Sovereignty and underdevelopment: Juridical statehood in the African crisis. *The Journal of Modern African Studies* 24(1): 1–31.

Jacobsen E and Rao U (2018) The truth of the error: Making identity and security through biometric discrimination. In: Maguire M, Rao U, and Zurawski N (eds) *Bodies as Evidence: Security, Knowledge, and Power*. Durham, NC: Duke University Press, pp. 24–42.

Jacobsen K (2015) *The Politics of Humanitarian Technology: Good Intentions, Unintended Consequences and Insecurity*. Abingdon: Routledge.

Jaffe R and Pilo' F (2023) Security technology, urban prototyping, and the politics of failure. *Security Dialogue* 54(1): 76–93.

Jasanoff S (2004a) Afterword. In: Jasanoff S (ed.) *States of Knowledge: The Co-Production of Science and Social Order*. Abingdon: Routledge, pp. 274–282.

Jasanoff S (2004b) The idiom of co-production. In: Jasanoff S (ed.) *States of Knowledge: The Co-Production of Science and Social Order*. Abingdon: Routledge, pp. 1–12.

Jeandesboz J (2016) Smartening border security in the European Union: An associational inquiry. *Security Dialogue* 47(4): 292–309.

Joh EE (2017) The undue influence of surveillance technology companies in policing. *New York University Law Review Online* 92: 19–47.

Johansen NB (2013) Governing the funnel of expulsion: Agamben, the dynamics of force, and minimalist biopolitics. In: Franko Aas K and Bosworth M (eds) *The Borders of Punishment: Citizenship, Migration, and Social Exclusion*. Oxford: Oxford University Press, pp. 257–272.

Johansen TK (2021) Introduction. In: Johansen TK (ed.) *Productive Knowledge in Ancient Philosophy*. Cambridge: Cambridge University Press, pp. 1–14.

Johnson TL, Johnson NN, McCurdy D, et al. (2022) Facial recognition systems in policing and racial disparities in arrests. *Government Information Quarterly* 39(4): 101753.

Jones R (2009) Checkpoint security: Gateways, airports and the architecture of security. In: Franko Aas K, Gundhus HO, and Lomell HM (eds) *Technologies of Insecurity: The Surveillance of Everyday Life*. Abingdon: Routledge, pp. 81–101.

Jordaan E (2003) The concept of a middle power in international relations: Distinguishing between emerging and traditional middle powers. *Politikon* 30(1): 165–181.

Kalir B (2019) The uncomfortable truth about luck: Reflections on getting access to the Spanish state deportation field. *Social Anthropology* 27(S1): 84–99.

Kalir B, Achermann C, and Rosset D (2019) Re-searching access: What do attempts at studying migration control tell us about the state? *Social Anthropology/Anthropologie sociale* 27(S1): 5–16.

Kane S (2004) The unconventional methods of cultural criminology. *Theoretical Criminology* 8(3): 303–321.

Kaufman E (2015) *Punish & Expel*. Oxford: Oxford University Press.

Kaufman E (2022) Territoriality in American criminal law. *Michigan Law Review* 121(3): 353–408.

Kaufmann M (2019) Who connects the dots? Agents and agency in predictive policing. In: Hoijtink M and Leese M (eds) *Technology and Agency in International Relations*. Abingdon: Routledge, pp. 141–163.

Kaufmann M, Egbert S, and Leese M (2019) Predictive policing and the politics of patterns. *British Journal of Criminology* 59(3): 674–692.

Kaushik V and Walsh C (2019) Pragmatism as a research paradigm and its implications for social work research. *Social Sciences* 8(9): 255.

Kayode I (2016) Repositioning Nigeria foreign policy for national development: Issues, challenges and policy options. *Afro Asian Journal of Social Sciences* 7(2): 1–14.

Kendall M (2021) *Hood Feminism: Notes from the Women White Feminists Forgot*. London: Bloomsbury Publishing.

Keohane R and Nye J (2002) The club model of multilateral cooperation and problems of democratic legitimacy. In: Keohane R (ed) *Power and Governance in a Partially Globalized World*. Abingdon: Routledge, pp. 219–244.

Klabbers J (2019) Notes on the ideology of international organizations law: The International Organization for Migration, state-making, and the market for migration. *Leiden Journal of International Law* 32(3): 383–400.

Koch A (2014) The politics and discourse of migrant return: The role of UNHCR and IOM in the governance of return. *Journal of Ethnic and Migration Studies* 40(6): 905–923.

Koh JL (2016) Crimmigration and the void for vagueness doctrine. *Immigration and Nationality Law Review* 37: 403–460.

Korneev O (2018) Self-legitimation through knowledge production partnerships: International Organization for Migration in Central Asia. *Journal of Ethnic and Migration Studies* 44(10): 1673–1690.

Krause U (2021) Colonial roots of the 1951 Refugee Convention and its effects on the global refugee regime. *Journal of International Relations and Development* 24(3): 599–626.

Ku J and Yoo J (2013) Globalization and sovereignty. *Berkeley Journal of International Law* 31: 210–235.

Kubal A (2014) Struggles against subjection. Implications of criminalization of migration for migrants' everyday lives in Europe. *Crime, Law and Social Change* 62(2): 91–111.

Kuhn T (2012) *The Structure of Scientific Revolutions*. 4th ed. Chicago, IL: The University of Chicago Presss.

Landau L (2005) Immigration and the state of exception: Security and sovereignty in East and Southern Africa. *Millennium: Journal of International Studies* 34(2): 325–348.

Larner W and Walters W (2004) Globalization as governmentality. *Alternatives: Global, Local, Political* 29(5): 495–514.

Lavenex S (2016) Multilevelling EU external governance: The role of international organizations in the diffusion of EU migration policies. *Journal of Ethnic and Migration Studies* 42(4): 554–570.

Law J (2009) Actor Network Theory and material semiotics. In: Turner B (ed.) *The New Blackwell Companion to Social Theory*. Chichester: Wiley-Blackwell, pp. 141–158.

Law J and Singleton V (2000) Performing technology's stories: On social constructivism, performance, and performativity. *Technology and Culture* 41(4): 765–775.

Lazaridis G and Skleparis D (2016) Securitization of migration and the far right: The case of Greek security professionals. *International Migration* 54(2): 176–192.

Leader K (2020) The trial's the thing: Performance and legitimacy in international criminal trials. *Theoretical Criminology* 24(2): 241–257.

Leander A (2021) Locating (new) materialist characters and processes in global governance. *International Theory* 13(1): 157–168.

Lee M (2013) Human trafficking and border control in the Global South. In: Franko Aas K and Bosworth M (eds) *Borders of Punishment: Migration, Citizenship, and Social Exclusion*. Oxford: Oxford University Press, pp. 128–145.

Lee M (2022) The externalization of border control in the global South: The cases of Malaysia and Indonesia. *Theoretical Criminology* 26(4): 537–556.

Leerkes A, Bachmeier JD, and Leach MA (2013) When the border is "everywhere": State-level variation in migration control and changing settlement patterns of the unauthorized immigrant population in the United States. *International Migration Review* 47(4): 910–943.

Leese M (2014) The new profiling: Algorithms, black boxes, and the failure of anti-discriminatory safeguards in the European Union. *Security Dialogue* 45(5): 494–511.

Leese M (2022) Fixing state vision: Interoperability, biometrics, and identity management in the EU. *Geopolitics* 27(1): 113–133.

Leese M and Ugolini V (2024) Politics of creep: Latent development, technology monitoring, and the evolution of the Schengen Information System. *European Journal of International Security* 9(3): 340–356.

Lefebvre C (2011) We have tailored Africa: French colonialism and the 'artificiality' of Africa's borders in the interwar period. *Journal of Historical Geography* 37(2): 191–202.

Lefebvre H (2009) *State, Space, World* (eds N Brenner and S Elden). Minneapolis, MN: University of Minnesota Press.

Lemberg-Pedersen M (2012) Private security companies and the European borderscapes. In: Gammeltoft-Hansen T and Nyberg Sørensen N (eds) *The Migration Industry and the Commercialization of International Migration*. Abingdon: Routledge, pp. 152–172.

Lemberg-Pedersen M (2019) Manufacturing displacement: Externalization and postcoloniality in European migration control. *Global Affairs* 5(3). 3: 247–271.

Lemberg-Pedersen M and Haioty E (2020) Re-assembling the surveillable refugee body in the era of data-craving. *Citizenship Studies* 24(5). Routledge: 607–624.

Lemke T (2018) An alternative model of politics? Prospects and problems of Jane Bennett's Vital Materialism. *Theory, Culture & Society* 35(6): 31–54.

Leonard P (2005) *Nationality Between Poststructuralism and Postcolonial Theory: A New Cosmopolitanism*. Basingstoke: Palgrave Macmillan.

Liboiron M (2021) Firsting in research. Available at: https://discardstudies.com/2021/01/18/firsting-in-research/ (accessed 3 May 2022).

Lie J (2013) Challenging anthropology: Anthropological reflections on the ethnographic turn in International Relations. *Millennium: Journal of International Studies* 41(2): 201–220.

Linz J and Secor A (2021) Undoing mastery: With ambivalence? *Dialogues in Human History* 11(1): 108–111.

Lisle D (2018) Failing worse? Science, security and the birth of technology. *European Journal of International Relations* 24(4): 887–910.

Littoz-Monnet A (2022) Exclusivity and circularity in the production of global governance expertise: The making of 'global mental health' knowledge. *International Political Sociology* 16(2). olab035.

Lloyd-Damnjanovic I (2022) Criminalization of search-and-rescue operations in the Mediterranean has been accompanied by rising migrant death rate. Available at: https://www.migrationpolicy.org/article/criminalization-rescue-operations-mediterranean-rising-deaths (accessed 26 July 2022).

Loader I and Sparks R (2010) *Public Criminology?* Abingdon: Routledge.

Lohne K (2020) Penal humanitarianism beyond the nation state: An analysis of international criminal justice. *Theoretical Criminology* 24(2): 145–162.

Lohne K and Sandvik KB (2017) Bringing law into the political sociology of humanitarianism. *Oslo Law Review* 4(1): 4–27.

Longo M (2018) *The Politics of Borders: Sovereignty, Security, and the Citizen after 9/11*. Cambridge: Cambridge University Press.

Loyle CE (2018) Transitional justice and political order in Rwanda. *Ethnic and Racial Studies* 41(4). Routledge: 663–680.

Lumsden K and Goode J (2018) Public criminology, reflexivity and the enterprise university: Experiences of research, knowledge transfer work and co-option with police forces. *Theoretical Criminology* 22(2): 243–257.

Lumsden K and Winter A (eds) (2014) *Reflexivity in Criminological Research: Experiences with the Powerful and the Powerless*. Basingstoke: Palgrave Macmillan.

Lynch M, Cole S, McNally R, et al. (2008) *Truth Machine: The Contentious History of DNA Fingerprinting*. Chicago, IL: University of Chicago Press.

Lyon D (ed.) (2003) *Surveillance as Social Sorting: Privacy, Risk, and Digital Discrimination*. Abingdon: Routledge.

Lyon D (2009) Identification oractices: State formation, crime control, colonialism and war. In: Franko Aas K, Gundhus HO, and Lomell HM (eds) *Technologies of Insecurity: The Surveillance of Everyday Life*. Abingdon: Routledge, pp. 42–58.

Mabry L (2008) Case study in social research. In: Alasuutari P, Bickman L, and Brannen J (eds) *The SAGE Handbook of Social Research Methods*. London: SAGE Publications, pp. 214–227.

MacAskill W (2022) *What We Owe the Future*. New York, NY: Basic Books.

Mackenzie S and Green P (2008) Performative regulation: A case study in how powerful people avoid criminal labels. *British Journal of Criminology* 48(2): 138–153.

MacLean S (2001) Challenging Westphalia: Issues of sovereignty and identity in Southern Africa. In: Dunn K and Shaw T (eds) *Africa's Challenge to International Relations Theory*. Basingstoke: Palgrave, pp. 146–162.

Madianou M (2019) The biometric assemblage: Surveillance, experimentation, profit, and the measuring of refugee bodies. *Television & New Media* 20(6): 581–599.

Maguire M (2009) The birth of biometric security. *Anthropology Today* 25(2): 9–14.

Malkki L (1992) National Geographic: The rooting of peoples and the territorialization of national identity. *Cultural Anthropology* 7(1): 24–44.

Mamdani M (2010) Responsibility to Protect or right to punish? *Journal of Intervention and Statebuilding* 4(1): 53–67.

Manning P (2008) *The Technology of Policing: Crime Mapping, Information Technology, and the Rationality of Crime Control.* New York, NY: New York University Press.

Marelli L, Kieslich K and Geiger S (2022) COVID-19 and techno-solutionism: Responsibilization without contextualization? *Critical Public Health* 32(1): 1–4.

Marin L and Spena A (2016) Introduction: The criminalization of migration and European (dis)integration. *European Journal of Migration and Law* 18(2): 147–156.

Markelius A, Wright C, Kuiper J, et al. (2024) The mechanisms of AI hype and its planetary and social costs. *AI and Ethics*. DOI: 10.1007/s43681-024-00461-2.

Markó FD (2016) 'We are not a failed state, we make the best passports': South Sudan and biometric modernity. *African Studies Review* 59(2): 113–132.

Martin A and Taylor L (2021) Exclusion and inclusion in identification: Regulation, displacement and data justice. *Information Technology for Development* 27(1): 50–66.

Martin L (2017) Discretion, contracting and commodification: Privatisation of US immigration detention as a technology of government. In: Conlon D and Hiemstra N (eds) *Intimate Economies of Immigration Detention: Critical Perspectives*. Abingdon: Routledge, pp. 32–50.

Martin-Mazé M and Perret S (2021) Designs of borders: Security, critique, and the machines. *European Journal of International Security* 6(3): 278–300.

Martins BO and Jumbert MG (2022) EU Border technologies and the co-production of security 'problems' and 'solutions'. *Journal of Ethnic and Migration Studies* 48(6): 1430–1446.

Matthewman S (2011) *Technology and Social Theory*. Basingstoke: Palgrave Macmillan.

Maxfield M and Babbie E (2015) *Research Methods for Criminal Justice and Criminology*. 7th ed. Stamford, CT: Cengage Learning.

Mbembe A (2000) At the edge of the world: Boundaries, territoriality, and sovereignty in Africa. *Public Culture* 12(1): 259–284.

Mbembe A (2001) *On the Postcolony*. Oakland, CA: University of California Press.

Mbembe A (2011) Provincializing France? *Public Culture* 23(1): 85–119.

McCarthy D (2018) Introduction: Technology in world politics. In: McCarthy D (ed.) *Technology and World Politics: An Introduction*. Abingdon: Routledge, pp. 1–21.

McDermott MJ (2002) On moral enterprises, pragmatism, and feminist criminology. *Crime & Delinquency* 48(2): 283–299.

McGuire MR and Renaud K (2023) Harm, injustice & technology: Reflections on the UK's subpostmasters' case. *The Howard Journal of Crime and Justice* 62(4). John Wiley & Sons, Ltd: 441–461.

McKay C (2022) The carceral automaton: Digital prisons and technologies of detention. *International Journal for Crime, Justice and Social Democracy* 11(1): 100–119.

McLaughlin A (2024) Existential risk, climate change, and nonideal justice. *The Monist* 107(2): 190–206.

McWhinney E (2008) Declaration on the granting of independence to colonial countries and people. *United Nations Audiovisual Library of International Law*. Available at: https://legal.un.org/avl/pdf/ha/dicc/dicc_e.pdf (accessed 29 September 2024).

Mechlinski T (2010) Towards an approach to borders and mobility in Africa. *Journal of Borderlands Studies* 25(2): 94–106.

Mehta R (2016) Borders: A view from 'nowhere'. *Criminology & Criminal Justice* 16(3): 286–300.

Mehta R (2020) *Women, Mobility and Incarceration: Love and Recasting of Self across the Bangladesh–India Border*. Abingdon: Routledge.

Menjívar C, Gómez Cervantes A and Alvord D (2018) The expansion of 'crimmigration,' mass detention, and deportation. *Sociology Compass* 12(4): 1–15.

Metcalfe P and Dencik L (2019) The politics of big borders: Data (in)justice and the governance of refugees. *First Monday* 24(4). DOI: 10.5210/fm.v24i4.9934.

Mignolo W and Walsh C (2018) *On Decoloniality: Concepts, Analytics, Praxis*. Durham, NC: Duke University Press.

Milan S (2020) Techno-solutionism and the standard human in the making of the COVID-19 pandemic. *Big Data & Society* 7(2): 2053951720966781.

Milivojevic S (2019a) *Border Policing and Security Technologies: Mobility and the Proliferation of Borders in the Western Balkans*. Abingdon: Routledge.

Milivojevic S (2019b) 'Stealing the fire', 2.0 style? Technology, the pursuit of mobility, social memory and de-securitization of migration. *Theoretical Criminology* 23(2): 211–227.

Milivojevic S (2021) *Crime and Punishment in the Future Internet: Digital Frontier Technologies and Criminology in the Twenty-First Century*. Abingdon: Routledge.

Milivojevic S and Radulski EM (2020) The 'future internet' and crime: Towards a criminology of the Internet of Things. *Current Issues in Criminal Justice* 32(2): 193–207.

Miller T (2019) *Empire of Borders: The Expansion of the U.S. Border Around the World*. London: Verso.

Molnar P (2019) Technology on the margins: AI and global migration from a human rights perspective. *Cambridge International Law Journal* 8(2): 305–330.

Molnar P (2021) Surveillance sovereignty: Migration management technologies and the politics of privatization. In: Hudson G and Atak I (eds) *Migration, Security, and Resistance*. Abingdon: Routledge, pp. 66–82.

Molnar P (2024) *The Walls Have Eyes: Surviving Migration in the Age of Artificial Intelligence*. New York, NY: The New Press.

Moore D and Hirai H (2014) Outcasts, performers and true believers: Responsibilized subjects of criminal justice. *Theoretical Criminology* 18(1): 5–19.

Morales DI (2014) Crimes of migration. *Wake Forest Law Review* (5): 1257–1324.

Morgan D (2013) Pragmatism as a paradigm for social research. *Qualitative Inquiry* 20(8): 1045–1053.

Morozov E (2013) *To Save Everything, Click Here: The Folly of Technological Solutionism*. Philadelphia, PA: Perseus Books.

Mountz A (2020) *The Death of Asylum: Hidden Geographies of the Enforcement Archipelago*. Minneapolis, MN: University of Minnesota Press.

Muller B (2009) Borders, risks, exclusions. *Studies in Social Justice* 3(1): 67–78.

Muller B (2010) *Security, Risk and the Biometric State: Governing Borders and Bodies*. Abingdon: Routledge.

Muller BJ (2004) (Dis)qualified bodies: securitization, citizenship and 'identity management'. *Citizenship Studies* 8(3): 279–294.

Müller F and Richmond M (2023) The technopolitics of security: Agency, temporality, sovereignty. *Security Dialogue* 54(1). 1: 3–20.

Müller M (2015) Assemblages and actor-networks: Rethinking socio-material power, politics and space. *Geography Compass* 9(1): 27–41.

Muncie J (2005) The globalization of crime control—the case of youth and juvenile justice. *Theoretical Criminology* 9(1): 35–64.

Murad M (2020) How the 'Big Three' biometrics compare. Available at: https://www.irisid.com/how-the-big-three-biometrics-compare/?utm_source=rss&utm_medium=rss&utm_campaign=how-the-big-three-biometrics-compare (accessed 30 July 2022).

Newburn T (2017) *Criminology*. 3rd ed. Abingdon: Routledge.

Newman D (2010) Territory, compartments and borders: Avoiding the trap of the territorial trap. *Geopolitics* 15(4): 773–778.

Nichols R (2014) The colonialism of incarceration. *Radical Philosophy Review* 17(2): 435–455.

Nigeria Civil Aviation Authority (2024) Implementation of Advance Passenger Information (API) system – The Nigeria experience. Available at: https://www.icao.int/WACAF/Documents/Meetings/2024/Webinar-FAL/API%20PNR%20_NIGERIA.pdf (accessed 25 September 2024).

Nigerian Immigration Service (2022) Visa on arrival FAQs. Available at: https://portal.immigration.gov.ng/pages/visaOnArrivalFaq#:~:text=Upon%20arrival%20at%20the%20port,in%20Nigeria%20and%20return%20ticket. (accessed 18 July 2022).

NIS (2024) NIS history. Available at: https://immigration.gov.ng/home-2/nis-history/ (accessed 29 September 2024).

Nisancioglu K (2020) Racial Sovereignty. *European Journal of International Relations* 26(S1): 39–63.

Nkrumah K (1965) *Neo-Colonialism: The Last Stage of Imperialism*. New York, NY: International Publishers.

Novick G (2008) Is there a bias against telephone interviews in qualitative research? *Research in Nursing and Health* 31: 391–398.

Obendiek AS and Seidl T (2023) The (false) promise of solutionism: ideational business power and the construction of epistemic authority in digital security governance. *Journal of European Public Policy* 30(7): 1305–1329.

Obiowo C (2024) Nigeria Immigration Services implements API PNR technology, integrates with INTERPOL 24/7, MIDAS databases. Available at: https://nairametrics.com/2024/06/23/nigeria-immigration-services-implements-api-pnr-technology-integrates-with-interpol-24-7-midas-databases/ (accessed 29 September 2024).

OHCHR (2020) Report of the Special Rapporteur on contemporary forms of racism, racial discrimination, xenophobia and related intolerance. Available at: https://www.ohchr.org/EN/newyork/Documents/A-75-590-AUV.docx (accessed 29 September 2024).

OHCHR (2022) The right to privacy in the digital age: Report of the Office of the United Nations High Commissioner for Human Rights. Available at: https://documents.un.org/doc/undoc/gen/g22/442/29/pdf/g2244229.pdf (accessed 29 September 2024).

Oksanen A-A (2021) The indigenous dimension of the intersocietal: Dussel, exteriority and the Sámi People. *Millennium: Journal of International Studies* 50(1): 83–109.

Okunade SK and Ogunnubi O (2021) A "Schengen" Agreement in Africa? African agency and the ECOWAS Protocol on Free Movement. *Journal of Borderlands Studies* 36(1): 119–137.

Olonisakin T, Ogunleye A, and Adebayo S (2018) The Nigeria criminal justice system and its effectiveness in criminal behaviour control: A social–psychological analysis. *International Journal of Accounting Research* 3(6): 28–44.

Olwig K, Grünenberg K, Møhl P, et al. (2020) *The Biometric Border World: Technologies, Bodies and Identities on the Move*. Abingdon: Routledge.

Onapajo H and Uzodike U (2012) Boko Haram terrorism in Nigeria: Man, the state, and the international system. *African Security Review* 21(3): 24–39.

O'Neil C (2016) *Weapons of Math Destruction: How Big Data Increases Inequality and Threatens Democracy*. New York, NY: Crown.

Onuoha G (2011) Contesting the space: The 'New Biafra' and ethno-territorial separatism in South-Eastern Nigeria. *Nationalism and Ethnic Politics* 17(4): 402–422.

Osiander A (2001) Sovereignty, international relations, and the Westphalian myth. *International Organization* 55(2): 251–287.

Otu N (1999) Colonialism and the criminal justice system in Nigeria. *International Journal of Comparative and Applied Criminal Justice* 23(2): 293–306.

Oxford Law Faculty (2023) Translating universal rights into local practices: Privacy, technology, and postcoloniality in Nigeria's legal regime for data governance. Available at: https://www.law.ox.ac.uk/content/event/translating-universal-rights-local-practices-privacy-technology-and-postcoloniality (accessed 13 September 2024).

Pali B and Schuilenburg M (2020) Fear and fantasy in the smart city. *Critical Criminology* 28(4): 775–788.

Pallister-Wilkins P (2022a) *Humanitarian Borders: Unequal Mobility and Saving Lives*. London: Verso.

Pallister-Wilkins P (2022b) Whitescapes: A posthumanist political ecology of Alpine migrant (im)mobility. *Political Geography* 92: 102517.

Palmer N (2021) Immigration trials and international crimes: Expressing justice and performing race. *Theoretical Criminology* 25(3): 419–436.

Paquette D (2021) Gunmen kidnap six in rare attack on university in Nigeria's capital. *The Washington Post*, 2 November. Available at: https://www.washingtonpost.com/world/2021/11/02/nigeria-abuja-university-kidnapping/ (accessed 3 March 2022).

Parmar A (2018) Policing belonging: Race and nation in the UK. In: Bosworth M, Parmar A, and Vázquez Y (eds) *Race, Criminal Justice, and Migration Control: Enforcing the Boundaries of Belonging*. Oxford: Oxford University Press, pp. 108–124.

Parmar A (2019) Policing migration and racial technologies. *British Journal of Criminology* 59(4): 938–957.

Parsanoglou D (2015) Organizing an international migration machinery: The Intergovernmental Committee for European Migration. In: Venturas L (ed.) *International 'Migration Management' in the Early Cold War: The Intergovernmental Committee for European Migration*. Corinth: University of the Peloponnese Press, pp. 55–85.

Patz R and Thorvaldsdottir S (2020) Drivers of expenditure allocation in the IOM: Refugees, donors, and international bureaucracy. In: Geiger M and Pécoud A (eds) *The International Organization for Migration: The New 'UN Migration Agency' in Critical Perspective*. Cham: Palgrave Macmillan, pp. 75–98.

Pécoud A (2018) What do we know about the International Organization for Migration? *Journal of Ethnic and Migration Studies* 44(10): 1621–1638.

Pécoud A (2020) Introduction: The International Organization for Migration as the new 'UN Migration Agency'. In: Geiger M and Pécoud A (eds) *The International Organization for Migration: The New 'UN Migration Agency' in Critical Perspective*. Cham: Palgrave Macmillan, pp. 1–27.

Peiffer C and Englebert P (2012) Extraversion, vulnerability to donors, and political liberalization in Africa. *African Affairs* 111(444): 355–378.

Peirce CS (1998) *The Essential Peirce: Selected Philosophical Writings, Vol. 2 (1893–1913)*. Bloomington, IN: Indiana University Press.

Perez C (2024) What is AI's place in history? Available at: https://www.project-syndicate.org/magazine/ai-is-part-of-larger-technological-revolution-by-carlota-perez-1-2024-03? (accessed 24 July 2024).

Peter M and Strazzari F (2017) Securitisation of research: Fieldwork under new restrictions in Darfur and Mali. *Third World Quarterly* 38(7): 1531–1550.

Petintseva O, Faria R, and Eski Y (2020) *Interviewing Elites, Experts and the Powerful in Criminology*. Cham: Palgrave Macmillan.

Pickering S and Weber L (2006a) Borders, mobility and technologies of control. In: Pickering S and Weber L (eds) *Borders, Mobility and Technologies of Control*. Dordrecht: Springer, pp. 1–19.

Pickering S and Weber L (2006b) De-territorializing criminology. In: Pickering S and Weber L (eds) *Borders, Mobility and Technologies of Control*. Dordrecht: Springer, pp. 207–212.

Pickering S, Bosworth M, and Franko Aas K (2015) The criminology of mobility. In: Pickering S and Ham J (eds) *The Routledge Handbook on Crime and International Migration*. Abingdon: Routledge, pp. 382–395.

Pickles J (2004) *A History of Spaces: Cartographic Reason, Mapping and the Geo-Coded World*. London: Routledge.

Pihlström S (2021) *Ihmisen maailma: Esseitä humanismista, totuudesta ja ajattelun tilasta*. Tampere: niin & näin.

Pollock E (2009) Researching white supremacists online: Methodological concerns of researching hate 'speech'. *Internet Journal of Criminology*: 1–19. Available at: https://media.wix.com/ugd/b93dd4_3686f65909044639a07b17e644b64f92.pdf (accessed 9 June 2025).

Pope PJ and Garrett TM (2012) America's homo sacer: Examining U.S. deportation hearings and the criminalization of illegal immigration. *Administration & Society* 45(2): 167–186.

Preissle J and Han Y (2012) Feminist research ethics. In: Hesse-Biber SN (ed.) *Handbook of Feminist Research: Theory and Praxis*. 2nd ed. London: SAGE Publications, pp. 583–605.

Privacy International (2019) New report underlines the EU's strategy in the war on migration: Border externalisation. Available at: https://privacyinternational.org/news-analysis/3224/new-report-underlines-eus-strategy-war-migration-border-externalisation (accessed 29 September 2024).

Privacy International (2024) When spiders share webs: The creeping expansion of INTERPOL's interoperable policing and biometrics entrench externalised EU borders in West Africa. Available at: https://privacyinternational.org/sites/default/files/2024-09/PI%20Briefing_When%20Spiders%20Share%20Webs_September24.pdf (accessed 29 September 2024).

Provine D and Zatz M (2015) Borders, crime and justice. In: Pickering S and Ham J (eds) *The Routledge Handbook on Crime and International Migration*. Abingdon: Routledge, pp. 353–366.

Queiroz M (2019) The impact of EURODAC in EU migration law: The era of crimmigration? *Market and Competition Law Review* 3(1): 157–183.

Quijano A (2007) Coloniality and modernity/rationality. *Cultural Studies* 21(2–3): 168–178.

Ragazzi F, Kuskonmaz E, Plájás I, et al. (2021) *Biometric and Behavioural Mass Surveillance in EU Member States*. Report for the Greens/EFA in the European Parliament. Available at: https://www.greens-efa.eu/biometricsurveillance/ (accessed 9 June 2025)

Ramachandran S (2019) The contours of crimmigration control in India. *Global Detention Project Working Paper No. 25*. Available at: https://www.globaldetentionproject.org/wp-content/uploads/2019/08/GDP-Working-Paper-25-The-Contours-of-Crimmigration-Control-in-India.pdf (accessed 9 June 2025)

Rhodes R (1994) The hollowing out of the state: The changing nature of the state in Britain. *Political Quarterly* 65: 138–151.

Ribeiro S and Soromenho-Marques V (2022) The techno-optimists of climate change: Science communication or technowashing? *Societies* 12(2): 64.

Richardson J, Godfrey B, and Walklate S (2021) Rapid, remote and responsive research during COVID-19. *Methodological Innovations* 14(1): 20597991211008581.

Robinson C (2018) Making migration knowable and governable: Benchmarking practices as technologies of global migration governance. *International Political Sociology* 12(4): 418–437.

Rorty R (1991) *Essays on Heidegger and Others: Philosophical Papers*. Cambridge: Cambridge University Press.

Rorty R (2017) *Philosophy and the Mirror of Nature*. Princeton, NJ: Princeton University Press.

Rorty R (2021) *Pragmatism as Anti-Authoritarianism*. Cambridge, MA: Harvard University Press.

Rose G (2017) Posthuman agency in the digitally mediated city: Exteriorization, individuation, reinvention. *Annals of the American Association of Geographers* 107(4): 779–793.

Rother S (2013) Global migration governance without migrants? The nation-state bias in the emerging policies and literature on global migration governance. *Migration Studies* 1(3): 363–377.

Ruggie J (1993) Territoriality and beyond: Problematizing modernity in International Relations. *International Organization* 47(1): 139–174.

Sager A (2016) Methodological nationalism, migration and political theory. *Political Studies* 64(1): 42–59.

Said E (1979) *Orientalism*. New York, NY: Vintage Books.

Šalamon NK, Frett B, and Stark Ketchum E (2020) Global crimmigration trends. In: Šalamon NK (ed.) *Causes and Consequences of Migrant Criminalization*. Cham: Springer, pp. 3–25.

Saleh-Hanna V (2008) *Colonial Systems of Control: Criminal Justice in Nigeria*. Ottawa: University of Ottawa Press.

Salter M (2013a) Research design. In: Salter M and Mutlu C (eds) *Research Methods in Critical Security Studies: An Introduction*. Abingdon: Routledge, pp. 15–24.

Salter M (2013b) To make move and let stop: Mobility and the assemblage of circulation. *Mobilities* 8(1): 7–19.

Salter M (2015) Passport photos. In: Salter M (ed.) *Making Things International 1: Circuits and Motion*. Minneapolis, MN: University of Minnesota Press, pp. 18–35.

Sassen S (2007) *A Sociology of Globalization*. New York, NY: W.W. Norton & Co.

Sayes E (2014) Actor-network theory and methodology: Just what does it mean to say that nonhumans have agency? *Social Studies of Science* 44(1): 134–149.

Schaible LM (2012) Overcoming the neglect of social process in cross-national and comparative criminology. *Sociology Compass* 6(10): 793–807.

Scheel S and Tazzioli M (2022) Who is a migrant? Abandoning the nation-state point of view in the study of migration. *Migration Politics* 1(2): 1–23.

Scheel S and Ustek-Spilda F (2019) The politics of expertise and ignorance in the field of migration management. *Environment and Planning D: Society and Space* 37(4): 663–681.

Scheel S, Ruppert E, and Ustek-Spilda F (2019) Enacting migration through data practices. *Environment and Planning D: Society and Space* 37(4): 579–588.

Scott JC (1998) *Seeing Like a State: How Certain Schemes to Improve the Human Condition Have Failed*. New Haven, CT: Yale University Press.

Seale C, Gobo G, Gubrium J, et al. (2004) Introduction: Inside qualitative research. In: Seale C, Gobo G, Gubrium J, et al. (eds) *Qualitative Research Practice*. London: SAGE Publications, pp. 1–12.

Sengoopta C (2003) *Imprint of the Raj: How Fingerprinting Was Born in Colonial India*. London: Pan Macmillan.

Seymour L (2013) Sovereignty, territory and authority: Boundary maintenance in contemporary Africa. *Critical African Studies* 5(1): 17–31.

Shaffer G (2005) Power, governance, and the WTO: A comparative institutional approach. In: Barnett M and Duvall R (eds) *Power in Global Governance*. Cambridge: Cambridge University Press, pp. 130–160.

Shah N (2012) The territorial trap of the territorial trap: Global transformation and the problem of the state's two territories. *International Political Sociology* 6(1): 57–76.

Shapin S and Schaffer S (1985) *Leviathan and the Air-Pump: Hobbes, Boyle, and the Experimental Life*. Princeton, NJ: Princeton University Press.

Sharma N (2020) *Home Rule: National Sovereignty and the Separation of Natives and Migrants*. Durham, NC: Duke University Press.

Sharma N (2022) National citizenship and postcolonial racism. *Citizenship Studies* 26(4–5): 638–649.

Shiffman J, Kunnuji M, Shawar YR, et al. (2018) International norms and the politics of sexuality education in Nigeria. *Globalization and Health* 14(1): 63.

Shukla N (ed.) (2016) *The Good Immigrant: 21 Writers Reflect on Race in Contemporary Britain*. London: Unbound.

Simmel G (1950) *The Sociology of Georg Simmel* (ed. Kurt Wolff). Glencoe, IL: The Free Press.

Singh J (2018) *Unthinking Mastery: Dehumanism and Decolonial Entanglements*. Durham, NC: Duke University Press.

Singler S (2021) Biometric statehood, transnational solutionism and security devices: The performative dimensions of the IOM's MIDAS. *Theoretical Criminology* 25(3): 454–473.

Singler S (2023) Performativity, pragmatism, and border control technologies: Democratising the ontologies of border criminology. *International Journal for Crime, Justice and Social Democracy* 12(2): 13–24.

Singler S (2024a) 'Do it yourself!' Pedagogical performances, technical expertise, and crimmigration control in the IOM's capacity-building practices in Nigeria. *Geopolitics*. DOI: 10.1080/14650045.2024.2331802.

Singler S (2024b) How to rethink tech in migration. Available at: https://algorithmwatch.org/en/how-to-rethink-tech-in-migration/ (accessed 11 November 2024).

Singler S and Babalola O (2024) Digital colonialism beyond surveillance capitalism? Coloniality of knowledge in Nigeria's emerging privacy rights legislation and border surveillance practices. *Social & Legal Studies*. DOI: 10.1177/09646639241287022.

Singler S and Milivojevic S (2024) The technopolitics of crimmigration control: Targeting bodies and re-scaling borders. In: Bosworth M, Franko K, Lee M, et al. (eds) *Handbook on Border Criminology*. Cheltenham: Edward Elgar Publishing, pp. 189–204.

Sipos A (2023) *Milde's International Air Law and ICAO: Revised by Attila Sipos*. 4th ed. The Hague: Eleven.

Sivandan A (2002) The contours of global racism. *Institute of Race Relations*. Available at: http://www.irr.org.uk/news/the-contours-of-global-racism/ (accessed 29 September 2024).

Smith K (2006) Problematising power relations in 'elite' interviews. *Geoforum* 37: 643–653.

Sokhi-Bulley B (2019) *Governing (Through) Rights*. Oxford: Hart.

Soliman F (2019) States of exception, human rights, and social harm: Towards a border zemiology. *Theoretical Criminology* 25(2): 228–248.

Soper K (2012) The humanism in posthumanism. *Comparative Critical Studies* 9(3): 365–378.

Sørensen NN (2012) Revisiting the migration–development nexus: From social networks and remittances to markets for migration control. *International Migration* 50(3): 61–76.

Sørensen NN and Gammeltoft-Hansen T (2012) Introduction. In: Gammeltoft-Hansen T and Sørensen NN (eds) *The Migration Industry and the Commercialization of International Migration*. Abingdon: Routledge, pp. 1–23.

Spivak GC (2013) Can the subaltern speak? In: Williams P and Chrisman L (eds) *Colonial Discourse and Post-Colonial Theory: A Reader*. Abingdon: Routledge, pp. 66–111.

Squire V (2014) Desert 'trash': Posthumanism, border struggles, and humanitarian politics. *Political Geography* 39(1): 11–21.

Squire V (2017) Unauthorised migration beyond structure/agency? Acts, interventions, effects. *Politics* 37(3): 254–272.

Srivastava S (2013) Assembling international organizations. *Journal of International Organization Studies* 3(1): 72–83.

Stambøl EM (2021a) Borders as penal transplants: Control of territory, mobility and illegality in West Africa. *Theoretical Criminology* 25(3): 474–492.

Stambøl EM (2021b) Neo-colonial penality? Travelling penal power and contingent sovereignty. *Punishment & Society* 23(4): 536–556.

Stambøl EM and Solhjell R (2021) Embodiments and frictions of statehood in transnational criminal justice. *Theoretical Criminology* 25(3): 493–510.

Steger MB and James P (2013) Levels of subjective globalization: Ideologies, imaginaries, ontologies. *Perspectives on Global Development and Technology* 12(1–2): 17–40.

Stock I, Üstübici A, and Schultz SU (2019) Externalization at work: responses to migration policies from the Global South. *Comparative Migration Studies* 7(1): 48.

Stricker Y (2019) 'International Migration' between empire and nation: The statistical construction of an ambiguous global category in the International Labour Office in the 1920s. *Ethnicities* 19(3): 469–485.

Stumpf J (2006) The crimmigration crisis: Immigration, crime, and sovereign power. *American University Law Review* 56(2): 367–420.

Stumpf J (2010) Doing time: Crimmigration law and the perils of haste. *UCLA Law Review* 58: 1705–1748.

Sud N and Sánchez-Ancochea D (2022) Southern discomfort: Interrogating the category of the Global South. *Development and Change* 53(6): 1123–1150.

Sullivan G (2022) Law, technology, and data-driven security: Infra-legalities as method assemblage. *Journal of Law and Society* 49(S1): S31–S50.

Sullivan J (2012) Skype: An appropriate method of data collection for qualitative interviews? *The Hilltop Review* 6(1): 54–60.

Sullivan S (2001) *Living Across and Through Skins: Transactional Bodies, Pramgatism, and Feminism*. Bloomington, IN: Indiana University Press.

Sultana F (2007) Reflexivity, positionality and participatory ethics: Negotiating fieldwork dilemmas in international research. *ACME: An International E-Journal for Critical Geographies* 6(3): 374–385.

Sundberg J (2011) Diabolic Caminos in the desert and cat fights on the Río: A posthumanist political ecology of boundary enforcement in the United States-Mexico borderlands. *Annals of the Association of American Geographers* 101(2): 318–336.

Sutherland E (1939) *Principles of Criminology*. 3rd ed. Chicago, IL: J.B. Lippincott Company.

Swatuk L (2001) The brothers grim: Modernity and 'international' relations in Southern Africa. In: Dunn K and Shaw T (eds) *Africa's Challenge to International Relations Theory*. Basingstoke: Palgrave, pp. 163–182.

Swyngedouw E and Ernstson H (2018) Interrupting the anthropo-obscene: Immuno-biopolitics and depoliticizing ontologies in the Anthropocene. *Theory, Culture & Society* 35(6): 3–30.

Taffel S (2018) Hopeful extinctions? Tesla, technological solutionism and the Anthropocene. *Culture Unbound* 10(2): 163–184.

Tagliapietra A (2022) More connected, less protected? How the EU Interoperability Framework will affect the European migration space. Available at: https://www.gmfus.org/news/more-connected-less-protected-how-eu-interoperability-framework-will-affect-european-migration (accessed 31 July 2024).

Tawil-Souri H (2014) Cinema as the space to transgress Palestine's territorial trap. *Middle East Journal of Culture and Communication* 7(2): 169–189.

Taylor L (2016) No place to hide? The ethics and analytics of tracking mobility using mobile phone data. *Environment and Planning D: Society and Space* 34(2): 319–336.

The Engine Room and Oxfam (2018) Biometrics in the humanitarian sector. Available at: https://www.theengineroom.org/wp-content/uploads/2018/03/Engine-Room-Oxfam-Biometrics-Review.pdf (accessed 28 July 2022).

Tilly C (1992) *Coercion, Capital, and European States, AD 990–1992*. Oxford: Blackwell.

Tomaszycki K (2018) The interoperability of European information systems for border and migration management and for ensuring security. *Facta Universitatis, Series: Law and Politics* 16(3): 195–212.

Torpey J (2000) *The Invention of the Passport: Surveillance, Citizenship and the State*. Cambridge: Cambridge University Press.

Torres É (2024) What 'longtermism' gets wrong about climate change. Available at: https://thebulletin.org/2022/11/what-longtermism-gets-wrong-about-climate-change/ (accessed 31 July 2024).

Transparency International (2021) Corruption Perceptions Index. Available at: https://www.transparency.org/en/cpi/2021 (accessed 28 May 2022).

Trauttmansdorff P (2022) Borders, migration, and technology in the age of security: Intervening with STS. *Tecnoscienza* 13(2): 133–154.

Tsui Q, Perosa T, and Singler S (2023) *Biometrics in the Humanitarian Sector: A Current Look at Risks, Benefits and Organisational Policies.* London: Engine Room.

Tuck E and Yang KW (2012) Decolonization is not a metaphor. *Decolonization: Indigeneity, Education & Society* 1(1): 1–40.

Tucker K (2018) Unraveling coloniality in International Relations: Knowledge, relationality, and strategies for engagement. *International Political Sociology* 12(3): 215–232.

Tzanou M (2010) The EU as an emerging 'surveillance society': The function creep case study and challenges to privacy and data protection. *ICL Journal* 4(3): 407–427.

Ugelvik T (2014) The incarceration of foreigners in European prisons. In: Pickering S and Ham J (eds) *The Routledge Handbook on Crime and International Migratoin.* Abingdon: Routledge, pp. 107–120.

UK Border Force (2021) Guide to faster travel through the UK border. Available at: https://www.gov.uk/government/publications/coming-to-the-uk/faster-travel-through-the-uk-border (accessed 26 July 2022).

UK Government (2024) Digital development strategy 2024–2030. Available at: https://assets.publishing.service.gov.uk/media/6613e7f7c4c84d4b31346a68/FCDO-Digital-Development-Strategy-2024-2030.pdf (accessed 29 July 2024).

UK Government (n.d.) Registered Traveller: Faster entry through the UK border. Available at: https://www.gov.uk/registered-traveller (accessed 26 July 2022).

UK Home Office (2022) New deal with Nigeria to deter illegal migration. Available at: https://www.gov.uk/government/news/new-deal-with-nigeria-to-deter-illegal-migration--2 (accessed 28 July 2022).

Ullrich L (2024) *Victims and the Labour of Justice at the International Criminal Court: The Blame Cascade.* Oxford: Oxford University Press.

UN CTITF (2012) CTITF launches counter-terrorism projects in Nigeria. Available at: https://www.un.org/counterterrorism/sites/www.un.org.counterterrorism/files/ctitf_beam-no5-web.pdf (accessed 29 September 2024).

UNDP (2024a) Legal identity. Available at: https://www.undp.org/governance/legal-identity (accessed 31 July 2024).

UNDP (2024b) *The Politics of Inequality: Why Are Governance Systems Not More Responsive to the Unequal Distribution of Income and Wealth?* New York, NY: United Nations Development Program.

UNHCR (2017) The people working for UNHCR. Available at: https://reporting.unhcr.org/sites/default/files/The%20people%20working%20for%20UNHCR%20-%20November%202017.pdf (accessed 29 September 2024).

UNHCR (2024a) Division of human resources. Available at: https://reporting.unhcr.org/sites/default/files/2023-12/DHR_organigram.pdf (accessed 29 September 2024).

UNHCR (2024b) Funding UNHCR's programmes: Global report 2023. Available at: https://reporting.unhcr.org/sites/default/files/2024-09/Global%20Report%202023%20-%20Funding%20Overview.pdf (accessed 29 September 2024).

United Nations (2021) Drowning of 27 migrants in English Channel is worst disaster on record: IOM. Available at: https://news.un.org/en/story/2021/11/1106562 (accessed 1 May 2021).

UNOCT (n.d.) goTravel software solution. Available at: https://www.un.org/cttravel/goTravel (accessed 28 July 2022).

UNODC (2020) World Day against Trafficking in Persons: Nigerian liaison magistrates deployed in Italy and Spain strengthen international cooperation to prosecute cases of human trafficking. Available at: https://www.unodc.org/nigeria/en/nigerian-liaison-magistrates-deployed-in-italy-and-spain-strengthen-international-cooperation-to-prosecute-cases-of-human-trafficking.html (accessed 28 July 2022).

UNSD (2022) United Nations Legal Identity Agenda. Available at: https://unstats.un.org/legal-identity-agenda/ (accessed 28 January 2022).

Valdivia A, Aradau C, Blanke T, et al. (2022) Neither opaque nor transparent: A transdisciplinary methodology to investigate datafication at the EU borders. *Big Data & Society* 9(2): 20539517221124586.

Valverde M (2011) Questions of security: A framework for research. *Theoretical Criminology* 15(1): 3–22.

van Berlo P (2015) Australia's Operation Sovereign Borders: Discourse, power, and policy from a crimmigration perspective. *Refugee Survey Quarterly* 34: 75–104.

van der Woude M and van der Leun J (2017) Crimmigration checks in the internal border areas of the EU: Finding the discretion that matters. *European Journal of Criminology* 14(1): 27–45.

van der Woude MAH, van der Leun JP, and Nijland JA (2014) Crimmigration in the Netherlands. *Law & Social Inquiry* 39(3): 560–579.

Van Rythoven E (2021) A feeling of unease: Distance, emotion, and securitizing indigenous protest in Canada. *International Political Sociology* 15(2): 251–271.

van Wingerden E (2022) Unmastering research: Positionality and intercorporeal vulnerability in International Studies. *International Political Sociology* 16(2): olac008.

Vassor E (2023) *Access to Digital Identity for People on the Move in Europe*. Geneva: IOM.

Vavoula N (2021) Artificial Intelligence (AI) at Schengen Borders: Automated processing, algorithmic profiling and facial recognition in the era of techno-solutionism. *European Journal of Migration* 23: 457–484.

Vazquez Y (2015) Constructing crimmigration: Latino subordination in a 'post-racial' world. *Ohio State Law Journal* 76(3): 599–657.

Veridos (2021) Identity for all: Africa rises to the challenge of enfranchising citizens lacking legal identities. Available at: https://www.veridos.com/en/topictrends/identity-for-all-africa-rises-to-the-challenge-of-enfranchising-citizens-lacking-legal-identities.html (accessed 12 June 2024).

Vigneswaran D (2013) Making mobility a problem: How South African officials criminalize migration. In: Franko Aas K and Bosworth M (eds) *The Borders of Punishment: Migration, Citizenship, and Social Exclusion*. Oxford: Oxford University Press, pp. 111–127.

Villasenor J and Foggo V (2020) Artificial Intelligence, due process, and criminal sentencing. *2020 Michigan State Law Review* 2: 295–354.

Vukov T and Sheller M (2013) Border work: Surveillant assemblages, virtual fences, and tactical counter-media. *Social Semiotics* 23(2): 225–241.

Waasdorp J and Pahladsingh A (2017) Expulsion or imprisonment? Criminal law sanctions for breaching an entry ban in the light of crimmigration law. *Bergen Journal of Criminal Law & Criminal Justice* 4(2): 247–266.

Wach E and Wach R (2013) Learning about Qualitative Document Analysis. *IDS Practice Paper in Brief* 13. Available at: https://hdl.handle.net/20.500.12413/2989 (accessed 9 June 2025)

Walker RBJ (1993) *Inside/Outside: International Relations as Political Theory*. Cambridge: Cambridge University Press.

Walklate S (2018) Criminology, gender and risk: The dilemmas of Northern theorising for southern responses to intimate partner violence. *International Journal for Crime, Justice and Social Democracy* 7(1): 1–14.

Walsh J (2020) Report and deport: Public vigilance and migration policing in Australia. *Theoretical Criminology* 24(2): 276–295.

Weber C (1998) Performative states. *Millennium: Journal of International Studies* 27(1): 77–95.

Weber L (2002) The detention of asylum seekers: 20 reasons why criminologists should care. *Current Issues in Criminal Justice* 14(1): 9–30.

Weber L (2013) *Policing Non-Citizens*. Abingdon: Routledge.

Weber L and Bowling B (2004) Policing migration: A framework for investigating the regulation of global mobility. *Policing and Society* 14(3): 195–212.

Weber L and Bowling B (2008) Valiant beggars and global vagabonds. *Theoretical Criminology* 12(3): 355–375.

Weber L and Gelsthorpe L (2000) *Deciding to Detain: How Decisions to Detain Asylum Seekers Are Made at Ports of Entry*. University of Cambridge: Institute of Criminology.

Weber L and McCulloch J (2019) Penal power and border control: Which thesis? Sovereignty, governmentality, or the pre-emptive state? *Punishment & Society* 21(4): 496–514.

Weber M (2009) Politics as a vocation. In: Gerth HH and Wright Mills C (eds) *From Max Weber: Essays in Sociology*. Abingdon: Routledge, pp. 77–128.

Werth R (2019) Theorizing the performative effects of penal risk technologies: (Re)producing the subject who must be dangerous. *Social & Legal Studies* 28(3): 327–348.

Wheeldon J (2015) Ontology, epistemology, and irony: Richard Rorty and re-imagining pragmatic criminology. *Theoretical Criminology* 19(3): 396–415.

Wheeldon J and Heidt J (2007) Bridging the gap: A pragmatic approach to understanding critical criminologies and policy influence. *Critical Criminology* 15(4): 313–325.

Wienroth M and Amelung N (2023) 'Crisis', control and circulation: Biometric surveillance in the policing of the 'crimmigrant other'. *International Journal of Police Science & Management* 25(3): 297–312.

Wille K (2020) Unease as a feminist-pragmatist concept: Conceptualizing a powerful sentiment along with Charlotte Perkins Gilman. *European Journal of Pragmatism and American Philosophy* 12(2): 1–19.

Williams D (2010) Making a liberal state: 'Good governance' in Ghana. *Review of African Political Economy* 37(126): 403–419.

Williams D and Young T (2012) Civil society and the liberal project in Ghana and Sierra Leone. *Journal of Intervention and Statebuilding* 6(1): 7–22.

Williams K and Mountz A (2016) Rising tide: Analyzing the relationship between externalization and migrant deaths and boat losses. In: Zaiotti R (ed.) *Externalizing Migration Management: Europe, North America and the Spread of 'Remote Control' Practices*. Abingdon: Routledge, pp. 31–49.

Wilson D (2006) Biometrics, borders and the ideal suspect. In: Pickering S and Weber L (eds) *Borders, Mobility and Technologies of Control*. Dordrecht: Springer, pp. 87–109.

Wilson D (2015) Border militarization, technology and crime control. In: Pickering S and Ham J (eds) *The Routledge Handbook on Crime and International Migration*. Abingdon: Routledge, pp. 141–154.

Wilson J (2015) The word criminology: A philology and definition. *Criminology, Criminal Justice, Law & Society* 16(3): 61–82.

Wimmer A and Schiller N (2003) Methodological nationalism, the social sciences, and the study of migration: an essay in historical epistemology. *International Migration Review* 37(3): 576–610.

Wincup E (2017) *Criminological Research: Understanding Qualitative Methods*. London: SAGE Publications.

Wonders N (2006) Global flows, semi-permeable borders and new channels of inequality: Border crossers and border performativity. In: Pickering S and Weber L (eds) *Borders, Mobility and Technologies of Control*. Dordrecht: Springer, pp. 63–86.

Wonders NA and Jones LC (2018) Doing and undoing borders: The multiplication of citizenship, citizenship performances, and migration as social movement. *Theoretical Criminology* 23(2): 136–155.

Wood M (2021) Rethinking how technologies harm. *British Journal of Criminology* 61(3): 627–647.

World Bank (2024) Net official development assistance and official aid received (current US$) – Nigeria. Available at: https://data.worldbank.org/indicator/DT.ODA.ALLD.CD?locations=NG (accessed 29 September 2024).

Yar M (2012) Critical criminology, critical theory and social harm. In: Hall S and Winlow S (eds) *New Directions in Criminological Theory*. Abingdon: Routledge, pp. 52–65.

Zandonini G (2019) Biometrics: The new frontier of EU migration policy in Niger. *The New Humanitarian*, 6 June. Available at: https://www.thenewhumanitarian.org/news-feature/2019/06/06/biometrics-new-frontier-eu-migration-policy-niger (accessed 29 September 2024).

Zedner L (2009) Epilogue: The inescapable insecurity of security technologies? In: Franko Aas K, Gundhus H, and Lomell H (eds) *Technologies of Insecurity: The Surveillance of Everyday Life*. Abingdon: Routledge, pp. 257–270.

Zedner L (2010) Security, the state, and the citizen: The changing architecture of crime control. *New Criminal Law Review: In International and Interdisciplinary Journal* 13(2): 379–403.

Zedner L (2016) Penal subversions: When is a punishment not a punishment, who decides, and on what grounds? *Theoretical Criminology* 20(1): 3–20.

Zedner L (2019) The hostile border: Crimmigration, counter-terrorism, or crossing the line on rights? *New Criminal Law Review: An International and Interdisciplinary Journal* 22(3): 318–345.

Index

For the benefit of digital users, indexed terms that span two pages (e.g., 52–53) may, on occasion, appear on only one of those pages.